Carving Nature

Carving Nature

WILDLIFE STUDIES IN WOOD

Frank Fox-Wilson

Guild of Master Craftsman Publications Ltd

First published 2000 by
Guild of Master Craftsman Publications Ltd
Castle Place, 166 High Street,
Lewes, East Sussex BN7 1XU

Photographs on frontispiece and pages 3, 10, 14, 21, 30, 37, 42, 52, 64, 71, 72, 86, 103, 115, 130, 163 and 164 by Anthony Bailey
Other photographs by Frank Fox-Wilson except where otherwise stated
Drawing on page 16 by Frank Fox-Wilson
Other drawings by Richard Haynes after originals by Frank Fox-Wilson

Whilst every effort has been made to obtain permission from the copyright holders for all material used in this book, the publishers will be pleased to hear from anyone who has not been appropriately acknowledged, and to make the correction in future reprints.

ISBN 1 86108 156 1

The publishers and author can accept no legal responsibility for any consequences arising from the application of information, advice or instructions given in this publication.

A catalogue record for this book is available from the British Library.

Edited by Stephen Haynes
Designed by John Hawkins
Cover design by Graham Willmott at GMC Publications design studio
Cover photograph by Anthony Bailey

Set in Perpetua

Colour origination by Viscan Graphics (Singapore)
Printed and bound by Kyodo Printing (Singapore)

SAFETY

Woodcarving should not be a dangerous activity, provided that sensible precautions are taken to avoid unnecessary risk.

Always ensure that work is securely held in a suitable clamp or other device, and that the workplace lighting is adequate.

Keep tools sharp; blunt tools are dangerous because they require more pressure and may behave unpredictably. Store them so that you, and others, cannot touch their cutting edges accidentally.

Be particular about disposing of shavings, finishing materials, oily rags, etc., which may be a fire hazard.

Do not work when your concentration is impaired by drugs, alcohol or fatigue.

Do not remove safety guards from power tools; pay attention to electrical safety.

It is not safe to use a chainsaw without the protective clothing which is specially designed for this purpose, and attendance on a recognized training course is strongly recommended. Be aware that regulations governing chainsaw use are revised from time to time.

The safety advice in this book is intended for your guidance, but cannot cover every eventuality: the safe use of hand and power tools is the responsibility of the user. If you are unhappy with a particular technique or procedure, do not use it – there is always another way.

MEASUREMENTS

Although care has been taken to ensure that the metric measurements are true and accurate, they are only conversions from imperial; they have been rounded up or down to the nearest whole millimetre, or to the nearest convenient equivalent in cases where the imperial measurements themselves are only approximate. When following the projects, use either the metric or the imperial measurements; do not mix units.

Note that all the working drawings are printed on a grid of 1in (25mm) squares, to facilitate enlargement by the method described on page 174.

For Mavis, Sarah and Claire
who have heroically coped with years of noise and dust,
and my continual absence in the workshop

Contents

ACKNOWLEDGEMENTS

Every woodcarver owes whatever skill and art he or she possesses to countless others — to the worldwide fellowship of carvers both professional and amateur who have provided inspiration and technical knowledge. To make a list of those whose work has influenced me over the years would fill several pages, and I can only mention here the carvers who have contributed directly to the making of this book.

First and foremost is Rod Naylor, whose book *Woodcarving Techniques*, published in 1979, stimulated a consuming interest in carving and set me on the trail to discover how such wonderful sculptures could be produced. More recently Rod has been particularly encouraging and has provided pictures of his work which appear in Chapter 14.

A number of others have kindly supplied pictures or allowed access for photography of their inspirational work: Ray Gonzalez, Ben Harms, Bill Prickett, Brian Faggetter, Rob Perrott, Bob Pyett and Chris Coleman. Geoff Weald, who runs the Bentley Wildlife Carvers Association, has also provided all kinds of practical assistance and useful contacts.

The original drawing on which the John Dory carving is based appears by courtesy of the artist, Sheila Mackie, and the original drawing of the squirrel by courtesy of Crowood Press. The photograph of the Grinling Gibbons panel on page 169 is by courtesy of the Trustees of the Victoria & Albert Museum.

I owe a great debt of gratitude to the editorial staff at GMC Publications, who have given enormous help and encouragement to a new author; especially Stephen Haynes, whose attention to detail with the text, drawings and photographs has been invaluable.

Many friends and members of my family have given great moral support, particularly when the going became rough in finding the time and energy to hold together a demanding day job with the pressures of writing, carving and photography for these projects. Above all in this category I cannot find the words to express my gratitude to my wife Mavis, who has so often had to put up with a far greater sharing of affection with the workshop than a spouse should expect. Without her support, encouragement and endless patience the book would never have been started.

Introduction

I GET VERY excited about wood – not so much with painted or gilded timber which, however skilfully fashioned, makes you wonder whether you are looking at wood at all; it is the natural product which brings such fascination. Even sawn lengths of deal display something of the infinite variety of grain figure and texture formed in every tree, but the real thrill is to be confronted with a new or reclaimed chunk of seasoned hardwood. The eye alights on it and all kinds of questions spring to mind: 'Is it sound?' 'I wonder what the finished grain figure will look like?' 'What are the possibilities here?'

With any new carving project it is important to get a number of questions settled before making the first cut. The primary consideration is whether you are looking for a piece of timber suitable for the particular subject you have in mind, or the other way round: 'Here is a beautiful lump of wood – what can I make from it?' Either way, you will need to think about the strength and hardness of the wood: will these be adequate for the most delicate parts of the carving? The surface will need to be examined closely, which may entail shaping and finishing a small section to see the colour and grain pattern, finding out how it handles when cut across the grain. Is the grain open like oak, or fine like yew and able to take a more polished finish? These and other characteristics – such as the differences between dense and soft wood (some pine species exhibit both qualities in their grain), and the problems of splits or shakes, knots, incorrect seasoning, bacterial staining (spalting), etc. – will be examined in more detail in later chapters.

The main part of this book contains 17 detailed step-by-step carving projects reflecting natural subjects, produced by an enthusiastic amateur for other amateur carvers. Perhaps you have already tried your hand at carving and would like some ideas on carving nature. You might have your roots in another branch of woodwork and want to have a go at carving. Or maybe you are already an expert in some other sculptural medium and are now thinking about widening your skills. Whatever your starting point – welcome!

Most books on carving contain a significant section on tools, techniques and sharpening; there are even whole books on the subject, or just about timber (see the Select Bibliography on page 180), and there is no end of easily accessible information in trade catalogues and magazines. What is less often found is an in-depth discussion of the design stage of carving, or useful snippets of advice gathered over the years from experienced carvers. These subjects are covered in Chapters 13 and 14.

The projects described here are all derived from nature, and attempt to reflect the reality and beauty of creation using natural wood. There are various ways of doing this. One specialized branch of wildfowl carving takes realism to the ultimate, using paint or pyrography to achieve the perfect image of a teal or wader. One can only admire these carvers' skill and infinite attention to detail (see for example page 172), but such projects are outside the scope of this book. Other carvers will use driftwood and old timber to suggest a natural shape in a more abstract way. The Waves carving in Chapter 7 is an example of a more abstract style, and driftwood is used as a base to mount the Turtle (Chapter 9). Most of the time, though, carvers will use standard blocks of seasoned timber obtained commercially, and the majority of the carvings illustrated here came from that source.

All the projects which follow concentrate on fusing two natural things into one object: the living creature or plant which is the subject, and the wood which reflects certain characteristics of the subject, but does not produce a slavish copy. In fact, you can try and produce two 'identical' carvings using different types of timber, and each will have something different to say about the subject. Even carvings which have come from the same tree will show remarkable variety. This is one of the main reasons I am elated by wood – the possibilities for creative variety are endless; and wood is such a warm medium to work with. In contrast, for example, to messing about with stone or clay, or wrestling with wrought iron, timber has a distinctive homely feel to it; and, unlike those other media, every piece of wood is different.

But then wood can be very unforgiving. Come to grief with an object on the potter's wheel and it doesn't take long to start again; but split the delicate beak of a carved bird, and it may be difficult to mend without spoiling the entire carving. Spend hours working carefully towards the centre of a huge log, only to find an untreatable section of rot, and you may be left with a piece of firewood. In the project descriptions I have tried to be as honest as possible, and include the many small problems and occasional large disasters which face the amateur carver. Wood sculpture often involves significant adaptation as the carving progresses, and it is surprising how often one can get over what appears at first to be an insurmountable problem. As a general rule, avoid giving up on any piece too early, especially when an enormous amount of time – not to mention expenditure on timber – has already been invested. Even an unforeseen and nasty area of rotten wood can sometimes be rectified by cutting it right out and replacing with a carefully shaped offcut. Techniques for repairing problems and disasters are discussed in Chapter 13.

At the end of the day, it is always the wood which is in charge, not the craftsman. Master carvers and experienced amateurs may feel that their technical skills are sufficient to produce the required result whenever they use an appropriate piece of timber, and so they can – but the key word is *appropriate*. The spark of appreciation is seldom ignited simply by technical virtuosity; it takes this *plus* the unique characteristics of the piece of wood used. To succeed – and this is particularly important if you are hoping to sell your work – the carving must display a seamless blend of design and raw material. The examples of work by various experienced and professional carvers in Chapter 14 all show this essential quality.

For most amateur carvers, the stress will be on the beauty of the wood rather than on dazzling technique, and that is the emphasis of the step-by-step projects in this book. We begin with two straightforward carvings of fish which depend largely on the final appearance of the grain and surface texture. As skills and experience are developed, the balance can gradually shift towards more complex designs; but however long you have been carving, it is always the wood which determines the start and the finish of every project. The truly stunning and inspirational wood sculptures you see at major exhibitions all have one thing in common: technique and timber have been brought together in a unique and perfect marriage.

There is one other aspect of carving nature which is apparent to the viewer in every sculpture. Does the carver know and understand the subject he is carving? Has he or she caught the particular characteristics of the animal, bird or foliage? There is a world of difference between simple copying and the art of the sculptor. Does the pike look mean and hungry? Is the wren perky and almost cheeky? Does the tree frog capture that moment of watchful, frozen immobility? In the projects which follow you will be the judge, and where I have not succeeded in capturing the essence of the subject, ask yourself why. You can learn a great deal from other people's mistakes as well as from your own.

Whether any natural carving succeeds or not will depend on the carver's knowledge of the subject, even when the technique is largely abstract – indeed, more so then. Capturing the essence of a living being starts with knowing the facts about its existence. From there, the subsequent portrayal of those unique characteristics in wood (or any other medium) will affect every stage of the work. It will come into sharpest focus at those moments when you stop carving to look critically at some aspect of the work in hand. Do the fins look as if they are holding the fish stationary in moving water, or are they dull and lifeless? You can see the bird's beak and eye are not quite right; what needs to be changed to get the effect you are striving for? Is the frog balanced naturally on the branch and leaf, or does it look awkward?

In some ways, each project from start to finish is a question of putting right what is wrong. At the beginning, the turtle's body is square and needs to be round; later, the head is an oval blob and needs eyes and mouth; towards completion, the bird's primary feathers are too regular and need to be slightly disarranged. Finally a stage is reached where you may still see things that are not quite right, but to continue will either spoil the overall appearance, or require skills that you do not yet have. In the end, unless you want to work on one carving all your life, there is a point at which you have to stop. For you, at this point in time, that is the state of the art. Next time it will be better; or at least, it will be easier to reach this point and perhaps continue a little further. In a sense, all works of art from the simplest to the greatest are eventually abandoned, and experience will decide when that moment has come.

Whether you copy some of these projects, or simply use them as a source of ideas for your own designs, I hope that they will help to increase your enjoyment of this fabulous pastime of carving wood.

CHAPTER 1
Two fish

JOHN DORY

THE IDEA FOR this carving came from a wonderful series of pencil sketches by Sheila Mackie in a book on the history of Lindisfarne written by Magnus Magnussen (see the Select Bibliography on page 180), now unfortunately out of print.

The John Dory (*Zeus faber*) is a fish so ugly that it is positively beautiful, and an ideal subject for a relief carving. The fish is as tall as it is long, with a very thin body and extensive spiny fins. The narrow profile and peculiar upturned mouthparts are exploited by the Dory to stalk the smaller fish on which it feeds. It inches forward using hardly visible wavelike motions of the two rear fins. Then, within striking distance, the extendible mouth shoots forward and engulfs the unsuspecting prey. On occasion it also hunts by lying half-buried in the sand with the shaggy filaments of the dorsal fin waving gently. Smaller fish attracted to this bait are summarily dealt with. Behind the pectoral fin there is a circular black patch which has given rise to the legend that this was the fish caught by St Peter in the Sea of Galilee, in the mouth of which was a coin. The mark was supposed to have been made by the Apostle's thumb when he held the fish – a nice story, but highly unlikely for all the obvious reasons.

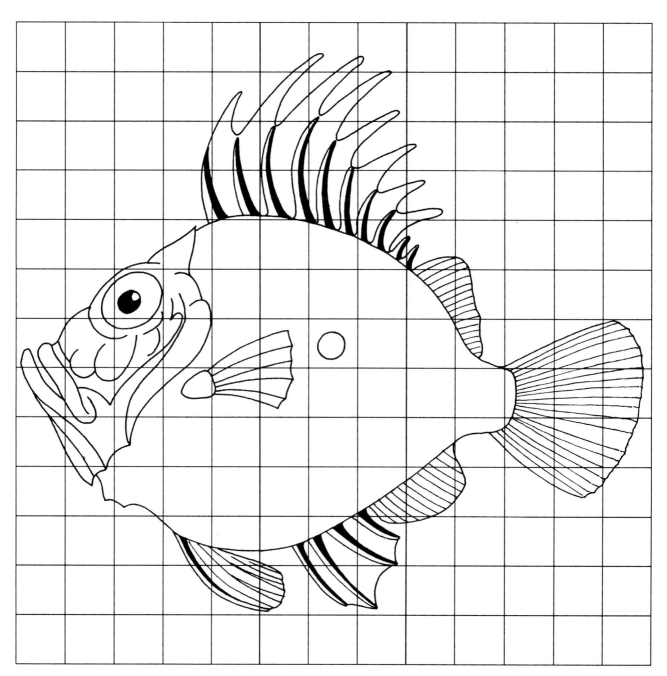

FIG 1.1*a* *John Dory: side elevation*

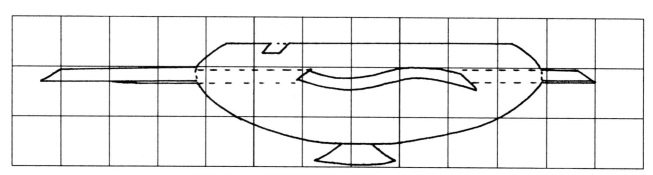

FIG 1.1*b* *Rear elevation*

Elm

The dark olive-brown colour of the Dory and its dappled markings suggested elm (*Ulmus procera*) as the ideal timber to use. The distinctive grain is a result of many small water-carrying pores, not only in the outer cambium layer, but scattered throughout the wood. They run through an interlocking grain which makes elm impossible to split in a straight line, if at all. For this reason it has been used in furniture-making and other crafts wherever this 'unsplittability' is required; examples include chair seats where the legs and back spindles are driven firmly into the wood, and the hubs of wooden cartwheels in which the spokes are inserted. Elm is also resistant to water damage, and is therefore useful for garden furniture and, traditionally, to make coffins. The swirling patterns generated by the interlocking grain have long been valued by woodturners and carvers.

The piece of elm used for the John Dory was 12 × 12 × 3in (305 × 305 × 76mm). One could easily get away with a piece 2in (51mm) thick, but the extra depth allows some curvature around the back so that the finished carving stands out more realistically from the wall.

Marking and cutting the outline (Fig 1.1*a* and *b*)

The original line drawing, some 3in (76mm) wide, was blown up on the photocopier to 12½in (318mm), the maximum size which would fit the timber. For this project the drawing is best angled at 45° to the grain direction, which allows a maximum size for the carving and also sets the trailing spines of the long dorsal fin along the grain (Fig 1.2). The picture can then be glued to another sheet of stiffer paper, and the outline shape cut out as a template. Both sides of the timber should be roughly planed to give some indication of the grain direction, particularly for orientation of the dorsal spines, and the outline is then drawn on the wood surface.

Allowing a margin of ⅛in (3mm), the timber is cut around the outline. This will take a fair time with a handsaw, and a bandsaw is far easier, if available.

FIG 1.3 *The vertical outline cut out, with the fins reduced in depth and their outlines re-marked*

Blocking out

The outlines of the fins and tail are marked for depth, allowing ¾in (19mm) for the fins and carefully removing the waste with a small handsaw on both the front and the back (Figs 1.3 and 1.4). At this stage a holding block roughly 6 × 2 × 1½in (150 × 150 × 38mm) is screwed to the back so that the piece can be held firmly in the vice as carving progresses (this can be seen clearly in Fig 1.5). Before shaping the shallow curve of the body, establish the highest point on the carving by marking the outline of the central pectoral fin and cutting round it with a V-chisel to a depth of ⅜in (10mm). The body can then be roughly

FIG 1.2 *The photocopied outline laid on the block of elm; it is oriented so as to place the delicate trailing dorsal fin along the grain*

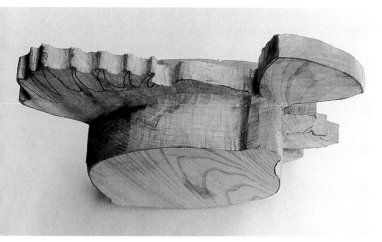

FIG 1.4 *Starting to reduce the level for the fins and tail. The body is left over-thick at this stage to allow for the projecting pectoral fin*

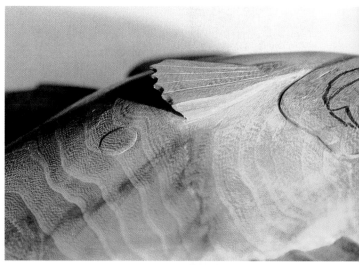

FIG 1.6 *The projecting pectoral fin and 'thumb' mark, shown at a slightly later stage. The slight swelling at the front of the fin represents the muscle*

FIG 1.5 *This view of the carving at a later stage shows the holding block screwed on with four coach screws (the nuts simply act as spacing washers), and the pencilled centre line which serves as a valuable reference when shaping the fins and body*

shaped using a large shallow gouge, cutting back to the base of the fins but allowing extra depth of wood for the area around the eye and mouthparts.

The fins and tail

More detailed work can now begin on the fins. In nature each one has a slightly different function, and this is reflected in their appearance and anatomy.

Because of the projecting pectoral fin and the curvature of the body, you will no longer be able to lay the original drawing over the carving to check the exact shape of the fins. If you make another copy of the picture and cut out each fin separately, the accurate fin outlines are now easily re-marked. You will find it helpful to draw a centre line right around the fish, including the fin outlines (Fig 1.5). The fins can be thinned and partly tapered to this line, allowing some extra thickness for the wavy rear fins and for the slight curve of the tail – even in relief carving, it is important to suggest some movement in order to bring the fish to life. Behind the fins you can allow extra thickness for strength. Providing the rear surface of the fin is bevelled off to an angle of less than 30°, observers of the finished carving will not perceive any distortion unless their face is almost hard up to the wall.

The pectoral fin can now be shaped accurately and undercut. The narrow grooves representing the spines are widely spaced, as are the serrations at the rear. The pectoral muscle is indicated by a slight projection at the front (Fig 1.6).

Coping with disaster

My average track record for unexpected problems (as the reader will become aware) is one minor disaster per project and a major one every five. This time, while holding the carving vertically in the vice to work on the dorsal fin, despite using a thick cushioning of old towel, insufficient care was taken to avoid pressure on the pectoral fin, and it split. However, the break was clean, and a repair with glue, using an awkward arrangement with a clamp and blocks of scrap wood, overcame the problem (Fig 1.7).

FIG 1.7 *Repair to the broken pectoral fin, using a Heath Robinson clamp arrangement to provide light pressure for gluing*

The main fins

The large dorsal and ventral fins have tapering spines which are quite chunky. Mark the shape of these spines, and of the trailing extensions on the dorsal fin. When these trailing parts are cut out, it is safest at first to leave webs between them for strength. To make the main spines stand out, cut back between them to a depth of about ⅛in (3mm), using a V-tool and shallow gouge. The spines are

FIG 1.8 *The dorsal fin, with work started on the projecting spines and the trailing appendages. For the sake of strength, the spaces between the long trailing parts will not be pierced right through until a much later stage*

then rounded and finished with abrasive paper and riffler files (Fig 1.8). In my own carving the lower level of the surface between the spines was extended straight out to the trailing parts, though on reflection it would have been better to make the trailing parts less uniform and give them a more wavelike, undulating surface.

Once the levels are right on the front of the dorsal fin, the back can be tapered more accurately and the strengthening webs removed using a small, deep gouge. The effect of this can be seen in Fig 1.10. However, because the dorsal fin is so fragile, this is best left until the rest of the carving is finished.

Other fins and tail

There are no protruding spines on the smaller rear fins, but these need to be given an undulating surface to suggest delicacy and movement. Again, the front levels are completed with a shallow gouge before the rear is tapered. Fine spines are indicated by cutting narrow parallel grooves with the V-tool. At the outer edge, a ¼in (6mm) no. 9 gouge is used to cut the tiny serrations between the spines (Fig 1.9).

Towards the tail, the body of the fish needs to extend into the tail fin, which is then shaped with a slight curve between top and bottom. Again the V-tool marks the spines and the serrations along the rear edge are cut out with a small, quick gouge. Fig 1.10 shows how the fins look on the completed carving.

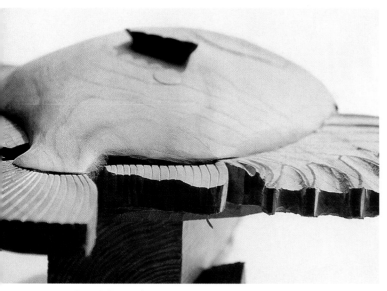

FIG 1.9 *Surface work completed on the tail and undulating rear fins*

FIG 1.10 *A rear view of the completed carving, showing the serrations of the tail and fins, and how the back edge is bevelled off to make the wood look much thinner than it really is*

FIG 1.11 *Face detail. Notice the overlapping gill flaps; the mouth has not been cut right through yet*

The main body can now be finally shaped and roughly sanded to fair all the curves and clean up the joints at the base of the fins and tail.

Carving the face

The face and mouthparts can now be tackled (Fig 1.11). Draw the outlines and study the picture carefully before starting to carve. The gill flaps need to look as if they overlap from front to back; this is achieved by cutting down with a V-tool along the rear edge of each flap, and levelling the adjacent surface using a small flat chisel. Note how the lips should protrude from the surrounding skin folds; and the surround to the eye is slightly raised. The eye itself is first carved as a shallow convex curve, and then the centre is cut out with a ⅜in (10mm) no. 7 gouge. Later the pupil can be stained with a dark brown wood stain to enhance the impression of depth. A more realistic effect can sometimes be given by retaining a narrow curved segment at the top, flush with the eye surface, which, when viewed from a distance, gives the impression of light reflecting from the lens (Fig 1.12).

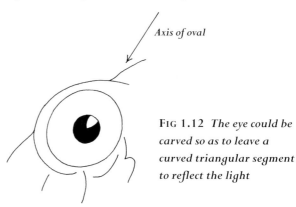

Axis of oval

FIG 1.12 *The eye could be carved so as to leave a curved triangular segment to reflect the light*

The gap between the lips is made by first drilling several small holes right through to the back, then joining these up with a fine Japanese saw to form a groove, and finally cleaning up with small shallow gouges and files.

Shaping the back

You can now match the body contours of the rear surface (behind the carving) to the curves and folds of the front (Fig 1.13). At this stage I realized that there was still about ½in (13mm) too much wood at the back – the rear curve of the body would almost meet at the centre, and a much wider flat area was needed to seat on the wall. The holding block was removed and some very careful and tedious

FIG 1.13 *A rear view of the completed carving, showing the rear of the body rounded and the edges of the fins tapered to retain strength. The holes left by the coach screws have yet to be plugged*

hand sawing undertaken to reduce the wood to the required thickness of around ⅜in (10mm) behind the fins.

Once the holding block has been removed, the screw holes can be filled in with plugs of elm. As the carving weighs very little, two small screws projecting from the wall are quite sufficient to support it, so two triangular holes are cut in the back of the carving to house the screws, with the top of each hole angled upwards to sit safely over the screw heads (Fig 1.14).

Finishing

The carving is now complete, and can be finished using increasingly fine grades of abrasive paper, followed by wire wool. Before applying any sealant, hold the piece at different angles to a strong light to show up any unnoticed blemishes which may require further sanding.

The fish needs a smooth but not glossy finish, so three coats of Danish oil are sufficient, using fine wire wool to de-nib and rub down between coats. After leaving for two or three days for final hardening, one coat of wax is applied, and polished an hour later to what could be described as a dull shine. The photograph of the finished carving shows how the swirling appearance of the elm grain enhances the final effect.

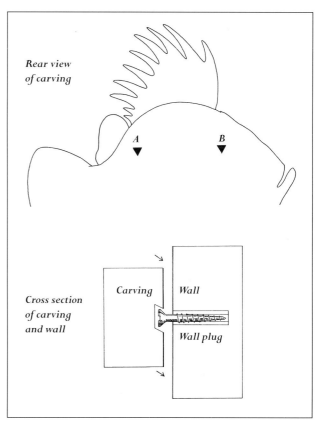

FIG 1.14 *Detail and position of the triangular holes (A and B) by which the carving is hung*

PIKE

Like the John Dory, the pike is designed as a hunter, though in a very different way. The long, powerful body and large rear fins provide a sudden and stupendous acceleration and the ability to turn at lightning speed. The pike feeds on almost any smaller creature in the water – not only fish, but swimming mammals like the water vole, occasional ducklings or even a fully grown mallard. It hunts mainly by sight, having a groove, rather like a gunsight, on the snout in front of each eye which helps its forward vision; though at night it can find an angler's deadbait by smell. The mouth bristles with small teeth, including some in the roof, and these are all attached by hinges, moving backwards towards the throat to assist swallowing and prevent any possibility of the victim's escape.

Various species of pike are found in most of the fresh waters of Europe, Asia and America. The common pike (*Esox lucius*) can live and grow for up to 15 years, the females reaching the largest size, sometimes over a metre (39in) long and weighing in excess of 50lb (22kg). The shape of the adult female changes considerably during the year due to spawning, when the roe can increase the body weight by a sixth. After early autumn spawning the belly and flanks become lean and flabby, and it can be caught and landed with scarcely a wag, but by the new year once again it has gained weight, changing to a creature of savage energy. This simple relief sculpture portrays a fully grown adult.

Ash

Any timber with bold grain would be suitable; in this case I used common ash (*Fraxinus excelsior*), obtained as a large, damaged offcut of 1⅜in (35mm) planking from the sawmill. Because of the rapid outburst of long leaves in late spring, the ash tree needs many large-pored vessels to carry quantities of sap up the stem. These appear as conspicuous irregular bands in the sawn timber, and between them lies the much harder, dense summer wood. The toughness and almost straight grain of the ash have made it an ideal wood for tool handles, ladder rungs, sports equipment, shafts for horse-drawn carts, and even weapons such as spears and arrows. Ash also features in

Fig 1.15
*Pike: side
elevation*

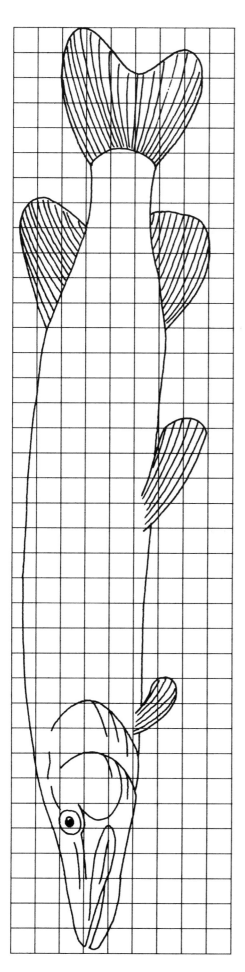

old colonial furniture, and is used for slats and hoops in chairs as it can be steamed and bent into a permanently curved shape.

When carving ash, the alternation of harder and softer wood requires a strong grip on chisels to avoid cutting too deeply into the soft grain. For the same reason, sanding will normally need a backing block – otherwise you end up with a wavy surface. The natural colour is almost white, though careful staining can produce a wonderful banded appearance, ideal for this subject. The technique for the pike carving is described here only briefly, as it is for the most part similar to the John Dory.

Making a start (Fig 1.15)

Working from a photograph or drawing, the outline is drawn to the required size using the grid or enlarged on the photocopier. My timber allowed a maximum height of 8½in (216mm) between the tips of the rear fins, which meant that a prize specimen 38in (965mm) long was possible, ideal for a dramatic impact when hung on the wall.

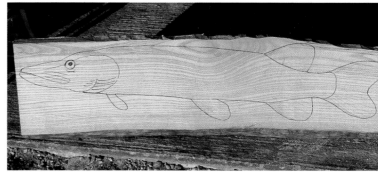

Fig 1.16 *The pike outline marked on to a 1⅜in (35 mm) plank of ash*

The outline is marked on the timber as before (Fig 1.16), and the edge cut all round to ⅛in (3mm) outside the line, preferably using a bandsaw. As I do not own one, I had to use the more traditional handsaw and chisel, which takes a little longer but helps to warm up on a cold morning start in the workshop (Fig 1.17).

Before you begin any cutting back to shape the body and fins, two preliminaries are necessary. First, fix a holding block underneath the plank; in this case a long 2 × 2in (51 × 51mm) strut was attached with four coach screws (Fig 1.18). Second, decide whether there should be any curvature in the fins – and particularly the tail – to suggest movement. Unless the timber is more than 1½in

FIG 1.17 *The outline sawn to shape*

FIG 1.18 *Temporary holding block attached with coach screws*

(38mm) thick, there is not much depth to play with, but even with just over 1in (25mm) I found it possible to angle the top of the tail fin and the body of the tail outwards.

The rear body and belly form the most bulky part of the fish, sloping back quickly from between the rear fins into the tail section. Roughly shape the whole body, cutting back the rear fins – but *not* the forward ones – to about ³⁄₈in (10mm) in thickness. With a carving of this size it takes quite some time to get the long body curves correct and smooth, joining all the fins at a convincing angle.

Fins and tail

It is not necessary to cut behind the rear dorsal and ventral fins; finish them to ¹⁄₄in (6mm) thick, except for a 30° chamfer at the back, towards the fin tips, to give a sharp edge. The pectoral and forward dorsal fins need a different treatment. Notice how they come out at an angle from the lower body: the tips are therefore near the upper surface of the plank, and they overlap the body, sloping downwards to join the body at some distance from the lower edge (Fig 1.19). Leave as much wood as possible behind these two fins, as the joints to the body are very short and on the cross grain. There is a play-off here between security and realism – the thinner and more natural the shape, the more delicate they become – you pays your money and takes your choice. At the base of each of these fins, leave a small protruding bump to represent the muscle which controls them. Shaping the curves of the body at the front can now be completed.

The numerous fine lines on each fin can then be cut with a V-tool or a triangular riffler file. At this stage the tool has to be held exceptionally firmly while cutting or filing over the alternating hard and soft grain, to avoid wobbles in the line's depth and width.

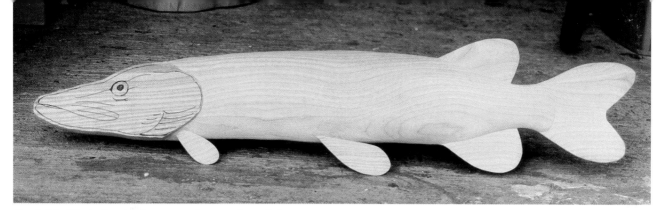

Fig 1.19 *The body and fins cut to shape and sanded*

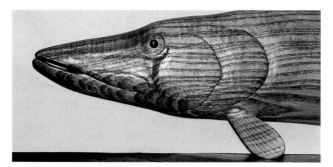

Fig 1.20 *The tooled surface of the head contrasts with the smooth body*

Head area

Once the body is sanded, the head and gill area is worked with gouges; I left it as a tooled surface to provide contrast and to suggest a bonier, more armoured appearance (Fig 1.20). Just the eye is sanded to a very smooth finish, the iris cut back quite deeply with a small gouge and stained dark. The mouth is drilled right through and can be cleaned up with a shallow gouge or a carving knife.

Staining and finishing

You can now remove the holding block and plug the screw holes with small dowels made from an earlier offcut. The size of the carving allows it to rest quite firmly on an old folded sheet or towel lying on the bench. While it is clamped face down, the angles at the back of the fins can be finished to give a uniform sharp edge round each fin. At this stage you may still need to reduce the thickness of the tail fin from the rear to provide a smoothly curved appearance (Fig 1.21).

Once the final sanding on both sides and the tooled finish to the head are complete, the carving can be brushed free of dust, the bench area cleared, and stain applied. As with all staining, test the colour on the largest offcut you can find – having ensured that it includes both a sanded and a tooled area. My first attempt used a colour which was called American Walnut; it looked just right on

the rag, but on the timber turned out far too red. Ash does not want to look like mahogany! Starting again with Medium Oak gave a far superior result. As a final check, the back of the pike is stained first. When dry, the carving can be turned over and the front stained. If desired, a second coat can be rubbed over the upper third (dorsal part) of the surface to make it a little darker – as a camouflage, most fish are lighter underneath, darker on top. Try not to allow any areas to dry before the staining is complete, as the edges may show darker.

Colouring or staining wood always requires great care. At this stage of a project all the carving work has been done, involving many hours of time and effort. If the staining then goes wrong, while it may not be a total disaster, it can be extremely difficult to rectify. Irregularly stained sections may require the wood which has been wrongly coloured to be removed, retooled or resanded. At worst, the entire surface of the carving may have to be reworked, which is never a welcome thought.

The carving is finished and sealed with two coats of Danish oil or similar. The pike does not need a glossy, varnished appearance; the oiled finish is quite adequate, though one final coat of wax may be used if required. Again, try it on the back first.

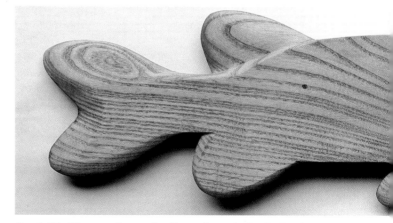

Fig 1.21 *The rear fins and tail seen from the back, showing how they are tapered so as to stand away from the wall*

CHAPTER 2
Plane-leaf bowl

THIS PROJECT looks fairly easy, but beware – it is not for the faint-hearted! To carve a flat leaf or a simple spray of leaves in relief on a background or base is not a difficult task, and is often given to the beginner as an exercise for the basic types of chisel. Here we are attempting something a little more ambitious: a leaf 'in the round'. Though it is not in essence much more difficult technically than a simple leaf outline, both the curves and the veins provide quite a challenge, not least because you are often working across the grain and exposing delicate, thin sections of wood around the edges.

THE INSPIRATION FROM NATURE

The idea came during an autumn holiday in southern France, staying in a town where the streets were lined with plane trees. I don't know whether leaves grow more vigorously in Mediterranean areas, but those falling to the ground appeared larger than I had ever seen before. As they dried they curled to form fascinating shapes, and the idea of trying to carve one became irresistible. I made drawings of the outline and of the crinkled shape (Figs 2.1a and 2.2), and tried to bring a leaf

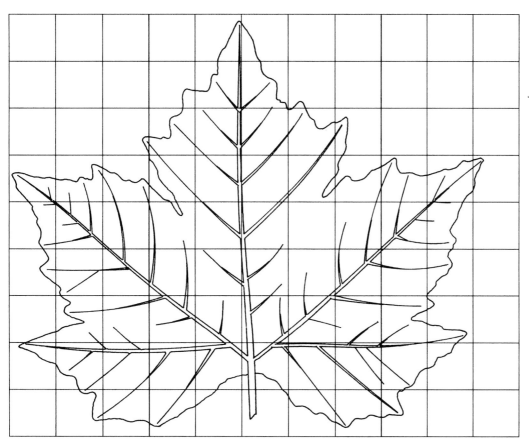

FIG 2.1*a* *Plane-leaf
bowl: plan view of the
flattened plane leaf,
used to mark out the
inside of the bowl*

FIG 2.1*b*
*Plan view of
the completed
bowl*

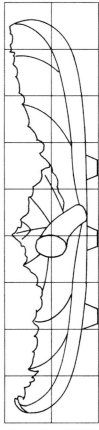

FIG 2.1*c*
End elevation

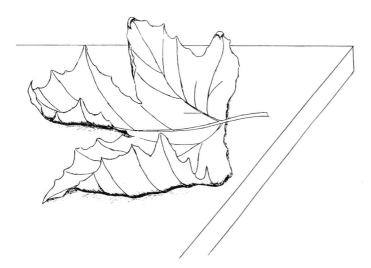

FIG 2.2 *My original sketch of the curling plane leaf*

FIG 2.3 *The flat leaf shape on the iroko block; at this stage it is about 10% oversize*

home, though it did not survive well in the luggage. It would have been interesting to try the sculpture in plane wood, which is used for carpentry in that area, but at home none was available, so the timber chosen was:

IROKO

Iroko (*Chlorophora excelsa*) is an African wood, the colour ranging from golden orange to mid-brown. It has durable interlocking grain and in some ways resembles teak, though the figure is more random and interesting. Both plane and iroko are ideal for external uses, such as garden furniture. For a carving like this, it might be better – certainly easier for the detail – to use a more close-grained timber, but then the finished carving might have a bland and disappointing appearance. Luckily, iroko grows extensively in West Africa and is widely available through sustainable sources. It also has more strength than teak and many other timbers, making it possible to carve the delicate edges necessary for the leaf, even in cross grain. The only problem sometimes encountered with iroko is the hard calcareous deposits found throughout the wood.

FIRST MAKE A BOWL

I felt that with this project it would be worth making the subject not only decorative but useful as well. The shape is ideal for a shallow bowl to hold light objects such as jewellery, and this has influenced the final design.

The piece of iroko available was 8½in (216mm) square and 3in (76mm) thick. The outline picture was adjusted, using a photocopier, to be about 10% oversize for the timber block (Fig 2.3; note that Fig 2.1a shows the drawing already enlarged). The reason for this is that once the block is shaped into a shallow curve it will have a greater surface area, and the drawing will then fit almost exactly. This is why I have found it necessary to give two different plans: one (Fig 2.1b) showing the final appearance of the bowl, to give the vertical outline; and the flat leaf plan (Fig 2.1a) which can be cut out and curved inside the bowl to give the correct angle for marking out the leaf serrations.

The top surface of the block is first cut down into the shape of a bowl. This can be done with mallet and gouges alone, but a quicker way is to rough it out first using a chainsaw or a power carving tool such as an Arbortech (Fig 2.4), and then finish the hollowing with gouges. Make the walls steep and the bottom a shallow curve, allowing enough wood at the rim where the leaf will curve over. The bowl is approximately 2in (51mm) deep to allow for the thickness of the leaf and the depth of the feet underneath, and is roughly circular; nothing has to be very accurate at this stage.

Place the drawing of the flattened leaf in the best position; the line from stem to tip and the major lateral

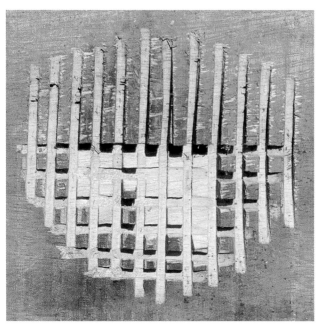

FIG 2.4 *This odd top view shows the 'FW rapid bowl excavation' technique. Numerous cuts have been made using the end of a chainsaw to remove waste prior to final hollowing with gouges.* IF THIS METHOD IS USED, THE WORK MUST BE SECURELY FIXED AND SUITABLE CHAINSAW SAFETY EQUIPMENT WORN. *Hollowing with mallet and gouges alone is equally satisfactory, but takes longer*

FIG 2.5 *The leaf plan is placed inside the bowl to determine where undercutting is required; this is indicated by the shaded areas*

curls need to be roughly along the grain, but not precisely. Mark where some thickness of wood needs to be left for the tighter curls around the edge (Fig 2.5). Undercut these with a reasonably large, almost semicircular gouge, ideally a frontbent gouge. It should now be possible to place the pattern entirely inside the bowl and draw the outline of the leaf all around.

HOLDING IN THE VICE

Before starting any external rounding, it will be necessary to make a projection from the base so that the piece can be held in the vice. It might be possible to screw a holding block on to the base, but then the screw holes would have to be filled later, so it is probably better to form a temporary hold for the vice by sawing a triangle about ⁵⁄₈in (16mm) deep around the position of the feet, with sides about 4in (100mm) long and with flattened apexes (Fig 2.6). The excess wood around the triangle can be cut away with saw and chisels; you can begin to shape the

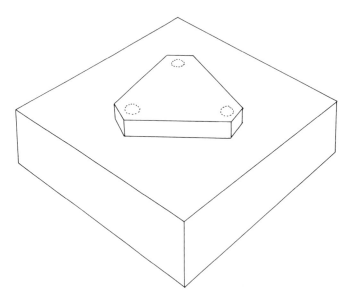

FIG 2.6 *A view of the underside, showing the vice-hold cut into the base; the dotted ovals indicate the eventual foot positions*

curvature of the base at this stage, but leave the leaf fairly thick at the moment. The carving can now be held securely in the vice in an upright position.

FIG 2.7 *The first stage in shaping the outside of the bowl:
the corners have been sawn off and the leaf outline roughly
cut out. Now the rounding process can be commenced*

FIG 2.8 *Veins on the top surface roughly set in. Most of
the leaf edge has been reduced in thickness, except at the
lower left*

FIG 2.9 *Another view of the same stage: the vice-hold below is clearly visible*

A BOWL BECOMES A LEAF

Now at last we can begin to see where we are. Cut out the shape of the stem with saw and chisels. Note that the stem has been unnaturally thickened for practical reasons: it will eventually form a handle for the bowl. Saw off the bulk of the waste on the outside, then cut around the leaf outline, leaving ⅛in (3mm) excess all around (Fig 2.7). It is best to use hand-held gouges rather than a mallet from now on. Next, work the outside (underneath) curves to match those inside, so that the thickness tapers from ⅜in (10mm) at the centre of the leaf to as thin as you dare around the edges, bearing in mind that before long more wood will need to be cut away on both sides to show the veins. Where the edges curl across the grain a fair amount of care is needed, using chisels as sharp as possible; hone the edges regularly as soon as the slightest dullness is noticed.

LEAF VEINS

Once the overall shape is satisfactory, begin work on the inside veins (Figs 2.8 and 2.9). On many natural leaves, the veins on the upper surface show almost as grooves; if you want an easier option, these can be shown on the carving as shallow grooves in the leaf surface. However, close inspection of the plane leaf reveals that the veins protrude on both sides, and for this project it was decided to make them stand out sufficiently to be clearly visible.

Use your original pattern to mark the position of the veins on the wood surface. Notice that although almost all natural living things are bilaterally symmetrical, they are not *exactly* so, and the vein patterns on opposite sides of the centre line do not need to match exactly.

The sides of the veins can now be cut carefully with a V-tool; this needs to be done with a fair degree of accuracy if they are to look anything like natural. Obviously they will taper slightly from the centre to the edges of the leaf. Start by making the veins too thick, particularly where they run across the grain; later they can more easily be trimmed to the correct width. The level between the veins now has to be lowered using an almost flat gouge. Near the centre of the leaf this is all straightforward, but where the edges curl over, things become more tricky. Life is made easier if you have several frontbent gouges and a curved V-tool. Right under the curl is very difficult to get

at, even to see what you are doing – but I did warn you that this project was not for those of a nervous disposition. The work is fairly tedious and may need to be carried out in shorter working sessions than normal over quite a long period. The slightest slip of a chisel or wrong angle of cut where the veins run across the grain could entail recutting at a lower level (if there is enough thickness available), and it is at this point that you may wish you had used a more close-grained timber!

WORKING THE LOWER SURFACE

Having completed the inside (top) of the leaf, the process is now duplicated underneath. However, now we face the problem of holding the carving upside down. I overcame this with an improvised arrangement of wood block and cloth inside the bowl, with the carving held down by a G-cramp. It didn't look too good, but worked quite well. (Parts of this apparatus can be seen in Fig 2.10.)

There is now no further need for the vice-hold underneath, so this can be sawn and chiselled away carefully, leaving the three conical feet intact (see Fig 2.11). The feet are carved so that they have a circular flat base ⅜in (10mm) wide and swell to a slightly larger diameter where they join the leaf. Now complete the curve of the leaf over the centre of the base between the feet.

The lower veins can now be marked (Fig 2.10). These must match the upper veins as precisely as possible – they are in reality the same vein in each case, seen from above

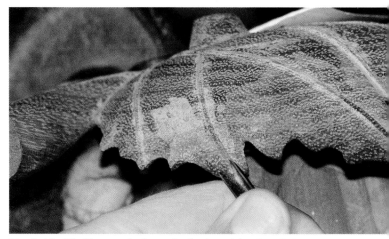

FIG 2.10 *Working on the lower leaf veins with a V-tool. One of the three conical feet is visible at the top. The padded block and G-cramp supporting the bowl can just be seen*

FIG 2.11 *The underside of the finished bowl. The feet are positioned as far apart as practicable for maximum stability*

FIG 2.12 *Top view. The veins form a strong, almost decorative pattern as the leaf curls upwards towards the edges*

and below. The lower veins are now cut and the interstices lowered in the same way as above. The nearer you work to the edges, the more careful you will need to be about the thickness. Too thick and it looks unnatural; too thin and there will be insufficient strength to withstand the slightest knock. Compromise is needed, and you can allow the curve towards the tip of each pointed section a little more thickness; this can be seen in the photograph on page 14.

FINISHING

I found that cleaning up all the veins, their edges, and the flatter curved sections between them could be continued indefinitely. On the whole I tried to avoid sanding, as I wanted to preserve a chiselled finish, but in some places the cross-grain veins needed very fine sanding. In the end, as with most carvings, you have to decide when continuing will only make things worse, and that enough is enough – this is the state of the art at the moment – time to move on. Certainly this project took longer than any other of similar size in the book, so don't be discouraged if it takes time to get it right.

Due to the oily nature of the wood, sealing and finishing was done simply with two coats of wax, each left to dry for rather longer than usual before buffing (Figs 2.11 and 2.12).

CHAPTER 3
Tree frog

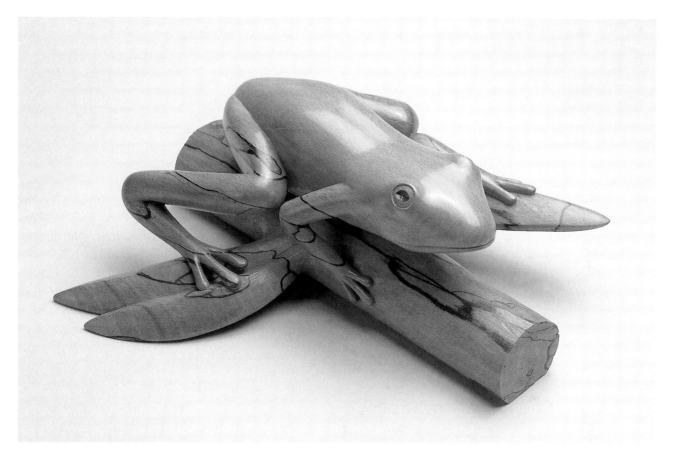

THE TAILLESS *Amphibia*, subclass *Anura*, come in all shapes and sizes, providing ideal subjects for the carver. Frogs range in size from the great North American bullfrog, with a body length of 7in (178mm), which will eat ducklings for breakfast, down to almost tadpole size. Few are more interesting than the tree frogs, which are found mainly in the South American rain forests, though species live in every continent, including Europe. Many are brightly coloured, and most have a smooth skin which shines with the permanent moisture of their surroundings. Their feet are seldom webbed, as they have little occasion for swimming, normally breeding in the small pools of standing water which form in tree boles. Instead, the toes are long, with the ends padded for getting a grip on the slippery leaves and branches. Most tree frogs catch their prey by a sudden extension of their long and remarkably sticky tongue. I have seen a wonderful carving which froze the moment when the extended tongue picked up a hapless bug, but this project is a little less ambitious.

BEECH

The timber used for this carving was European beech (*Fagus sylvatica*). Because of the strength of its close-grained structure, beech is used widely in furniture-making, particularly where strong mortise and tenon joints are required, or where the whole object is liable to receive rough handling (such as the old-fashioned classroom desk). Many carvers will own chisels fitted with beech handles. American beech (*F. grandifolia*) has

FIG 3.1*a Tree frog: plan view*

a coarser quality than the European species, and is normally a darker, reddish-brown colour. As a timber for carving, although beech will take fine detail, the grain is not particularly interesting. So, apart from the strength needed at the joints, it was only chosen for this project because the block I had was marked with veins of black

spalting. Spalting can produce beautiful patterns, but it does indicate the first signs of decay, so the wood may be softer than one would wish – or at worst, verging on the crumbly, which makes it impossible to carve accurately.

The section I had in stock was a 9in (229mm) cube, with evidence of two major shakes along the grain. The

FIG 3.1*b Right side elevation*

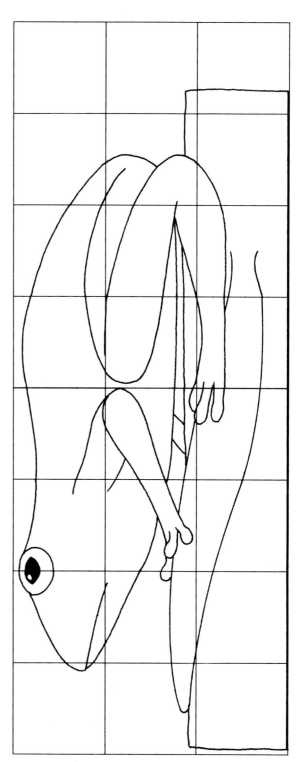

FIG 3.1*c Left side elevation*

timber was split with an axe along these two lines to produce a piece 9 × 9 × 4½in (229 × 229 × 114mm), approximately the required size for the carving. Any closed-grained timber could be used, ideally with some kind of exotic grain or colouring to add interest (see the frogs on page 164 for an example).

THE CONCEPT (Fig 3.1*a–e*)

The idea is to situate the frog on a small branch with thick side leaves. Three legs will rest on the leaves, and the other hold on to the branch. The final stage of carving will separate the body of the frog from the underlying branch

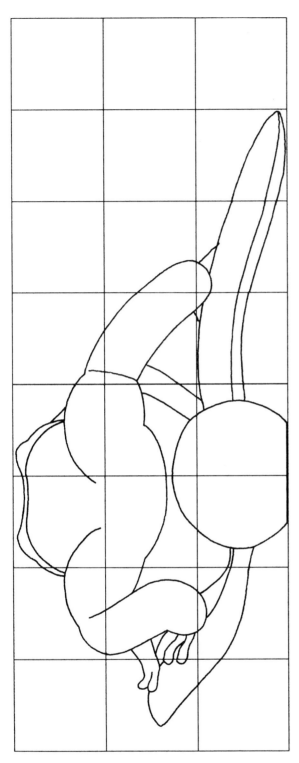

FIG 3.1d *Rear elevation*

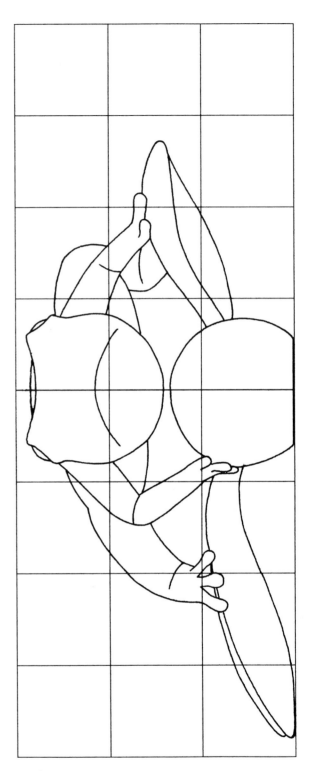

FIG 3.1e *Front elevation*

so the animal appears to be free-standing. To give stability, the leaves on one side will curl down slightly to provide part of the base. As they need to be reasonably strong, a shallow triangular 'fleshy' shape is used.

For this project I have chosen a larger size of tree frog for ease of carving, so the body is 5½in (140mm) long, the branch projects about an inch (25mm) either end, and the overall width is 7in (178mm). With any carving, the final

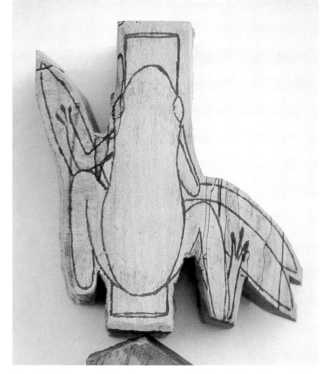

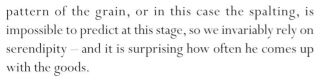

FIG 3.2 *The plan is marked on the surface of the piece of spalted beech*

FIG 3.3 *The vertical plan sawn and chiselled to about ⅛in (3mm) oversize*

pattern of the grain, or in this case the spalting, is impossible to predict at this stage, so we invariably rely on serendipity – and it is surprising how often he comes up with the goods.

Once the plan view has been marked (Fig 3.2), cut the timber roughly to the outline with mechanical or hand saw and trim with chisels, leaving at least ⅛in (3mm) of spare timber outside the lines (Fig 3.3). Before carving begins in earnest, turn the piece over and plane the base absolutely flat if necessary, then saw the ends of the branch parallel so that the piece can be held securely in the vice. As the base of the finished carving will be a relatively thin flat strip on the underside of the branch, it is not possible

or necessary to screw the piece to a carving stand. Clamping each end of the branch in the vice works very well, as the carving can easily be rotated through 360° or reversed end to end, giving every possible angle for working – later you will definitely need this flexibility.

STARTING TO CARVE

The main tool work now begins, and starting from the top downwards works very well. I found that this carving, more than most, was an experience of 'finding' the subject in the wood, like exposing a fossil encased in rock (Fig 3.4).

FIG 3.4 *View from the left, showing the upper body and limbs shaped*

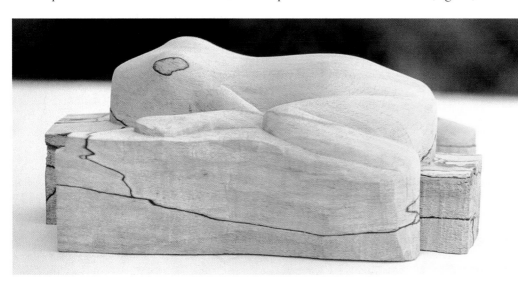

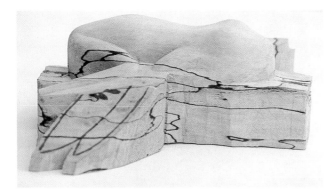

FIG 3.5 *The right-hand side at the same stage*

FIG 3.6 *A top view at the same stage shows the leg positions in relation to the body: rear right and fore left extended, the other two close*

Begin by shaping the curves of the head and back. I seldom use a mallet for small carvings, preferring hand-held tools to pare away the waste – mainly shallow gouges, and a medium-sized V-tool to define edges. The highest points are the eyes and the two ridges on either side of the backbone towards the tail. As you work downwards, begin to shape the upper surfaces of the limbs (Figs 3.5 and 3.6).

Before working on the two lower sections of the limbs, on either end of the squared branch draw a circle about 1¼in (32mm) in diameter, with a flattened base ½in (13mm) wide, to indicate the cross section of the branch. Draw the horizontal level of the leaves; the two leaves

together on the right will slope gently from the centre of the branch down to base level (Fig 3.7); that on the left will begin by curving upwards from the centre of the branch and then curve the other way, towards the horizontal, as if bent down slightly due to the pressure of the left forelimb (see Fig 3.9).

LIMB SHAPES

The lower parts of the limbs can now be carved, taking care to leave sufficient depth to form the acute angle of the joints at the knee and ankle. Notice that to add interest, the legs and arms on each side are set at different angles. Start with the right-hand side. Once the angles of the top surface of the limbs are correct, the oval shape of each limb can be carefully set in (Figs 3.7 and 3.8). At each leg joint a groove needs to be made between the inside angles. For the knees and left elbow this will be on the upper and lower surfaces – the joint is almost horizontal. For the ankles and right elbow the joint is vertical, and the grooves therefore fall on either side. (This can be seen most clearly in the pictures of the finished carving.) With each limb, leave plenty of wood just above the junction with the leaf for the toes to be carved later; bear in mind that the right forearm is resting on the branch rather than on one of the leaves (Fig 3.7).

While carving the lower limb sections, the leaves are roughly shaped so that the foot rests on them in a realistic way. Working inside and under the legs is in fact quite tricky; for some of the angles it is impossible to work with the grain. For cutting against the grain, an extremely sharp, long-bevelled chisel is required. It will also be easier if bent gouges are available for the most inaccessible

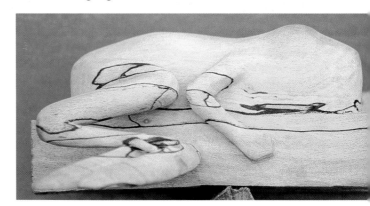

FIG 3.7 *Lower limbs are now set in. The rear leg rests on two joined leaves; the forelimb will hold the branch*

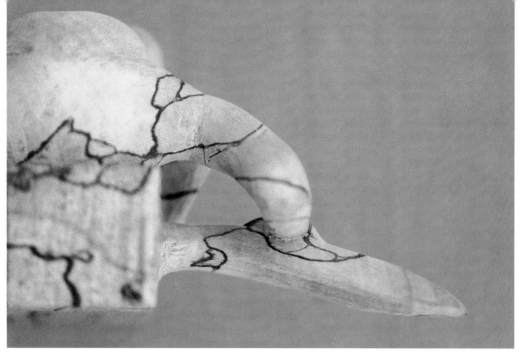

FIG 3.8 *This rear view of the right side shows the rear leg separated from the projecting leaves, which bend down to base level. At this stage the branch is still square and attached to the body*

places, together with an acute-angled skew chisel. Careful use of a drill with a long-shank bit may also help to separate the elbow from the body and the knee from the leaf below. The danger of drilling is either getting the angle wrong, or boring too deep. Either way you can all too easily produce a hole where there should be wood.

Once you are satisfied that the leg sections on the right are roughly the correct shape and at the proper angles, the underlying leaves can be tapered towards the branch, making sure enough wood is left at this cross-grain join to allow sufficient strength – remember the two leaf-to-branch joints will take the strain when the body is finally separated from the branch (Fig 3.8).

Now carve the left leg and arm in the same way. On this side all the angles are more acute, with the leg folded more closely, as both limbs rest on the one leaf (Fig 3.9).

All the limbs can now be rough-sanded and viewed from different directions to give a better idea of the correct taper for each section. Complete these adjustments, making sure each joint looks natural.

SEPARATING THE FROG FROM THE LOG

Before the limbs are fine-sanded and the toes carved, cut down at an angle under the mouth and behind the tail to the top level of the branch and begin to separate the body of the frog from the branch underneath. This is awkward, to say the least. The preliminary cuts can be made with a pointed Japanese saw. First saw almost through, working

inwards from either side just above the top of the branch. This leaves a long, thin wedge holding the body to the log to retain strength. The branch can then be carved to its approximately circular shape from each end, working under the body towards the centre. Underneath the branch, remember to leave about ½in (13mm) flat to act as a secure base. As the top of the branch is curved round, so the stomach of the frog can be shaped until only a thin line of wood is left joining frog and branch.

Once you are happy with the shape of the belly, the underside of the limbs and the branch, saw through the remaining wood, so separating the frog from the branch (Fig 3.9). The whole carving is now much more delicate; if it is still held in the vice at either end of the branch, very

FIG 3.9 *Left-side view of the completed carving, showing both limbs resting on one leaf. Notice the movement of the spine, the protruding eyes, and how the leaf on this side tilts upwards. A little more undercutting around the toes would have given a more realistic separation from the leaf*

little pressure can be placed on the animal. Clean up carefully underneath; in the most inaccessible places, very sharp tools may be needed to work against the grain. While working 'inside' the carving, the shanks of chisels can easily catch against the limbs and mark them; fishtail (thin-shanked) gouges are helpful here, if you have them. As with all complex carvings, the final details and sanding are done by starting from the most difficult places and gradually working outwards. This takes a fair amount of time and constant readjustment of the carving angle in the vice. With my own carving the statutory project disaster struck at this stage: slight pressure outwards on the right forearm caused a section of it to break completely along the spalting lines and ping off across the workshop. Fortunately it was recovered from amongst the shavings and could be glued back in place cleanly.

TOES

Although the toes are quite small, particularly on the forelimbs – in fact, *because* they are small – they will take a fair amount of time and care to get right (Fig 3.10). Start by making grooves between the toes, then slowly cut back with the smallest chisels available, taking care not to cut below the level of the leaf surface. Eventually the leaf should look unblemished under and around the toes; this will require careful use of riffler files, finally undercutting each toe so that it looks as if it is resting naturally on the leaf. Notice how the toes are splayed, with a rounded pad at the end.

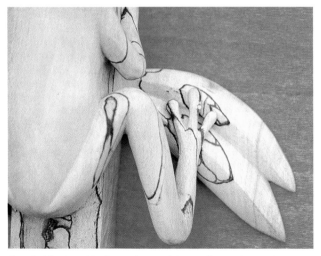

FIG 3.10 *Detail of rear leg and leaves from above. The toes are splayed, padded at the tips and resting on the leaves*

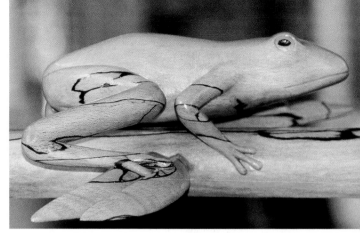

FIG 3.11 *Right view, carving complete. Happily the damage to the forearm is no longer visible. Note how the hollowed pupil adds depth to the eye*

EYES

Mark the positions of the two protruding bumps where the eyes will be situated, so that the line of sight will be slightly up and forward. Make sure the vertical and horizontal levels for both eyes are matched. On the carving illustrated, a dark patch was situated in just the right place for the left eye. When marking the eye circle, the position was fine-tuned so that this natural patch centred on the pupil. This looked fairly good, but made the opposite eye appear bland and lifeless; a better balance was obtained by staining the pupil on the right. Depth for the pupils is suggested by making two almost semicircular cuts around a centre line which is just off horizontal (Fig 3.11).

FINISHING

To finish the frog (but not the branch), a smooth and shiny appearance is required, so the whole of the animal needs to be sanded down using increasingly fine grits, ending with medium-grade wire wool (see the notes on finishing on pages 156–7). The branch, for contrast, is tooled lightly with a shallow gouge. Two coats of sanding sealer were applied over the whole piece, rubbing down with wire wool to de-nib after each coat. Note that sanding sealer can dry very quickly; in warm surroundings it may become tacky before the application of one coat is complete.

The frog was finished with two coats of polyurethane varnish, thinned slightly with white spirit (mineral spirit) to avoid any build-up or clogging between the toes (Figs 3.12–3.14).

FIG 3.12 *Front view of the finished carving, showing the angles of the limbs and leaves*

FIG 3.13
Rear view

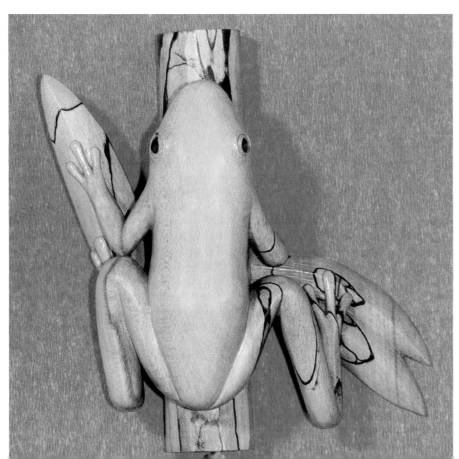

FIG 3.14 *The completed carving seen from the top. Back at the design stage, more 'life' might have been generated by placing the body at a slight angle to the branch*

CHAPTER 4
Butterflies
and moths

FIG 4.1 *Various timber samples, mainly offcuts, with colour and grain patterns which may be suitable for butterfly and moth wings*

BUTTERFLIES AND MOTHS together make up the order of insects called *Lepidoptera*, meaning 'scale wings'. The infinite variety of coloured wings, from glorious iridescent tropical butterflies to the dull brown of several temperate moths, is produced by the reflection of light from countless tiny scales which make up the surface above and below each wing. The array of colours and patterns is designed not only for display in mating, but also in many species for camouflage, or for mimicry of other, distasteful species. Male and female adults of the same species may be dramatically different in appearance.

Worldwide, there are some 150,000 known species of *Lepidoptera*; the division of the order into butterflies and moths is an artificial one based on various observable differences. In contrast to moths, butterflies tend to be more brightly coloured, fly by day rather than at night, hold their wings vertical instead of flat and generally have a more delicate body structure. Almost all butterflies have antennae which are slightly club-shaped, and are therefore known as *Rhopalocera* ('club-horned'), compared to the tapered or feathered antennae of moths, known as *Heterocera*. However, in each case there are occasional exceptions.

The life history of insects is one of the most incredible miracles of the natural world. Nearly all species move through four stages: egg, larva (grub or caterpillar), pupa (chrysalis), and imago or adult. The gradual emergence of an adult butterfly or moth from its drab, lifeless chrysalis is a phenomenon which has to be seen to be believed.

CARVING BUTTERFLIES AND MOTHS

Apart from beetles, butterflies and moths are probably the only other viable subjects among the insects suitable for woodcarving life-size – though some heroic carvers have succeeded with dragonflies, ants and others. Those of us living in temperate zones are thrilled at the summer appearance of their bright colours and variety of shapes, but these are nothing compared to the splendour of tropical species. One of the recurring features on wing surfaces is the dramatic 'eye' spots, strategically positioned so that they can be flashed at the approach of danger. These can be portrayed by judicious positioning of a suitably sized knot. Some promising timber samples can be seen in Fig 4.1.

Several carving techniques are described in this chapter, but the basic idea is to provide a mirror image between opposite wings, matching the pattern of colours to the figure of the wood. The technique of providing a mirror image of the grain pattern is based on that of children's paint-blob pictures, where a sheet of paper is folded and pressed on the wet blotches of paint, then unfolded and cut out as a butterfly. It is helpful to make a transparent working drawing so that the detail of the grain can be seen inside the outline (Fig 4.2).

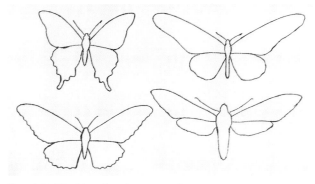

FIG 4.2 *Working drawings traced on to a transparent sheet, through which the grain and colour of the wood can be viewed*

Fig 4.3 Spalted beech with four adjacent bandsaw cuts, ready to explore the mirror-image grain figure. This piece was later abandoned, as the match proved unsuitable

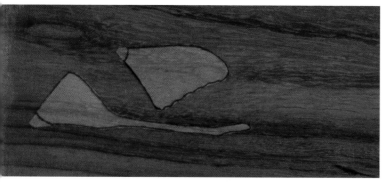

FIG 4.4 *Marking out wing shapes from a transparent sheet laid over the grain*

With carving, the procedure is to make a fine saw cut through an interesting grain figure (Fig 4.3), then open the two (or four) sawn sections like a book (the technical term for this process is 'bookmatching') and draw the wings so as to take best advantage of the grain pattern (Fig 4.4). The four wings can be carved separately (as in the Exotic moth project), in two sections (the Swallowtail), or even as one section with the body (the Hawk moth). In the latter case, the grain has to be remarkably kind to provide an acceptable match between the opposite sets of wings.

For each project, the outline shape is traced from a photograph on to paper or transparent film. If necessary, the size can be adjusted by a photocopier with a zoom facility, or by hand with the grid technique (see page 174). The subjects chosen are all tropical butterflies and moths – mainly because the shapes are more dramatic and the colours more brilliant than temperate species.

GIANT SWALLOWTAIL (Fig 4.5a–c)

Subject and timber

The shape, though not the coloration, is that of the African giant swallowtail (*Papilio antimachus*). This is in fact the largest butterfly found on that continent, with a wingspan of 10in (254mm). In the carving, to prevent things becoming unwieldy, the wingspan is scaled down to just over $5\frac{1}{2}$in (140mm).

The wood chosen is purpleheart or violetwood (*Peltogyne pubescens*), which comes from Central and South America. The figure is not particularly interesting, but the colour when freshly cut is a remarkable deep purple-violet which soon fades if it is not sealed. The grain is irregular, and care should be taken with cutting to prevent small splits, which can be disastrous at this scale. It is also extremely hard to work across the grain.

In this case, as the grain figure is very regular, the fore and rear wings can be cut from one $\frac{1}{4}$in (6mm) slice. The transparent outline is placed on the surface and moved around to find the grain pattern you think best for the wings. Mark the outline (Fig 4.6) and cut round with a small saw, or on a fine-bladed bandsaw. Offcuts are kept to one side for the body and antennae.

Wings

The wings are now in two sections: left and right, each comprising one fore and one rear wing. Each wing section is placed vertically in the vice and trimmed accurately to the outline using a small flat chisel. In the descriptions below, the body end of each wing will be referred to as the 'base'.

As the top surface of the wings is virtually flat, very little work is required here except to form the overlap between fore and rear wings. Mark a line where the wings join and, using a narrow V-tool, cut a groove along this line to a depth of about $\frac{1}{32}$in (1mm). This is done with the

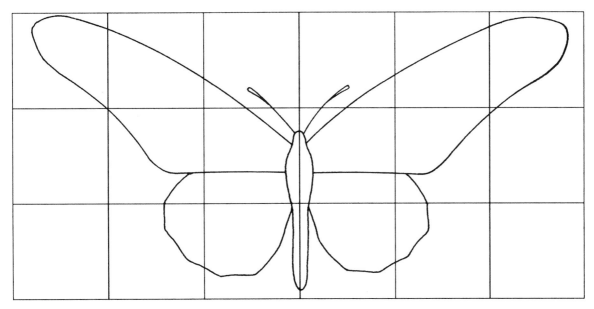

FIG 4.5a *Giant swallowtail: plan view with wings spread out flat*

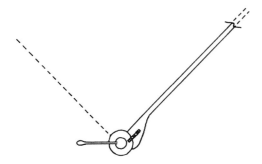

FIG 4.5b *Front view showing antenna* (left) *and wing joint with pin* (right)

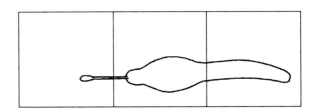

FIG 4.5c *Side elevation of body*

FIG 4.6 *Outline of swallowtail wings marked on the wood in a position which takes full advantage of the grain*

FIG 4.7 *Wings and body cut to shape; horizontal grooves represent the edges of the forewings where they overlap*

FIG 4.8 *Underside of wings. Reduction of the wing thickness has been started around the edges, leaving the base at its full thickness*

V-tool tilted so that the side of the groove adjoining the forewing is vertical, to give the impression of the forewing overlapping the rear wing. A flat chisel can then be used to reduce the rear wing surface slightly to the level of the V-cut (Fig 4.7).

In nature the undersurface is also flat, but where the base will be joined to the body we need to leave sufficient thickness to give the joint some strength. I find the easiest technique is to place the wing face down on a flat block held in the vice, then use a small clamp to hold the wing down – first at the base. Working with a small shallow gouge and flat chisel, pare away at the undersurface to reduce the wing thickness to about ⅛in (3mm) at the centre, curving slightly down to the edges, which will become almost sharp (Fig 4.8).

Move the clamp to the now reduced area of the wing in order to work on the base. Right at the base edge the thickness is left at ¼in (6mm), but it is reduced sharply at

a 45° angle down to the overall thickness of ⅛in (3mm)(Fig 4.9; see also Fig 4.5*b*). An incised groove, as before, represents the edge of the rear wing where it overlaps the forewing. Sand both surfaces to give a smooth finish (Fig 4.10).

When both wings have been carved to this stage, put them on one side while you work on the body.

BODY

An insect's body is composed of three sections: head, thorax and abdomen. These vary considerably in their relative proportions, and each subject needs to be studied carefully. If the body were simply represented as a long tube, this would spoil the appearance of the carving completely, making it resemble nothing so much as a small flying sausage.

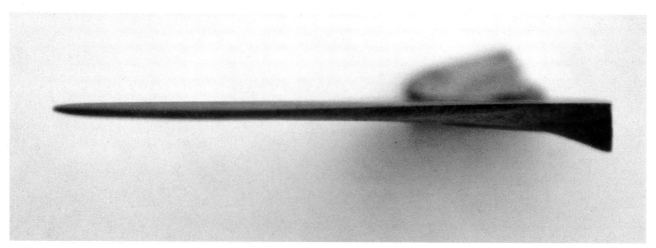

FIG 4.9 *A view of one wing from the front, showing how the thickness tapers from ¼in (6mm) at the base to an almost sharp edge*

FIG 4.10 *Underside of one wing, completed and sanded*

In most butterflies and moths the thorax (where the wings are anchored and the flight muscles operate) is the widest part, the abdomen the longest. Although in one sense separate, the three sections blend into each other with only a hint of constriction between them.

The offcut set aside earlier is cut to be $^5/_{16}$in (8mm) square in section and about twice as long as the body; the extra length provides a vice-hold during carving. The outline of the body is marked, and the body carved to shape. The procedure is really blocking out in miniature. Small gouges and chisels are required, and the shape must be checked from all angles so that it ends up bilaterally symmetrical in the vertical plane. The horizontal plane is shown in Fig 4.5*c*.

Matching wing to body

Shaping the base of each wing to fit the rounded body exactly can only be done by trial and error – though try to make the errors small. Basically, the small flat end of the wing has to be made concave to fit around the thorax. The critical point is where the top surface of the wing butts on to the body: eventually there should be no visible gap. As the thorax is convex in two planes, so the wing base must be concave to match. (Although it would be simpler to form flat areas on each side of the thorax instead, this would inevitably look unnatural.)

Before starting, decide at what angle the wings will be placed. With moths this is practically horizontal; butterflies at rest hold their wings vertical or at about 45°. The latter position will be used here, as wings held vertically would hide the top surface entirely.

Clamp the wing upright in the vice, base uppermost, protecting both sides with a small cloth. Using a ¼in (6mm) no. 7 or 8 gouge, cut out the concave shape, regularly offering up the body at the correct angle to check on progress. This is careful, painstaking work and cannot be hurried. When you are satisfied with the fit, repeat with the other wing.

Antennae

Here we are into microcarving, close-up spectacles and possibly a magnifying lens. The antennae are tiny! For a butterfly, remember that they are slightly club-shaped at the end, and in nature the shaft has the thickness of a hair. It is vital to use a tiny section of wood where the grain runs exactly down the length of each antenna. To make sure of this, split a small section with a chisel, but allow the split to form naturally by levering it apart after the initial incision. Repeat this procedure until you have a section about an inch (25mm) long and ⅛in (3mm) square – about the size of a match. Experiment until you find a piece that splits fairly straight.

In all honesty there is no way this can be clamped, so holding it with one hand, and resting on a flat surface, use a very small flat chisel to gradually pare away tiny slivers. Get the club end right first: this is slightly angled towards the wing. Then work at the shaft, using the chisel as much as you dare and then reducing the thickness further with abrasive paper. Eventually, when you cannot proceed any further, it's time to stop, and work on the second antenna. From a visual point of view the two should match as precisely as possible (Fig 4.11).

Assembly

The order of construction is: fix the wings to the body, followed by the antennae. Using the 'pin technique' described on page 154, a pin or needle is inserted into the base of each wing, with a matching hole drilled into the side of the body at 45° to the vertical (Fig 4.11; see also Fig 4.5*b*). The joint on one side is glued – ideally using a wood glue which has a thin consistency, or even superglue – then body and wing are clamped gently in the vice to give sufficient pressure until the glue is set. Any excess glue can be removed with a dampened cotton bud. The gluing is repeated for the other wing, and again the

FIG 4.11 *All the parts ready for assembly, with pin dowels inserted in each wing*

assembly is clamped; as the wings are set at 90° to each other, this does not cause any difficulty. Once the wings are set, any final cleaning up is done around the joints.

Short holes are now drilled in the head for the antennae, with a tiny drill bit the appropriate diameter for the shaft. This is quite a delicate operation, and again the holes have to be made at the appropriate angle so that the antennae sit almost parallel to the front line of the forewings, though in the same horizontal plane as the body (see Fig 4.5*b*). They are then fixed with a tiny drop of glue.

Finishing

To bring out the colour and sheen appropriate for a tropical butterfly, I found that the best finish was yacht varnish. The first coat is applied after thinning with 25% turpentine, and this takes a good 24 hours to dry. The surface is then carefully de-nibbed with fine wire wool, and one more neat coat of varnish applied. Apply this slowly and evenly to avoid tiny bubbles which will

mar the final 'iridescent' appearance, and during the long drying time rig up some kind of cover to protect the surface from dust.

Mounting

Needless to say, we have omitted an important part of the insect's anatomy – the legs. At this scale they are really too tiny to carve, and if sufficient care has been taken with the rest of the carving, only a rabid perfectionist could complain about their omission.

The butterfly can be mounted on any suitable base – a coloured pebble or a piece of bark, for example – by gluing the underside of the body to the mount. Or, using something like Blu-Tack, it can be fixed on a more temporary basis to any piece of furniture. It will look best set at a jaunty angle, for example on a shelf, or anything which is seldom disturbed by passing traffic.

The peacock butterfly in walnut, seen in the foreground of the photograph on page 30, is made in the same way as the swallowtail.

EXOTIC MOTH (Fig 4.12)

This is based on the Madagascan moon moth (*Argema mittrei*), one of the strikingly beautiful *Saturniidae* family. In real life this moth is bright yellow with a dominant eye spot on each wing, but I chose it for its splendid shape, particularly the trailing rear wings. The wood chosen is padauk (*Pterocarpus sp.*) – orange rather than yellow, but it is the overall effect of shape and bright colour, rather than slavish copying of the original, that we are looking for.

Padauk

There are various species of padauk wood, from Africa, Burma, Thailand and the Andaman Islands. The colour varies from blood-red, through orange to purple-brown, often with darker streaks. Like purpleheart, the grain is irregular and interlocking, requiring particular care when working detailed sections. I chose a piece which was an especially vivid orange colour.

Having given one butterfly project in detail, for the others I will describe each step only briefly, focusing on those points where the technique differs from the previous carving.

Making the exotic moth (Fig 4.12)

Working from two ¼in (6mm) slices, the positions of the four separate wing shapes are selected to take maximum advantage of the grain pattern (Fig 4.13). In this case the lower end of each forewing will extend by ¼in (6mm) to allow for a small rebate for joining to the hind wing (shown in Figs 4.12 and 4.14). The wings are cut out and trimmed to the outline as previously.

Before trimming the underside of the wings to shape, work on the overlap and rebate. Clamp the forewing on a flat surface, topside uppermost, mark the joint line and, using a V-tool, cut down a ¹⁄₁₆in (2mm) step on which the hind wing will sit. Next, working on the hind wing clamped upside down, mark the size of the forewing

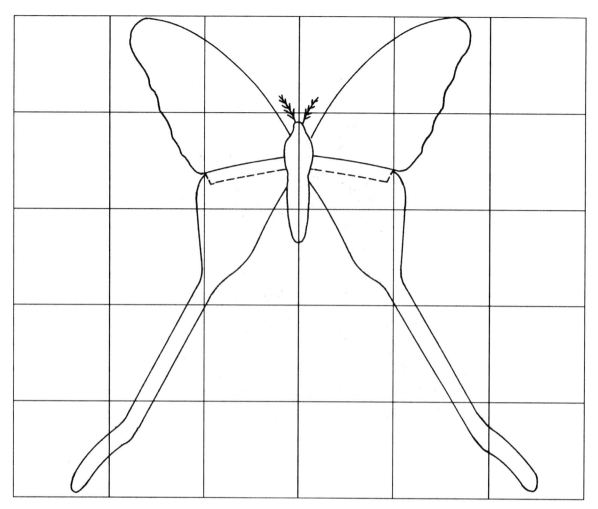

FIG 4.12 *Exotic moth: plan view with wings spread out flat*

FIG 4.13 *Fore and hind wings of the exotic moth marked on one of the bookmatched slices of padauk.*

rebate. Again using the V-tool and a small flat chisel, cut a step down (from the *lower* surface of the wing) to leave just ¹⁄₃₂in (1mm) of wood for the overlap. Now place the two wings together and trim the leading edge of the hind wing until it fits exactly into the rebate (Fig 4.14). During this process you may need to trim the back of the rebate in the hind wing. Once the match is satisfactory, glue the two wings together, pressing them together with a small

FIG 4.14 *Fore and hind wings with rebate cut and shaped*

clamp. Repeat the procedure for the opposite pair of wings. Now that there are two wing sections, the carving can proceed using the same techniques as for the Swallowtail project.

FIG 4.15 *The main components, with the wings ready for assembly. The body is roughly shaped and still has the long vice-hold*

FIG 4.16 *The left wing section fixed to the body. The right wings are ready for gluing, with pin dowel showing*

A few differences need to be borne in mind:

- Remember that, since this is a moth rather than a butterfly, the body is somewhat more bulky. Fig. 4.15 shows the body during carving, with a long vice-holding section which will be removed once the body shape is complete.

FIG 4.17 *An experiment in carving a feathered antenna. The antenna with its shaft is just under ½in (12mm) long*

- The wings are mounted horizontally rather than angled upwards (Fig 4.16). Having said that, on reflection my own attempt left the wings too flat, giving a lifeless or display-cabinet appearance. A slight upward, or downward, angle of a few degrees would be more natural in the resting moth.
- The antennae in this species are feathered rather than club-shaped. To carve them with a lifelike appearance is somewhat fiddly, but can be done using an extended length as a vice-hold (Fig 4.17). In order to avoid any glue showing around the base of each antenna, providing the strength of the joint is not critical, ordinary white glue can be mixed with fine padauk sawdust before it is applied (Fig 4.18).
- The surface appearance of this moth is less iridescent than that of the swallowtail butterfly so, rather than using varnish, it can be finished with three coats of sanding sealer before waxing.

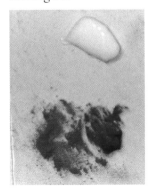

FIG 4.18 *White water-based glue mixed with fine padauk sawdust for use on the antennae*

HAWK MOTH

The hawk moths of the world all have a remarkably similar shape. They are strongly built and streamlined for swift flight. Many have a particularly long proboscis for extracting nectar from flowers with a tubular corolla. The subject for this project is Darwin's hawk moth (*Xanthopan morganii*) from Madagascar. The naturalist Charles Darwin postulated that a certain giant orchid with a flower almost a foot (300mm) long required an insect with an exceptionally long proboscis for pollination. Many years later, such a moth was discovered and named after him. Its general shape is almost identical to several temperate species, such as the privet hawk moth found in Britain.

Olivewood

The timber used is olive (*Olea hochstetteri*), chosen for its irregular, marbled figure, ideal for portraying the camouflage pattern of this moth. Olive is very easy to work, though like teak it is inclined to be oily and will quickly clog abrasive paper. It has a characteristic pleasant smell when freshly cut, and will finish to a distinctive natural sheen. It is most often seen in decorative objects carved or turned for the household – it is a safe material for bowls to contain food, for example. The timber is also used for attractive parquet flooring and smaller items of furniture.

Note in the photograph above how the grain pattern serendipitously marks the abdominal segments.

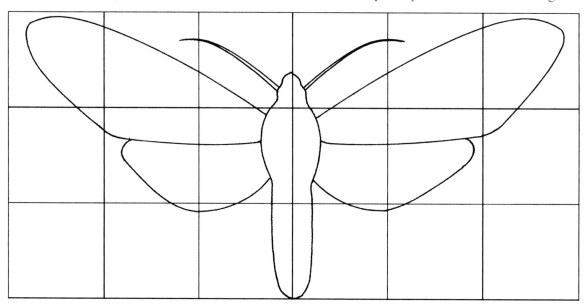

FIG 4.19 *Hawk moth: plan view with wings spread out flat*

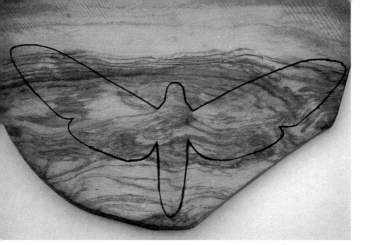

FIG 4.20 *The hawk moth outline marked on a ½in (13mm) section of olivewood, chosen for the grain match left and right*

FIG 4.21 *The outline has now been cut out, leaving a wide section around the abdomen for holding*

Making the hawk moth (Fig 4.19)

There are two major differences between this moth project and the others. First, it is carved from one piece of wood; and second, the top surface of the forewings is slightly curved from front to back, which in real life gives greater lift when flying at speed. If you have attempted either of the others, this will be comparatively easy. However, as the wings have to be matched from one length of timber, that piece may take a bit of finding.

Begin with a slice of wood ½in (13mm) thick. Choose where you can best match the grain left and right (Fig 4.20) – though the figure will change anyway as you carve the wing curves. I decided to let the grain run along the length of the wings rather than along the body. This results in a weak cross-grained abdomen, though it is thick enough to take a light knock. If the grain ran vertically, the thin section of the wings would be particularly vulnerable to damage.

Mark the outline on the surface, saw to the line and trim around the wings, leaving a wide section around the abdomen for holding (Fig 4.21). Working first on the top,

cut the semicircular shape of the top half of the body down to the wing surface, using a V-tool. From this level, trim the top surface of the forewings with a shallow gouge and flat chisel so that it curves very slightly both from base to tip, and from front to back.

Turning the piece over, reduce the wing thickness as far as practicable, starting at the wing tips and working towards the body. As the whole carving is in one piece and the grain is running along the wings, there is no need this time to leave a thick section at the base of each wing. Trim the underside of the thorax so that it curves round to the wing join (Fig 4.22). The abdomen can now be shaped all round; take extra care, as its length runs across the grain. The head is also cut to shape.

Even in this one-piece carving there is in fact some construction involved, because again the antennae (which in this case have a tapering profile) have to be carved separately and added at the end.

The finish for this moth was two coats of sanding sealer and one of wax. The photograph on page 40 shows the final result.

FIG 4.22 *A view of the finished carving from below, showing the thorax curving round to the underside of the wings*

CHAPTER 5
Wren

ALMOST THE SMALLEST of the British breeding birds, the wren is a fascinating subject for carving; its tiny size presents quite a challenge, particularly when it comes to the legs and feet. Nicknamed 'Jenny Wren' – a name which is applied to both male and female birds – the wren has always featured in folklore, and has in the past been subject to persecution through the annual St Stephen's Day hunt on 26 December – a cruel practice dating from the Bronze Age. The winter is in any case a difficult time for such a small bird, as they face serious problems keeping warm in icy weather. A hard winter means heavy losses.

Wrens are usually seen flitting between the branches of dense hedgerows, seldom still and therefore difficult to photograph; in fact the inspiration for this carving came from a painting rather than a photograph.

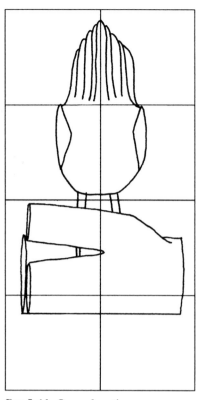

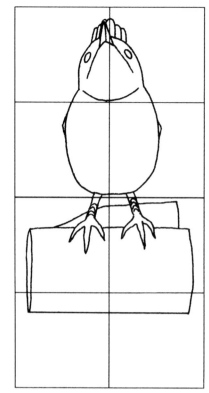

FIG 5.1a *Wren: side elevation*   FIG 5.1b *Rear elevation*   FIG 5.1c *Front elevation*

WALNUT

The wood chosen for this project is European walnut (*Juglans regia*) – though any walnut species or other dark brown, close-grained timber would be suitable. Walnut wood is hard and tough, but also elastic, which means that in small cross-grained sections it is stronger than most woods, bending under pressure before it breaks. This characteristic is particularly helpful with delicate and intricate carving such as that required here. The grain is highly figured and liable to change direction frequently, giving the surface a swirling appearance with bands of light and dark wood, aptly described as 'smoky-brown'. Walnut is therefore used extensively as a decorative veneer in furniture-making and for up-market car fascias, veneers from the stump and burr being particularly sought-after.

Apart from furniture, solid walnut is widely used for gunstocks, woodturning and, of course, carving.

North American walnut (*Juglans nigra*) is darker and of slightly coarser texture than the European, and is sometimes known as black walnut. The South American species (*Juglans neotropica*) is also dark, and polishes to a wonderful chocolate-brown sheen.

PLANNING THE CONSTRUCTION (Fig 5.1*a–c*)

Although it might just be possible to carve a wren from one piece of wood, realistically it is best done in two sections so that the body, then the legs and base are tackled separately. It is possible to buy metal birds' legs of various sizes from specialist suppliers, but these are only suitable if the sculpture is to be painted. Here we will attempt to design the log base so that the ultra-thin legs are given support from a branch underneath. The tiny claws will be carved directly on to the main log.

In choosing a piece of timber, try and find a piece for the body section where the grain is curved and can be aligned with the direction of the beak and also the upright tail. With the leg and base section, naturally the grain must run as closely as possible along the legs (Fig 5.2). Mark the lateral view of both sections on the wood and cut them out in block shape with hand- or bandsaw; using small gouges, trim to just outside the outline (Fig 5.3). The body needs to be 1¼in (32mm) wide, the base 1¾in (44mm) wide. A square piece of wood is left below the body as a vice-hold or, preferably, for screwing to the plate of a universal-joint carving stand.

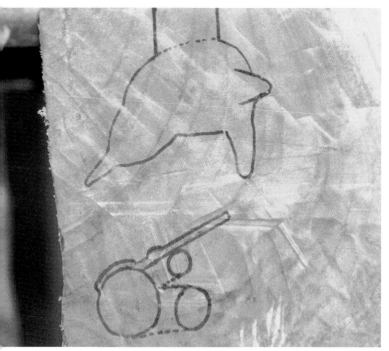

FIG 5.2 *The two sections marked in lateral view on a block of walnut. They are positioned so that the curved grain favours the beak, tail and legs*

FIG 5.3 *The body section cut to just outside the lateral outline, leaving a projecting vice-hold; head and wing details have been marked*

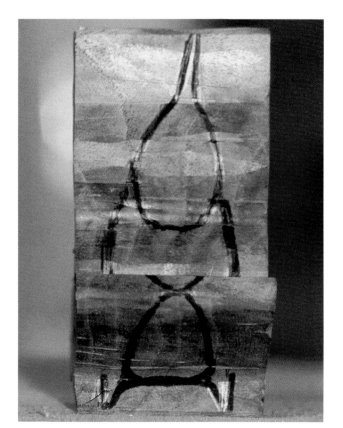

FIG 5.4 *The top view marked on the block; note the head tilted slightly to the right*

BLOCKING OUT THE BODY SECTION

Working first on the body and head, pencil a light central line above and below. It will give a little more character if the head is a little offset, so the centre line will kink slightly at the neck joint. Now mark the vertical view (Figs 5.4 and 5.5). The body is now cut to the vertical outline, leaving plenty of wood at the widest part, which is the wings. These can be left almost flat for the time being. The

FIG 5.5 *Top and side views marked out ready for carving*

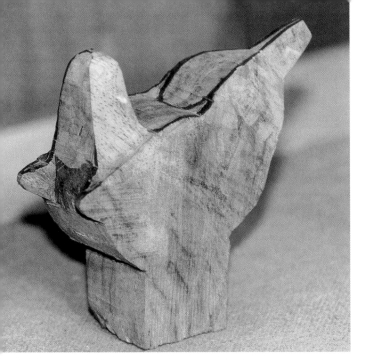

FIG 5.6 *The body section blocked out*

FIG 5.7 *Starting to round the body so as to leave the wings projecting either side*

tail feathers need to be cut into outline shape. Viewed from the front or back they form a long inverted U; viewed from the side they taper upwards and forwards in a slight curve almost to a point (Fig 5.6).

Whenever you use a saw on a vice-held carving, a good tip is always to saw *across* the vice rather than along. There is then less tendency for the piece to move if the vice has not been tightened sufficiently. If you are using any kind of mechanical saw, such as a hand-held jigsaw, extra care

is always required to avoid cutting into the top of the vice jaws; above all, keep well clear of any metal sections, which on contact could prove extremely dangerous.

BOSTING IN

Once the body section is blocked into shape, begin work on rounding the body with shallow gouges to form an almost circular shape around the chest, back and rear (Fig 5.7). Then start work on the head, making sure that both sides of the head have the same gentle curve towards the beak (Fig 5.8). The joint between head and body is quite a complex shape (see Fig 5.9) and the two sides will need to match accurately.

FIG 5.8 *Head, beak and tail approximately shaped. The bird is still too fat, to allow more detail to be added later*

OH NO!

All carving, and more particularly delicate carving, is fraught with hazards – although many textbooks omit to mention any disasters which were encountered before producing the impressive finished product illustrated on the page. As you know, that is not the policy of this book, in which I am trying above all to share the experience of carving, rather than to illustrate the production of perfect sculptures. Which is a long-winded way of saying that at this stage a nasty problem became apparent and then double disaster struck.

The nasty problem was the appearance of a significant crack at the base of the body. The more the lower chest was rounded, the wider the crack became. It was decided to leave this until later, when the shaping was almost complete and the temporary base could be removed to reveal how far the crack went. It was eventually filled with a sliver of wood shaped from an early offcut; but the hairline crack at the base of the wing can still be seen on close inspection, spoiling the lie of the secondary feathers (see Fig 5.18). Possibly, rubbing with a matching stick of filling wax might hide this, but in fact the crack at this point has no width, so there is nothing to fill. After finishing, I hope that, as the saying goes, 'a blind man would be glad to see it'.

The real disaster came in an unguarded moment while turning the carving around in the vice; it slipped straight out of my hands and spiralled to the concrete floor, clouting the beak and tail, both of which broke off. Unguarded words slipped out and the hunt was on among the chippings for the two broken fragments. The tail piece was found, but as far as I know the beak tip is still down there.

As it turned out, the head and beak were still too long and could be carved back so that the beak finished at the break. The tail, though, had to be mended. Perversely, the grain was not straight up the tail but sloping diagonally (it is very difficult with walnut to work out just where the grain is going at any one place); but it was a clean break. For strength, before the broken section was glued on, a short length from a household pin was inserted, point uppermost, into the base of the tail. Wood glue was applied, the top section pressed down on to the pin and an elastic band placed over the top of the tail and under the body to keep some pressure on while the glue dried. After later detailed work to the tail feathers, the join was invisible.

FROM BASIC BIRD SHAPE TO WREN

Once the general shape of the bird is complete, three areas of detail need to be addressed (Figs 5.9 and 5.10):

The face

Notice the shape of the blocks of feathers on the face around the eye. The beak fits back into the face almost to the eye, so that the (invisibly small) feathers around the

FIG 5.9 *Making a start on the face and eyes. Wing and tail feathers have also been set in*

FIG 5.10 *Detailed work in progress on the eye, using a ³⁄₁₆in (5mm) no. 9 gouge*

beak overlap on to it very slightly. The eye is set into the face but needs to protrude at the centre so that it is not lost. Later, the eyes can be stained almost black to give a more lifelike appearance. It is also possible as a finishing touch, after oil or some other matt finish has been applied to the whole carving, to apply a tiny spot of gloss varnish to highlight each eye. At this minuscule scale of carving, even the smallest chisel marks around the face can spoil the character, so once the shape is complete, it can be sanded with the finest sandpaper and finished with medium-grade wire wool.

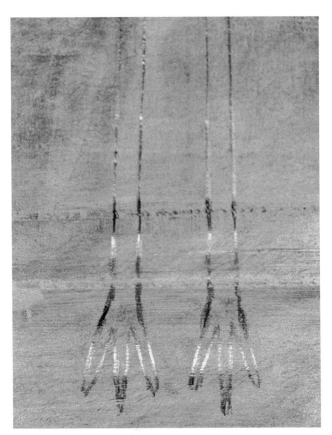

FIG 5.11 *Top view of the legs marked on to the lower section*

FIG 5.12 *Side view of the base with the legs and claws blocked out. Note the protruding hump just behind each foot*

The wings

The tiny secondary feathers are merely suggested by using a small gouge to stab the outline. Then pare back to the stabbed line with as much precision as you can manage, so that the long primary feathers will appear to emerge from underneath. With the primary feathers, the line of each join is first scored using a small skew chisel or carving knife. Then, with a V-tool or a tiny flat chisel, each feather is cut back so that it appears to overlap the one below. Behind each wing, where it projects from the back of the body, the inner line of the feathers is suggested with fine grooves (on the underside of a wing, the feathers overlap from bottom to top). The front of the wing projects slightly from the body and is approximately rounded to match the shape of the body underneath.

The tail

This is more difficult than the wings because of the curve, particularly where it is concave on the forward surface. Although walnut takes detail well, it is not the best wood for very fine detail, and the base of the tail feathers where they join the back is particularly difficult to get clean. Try to match the individual feathers front and back to give a realistic appearance to the tip and sides of the tail.

The rest of the bird can now be fine-sanded, if that has not been done, and if desired scraped over with a sharp chisel (or freshly cut glass, handled with great care) to give an exceptionally smooth surface.

BLOCKING OUT THE BASE SECTION

This second stage of the project is actually more difficult. Once the side outline has been cut out of the block, mark on the top surface the line of the legs (Fig 5.11). With a fine saw, cut these down almost as far as the intersection with the topmost branch. Continue with chisels to cut the legs in square section down to the small hump near the feet. Cut back around the outline of each foot to leave a pad which can later be detailed to form the claws (Fig 5.12).

FIG 5.13 *The branches are rounded and shaped before the legs*

FIG 5.14 *The base section complete. The legs remain joined to the smaller branch underneath*

IN AND AROUND THE BRANCHES

The branches are now shaped so that they appear to branch out from the log at one end (Fig 5.13). Getting the shape of the outside of the branches is fairly straightforward; the problems start with the inside, particularly where they join each other. The inside joints between the branches are inaccessible to say the least, and the difficulty is compounded not only by the legs, but also by the rear claw, which projects backwards from each foot. In fact, omitting the rear claws would make life a great deal easier, but if the finished carving is for a bird expert, beware!

A study of Figs 5.14–5.17 will show the inside structure, and it will be necessary to complete this difficult area of carving before working on the detail of the lower leg; otherwise the delicate leg can easily be damaged by the sides of chisels. It may be possible to use a mechanical burr for this work, but it is very hard to obtain a clean finish by this method. Piggling away with the smallest chisels – particularly skew and frontbent tools, all newly honed – is really the only way to clean up satisfactorily.

FIG 5.15 *Side view of the base section, showing the rear claws*

FIG 5.16 *A view from the opposite side. Strengthening pins inside the legs protrude slightly, and are left protruding when the legs are inserted into the body*

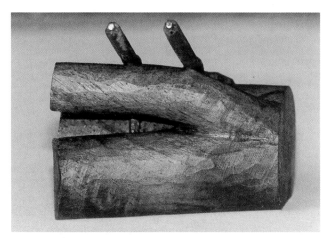

FIG 5.17 *Rear view of the base section. Note the tooled finish on the branches*

LEGS AND CLAWS

The legs can now be rounded and narrowed, leaving a small hump near each foot which is then lightly grooved. This 'knuckle' is anatomically part of the foot, as is the 'false shin' which forms the visible leg, up to the true ankle near the bird's body. It hardly needs repeating that at this stage the legs become extremely thin! As I was

worried that the grain did not run perfectly straight along the legs, I drilled a $^1/_{32}$in (1mm) hole down the centre of each leg as far as the knuckle and inserted an old carpet needle. This operation needs extreme care to ensure that the drill bit goes dead-centre down each leg. If you have not attempted this technique before, try it out on several matchsticks first. Where the leg rests on the rear branch, it needs to remain joined, but only just – as if just touching the branch.

Next cut out and shape the claws. Again, these are exceptionally tiny, but they will look far more realistic if they are not simply curved. The shape of each claw is made up of three short straight sections with knuckles between. If eyesight permits – or using a magnifying lamp – undercut each claw very slightly so that it stands naturally on the log (see especially Figs 5.14 and 5.15).

The cleaning up of claws and legs takes a fair amount of patience and time, but this will be rewarded by the final result.

ASSEMBLY

Finally, the two parts of the carving can be put together. Offer up the legs against the side of the body to ascertain the correct angle for the legs and their point of entry into the body (Fig 5.19 may help here). Pencil the entry line on the side of the body. Now place the upper ends of both legs at the intended insertion point and mark the exact position for each hole. Choose a drill bit the same size as the legs, and drill carefully at the correct angle to the required depth (Fig 5.18). This acute angle is critical and

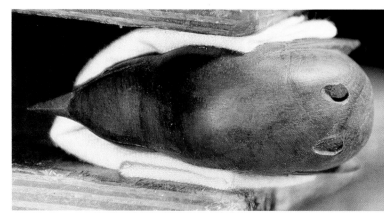

FIG 5.18 *Holes drilled into the body to receive the legs. The crack and repair described on pages 45–6 can just be seen in front of the left-hand (upper) hole*

FIG 5.19 *Throughout the carving process, aim for this 'Jenny Wren' pose which says: 'I'm not staying here long'*

will make or break the appearance of the carving. Take extreme care not to drill too far – that is, right through the body and out again near the tail section. Once the holes are the correct size and depth, the legs can be carefully inserted. With luck the fit may be so good that the two pieces will hold together without the need for glue. However, glue is always advisable in case of later wood movement, and should be applied before the legs are fitted; remember to wipe away any excess around the join immediately, using a damp cloth.

FIG 5.20 *The natural smoky-brown colour of walnut turned out to be ideal for this subject*

FIG 5.21 *When looking at a carving of any animal or bird, the observer's view should be drawn straight to the eye*

FINISHING

The carving is now complete (Figs 5.19–5.21). If you wish to stain the eyes darker, this can now be done with a fine artist's brush.

Seal with Danish oil or other oil finish – varnish would tend to clog the tiny details, though, as mentioned earlier, a final tiny drop of gloss varnish on each eye will help to bring it alive. Similarly, allowing one more coat on the bird than on the base may help it to stand out from the log, particularly in the case of the legs and claws.

Finally, rub down the entire piece with fine wire wool and apply one coat of wax using a small but stiff brush. When waxing delicate carvings, it is a good idea to have two 1/4in (6mm) paintbrushes set aside specially for this purpose, with the bristles cut right down to a length of about 1/4in: one is reserved for applying the wax, the other for polishing.

CHAPTER 6
A couple of sticks

FIG 6.1 *A wide range of different types of exhibition stick*

STICK-MAKING is a whole subject in itself (see the Select Bibliography on page 180), only partly related to carving – or at least to woodcarving – since many stick handles are made from animal horn or antler, while others, like the simple thumb sticks, are hardly carved at all. There are five traditional types of stick handle: thumb, crook, market, leg and half-head. Fig 6.1 shows a wide variety of sticks for sale at a wood exhibition.

Only a few types of tree produce branches straight enough and without large side shoots. The most widely used are hazel (*Corylus avellana*) and blackthorn (*Prunus spinosa*), though on occasion holly (*Ilex aquifolium*) and ash (*Fraxinus excelsior*) are seen. Though blackthorn is strong, it is heavier than hazel; the latter is the more popular, as it is more widely available and makes a light stick, more easily swung around.

Stick handles, particularly those of the crook shape, are more likely to be made of horn, antler, or even plastic than wood. This is because making the curve in timber poses the problem of cross grain. For this reason, wood for the handle needs to be dense, or burred (with random grain), or from a part of the tree producing naturally curved grain.

Dedicated stick-makers each have their own method for fitting the handle to the stick. Some prefer to use some kind of dowel: either a hardwood dowel inserted in drilled holes, or a metal rod such as a steel bar or headless nail, or a round tenon formed from the top of the stick to fit into the handle. Others use a double screw; this is first screwed into the stick, then the handle is screwed down on to it. On occasion a decorative spacer is inserted between handle and stick; this can be made of horn, hardwood or rings of leather.

A DECORATED CROOK

Of all the handle shapes, the crook presents the greatest challenge to the woodcarver. The curve required for a crook can seldom be achieved successfully by bending the timber by steaming and pressure; and if the bark is left on, wrinkles on the inside curve and splits on the outside are

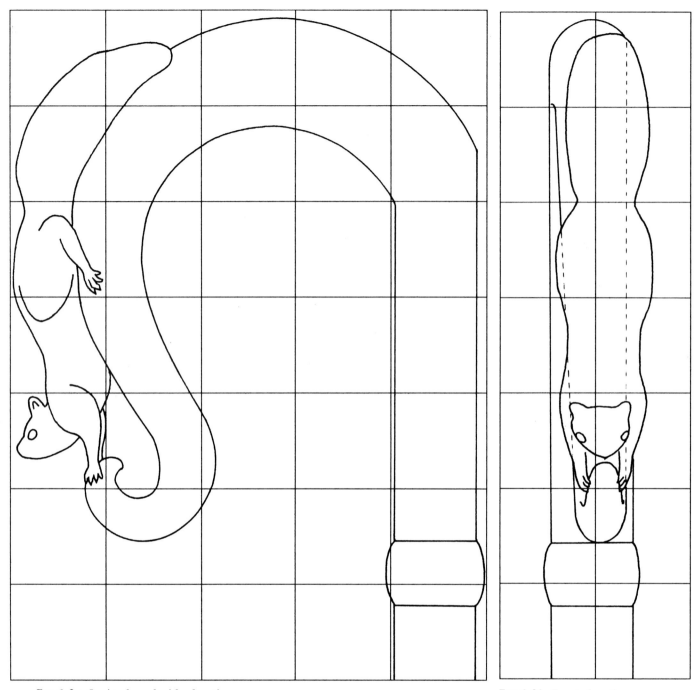

FIG 6.2a *Squirrel crook: side elevation*

FIG 6.2b *Front elevation*

inevitable. For this handle a large piece of laburnum fork was used; this had naturally curved grain which removed the need for bending.

Laburnum

Laburnum (*Laburnum anagyroides*) has chocolate-brown heartwood surrounded by creamy sapwood. The deep colouring, often combined with bold grain figure, has made it a favourite for woodturning, inlay work and small woodcarvings (large chunks are rarely available). Musical instruments have also been made from laburnum, benefiting from the wood's strength and ability to be drilled accurately; it is used, for example, in the making of bagpipe chanters. This project started with an overlarge fork from the main trunk of a garden laburnum.

Making a start (Fig 6.2a and b)

The idea for the subject came from a drawing by Frank Day in *The Craft of the Stickmaker* by Leo Gowan (see Bibliography). The fork was first sawn vertically to determine the layout of the grain. The original small drawing was enlarged to 6 × 5½in (152 × 140mm), then cut out as a template, and the outline marked on to the wood, matching the curved handle shape to the grain as advantageously as possible (Fig 6.3). Once you have drawn the outline on a suitable piece of timber, cut out ⅛in (3mm) outside the convex outline, ideally using a bandsaw, and across the base. The opposite face is sawn to make the blank 1¼in (32mm) thick. The inside curve can now be cut out. My method is to divide up the waste into narrow sections with several parallel saw cuts; one of the sections can then be removed with a V-tool or by drilling through it, and the others cut out with a small pointed saw.

The straight section of the crook, which forms an extension of the stick, is rounded using the inside face of a gouge of slightly larger curvature than the handle. Make sure the handle diameter is slightly larger than the hazel stick to be attached later. The top curve is also rounded as far as the squirrel's tail (Fig 6.4). At this point the outline of the squirrel needs to be marked accurately. The inside curve of the crook by the squirrel can now be gradually

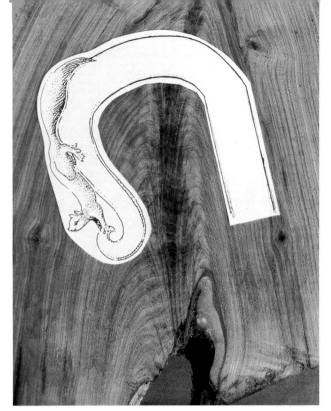

FIG 6.3 *Positioning the drawing to make best use of the curved grain*

tapered to a thickness of ½in (13mm) at the tip (Fig 6.5). The central hole at the end of the crook is carefully drilled through and the rough outline of the scroll carved to shape, leaving sufficient wood for the front legs to rest either side.

FIG 6.4 *The outline cut out and the plain part of the handle roughly rounded*

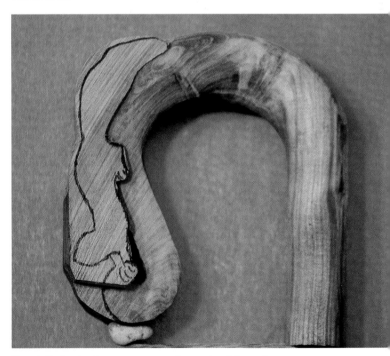

FIG 6.5 *Beginning to separate the squirrel from the tapered crook*

FIG 6.6 *A view of the front of the crook, with the plan view of the squirrel marked. The scroll of the crook has already been shaped*

Squirrels

In Britain there are two species of squirrel: the red (*Sciurus vulgaris*) and the grey (*Sciurus carolinensis*), which is the larger. The main physical differences, apart from the colour, are seen in the shape of the tail and the ears. On a larger carving more subtle differences, for example in the face, would become more important. For this project, as the more pointed ears of the red squirrel would be too fragile, I have gone for the grey – or more accurately, as the carving is so small, a sort of 'representative' squirrel.

Blocking out

Mark the outline of the squirrel as if looking from above the animal (Fig 6.6). Pare down the shape so that the outline is blocked out at right angles, using a small saw and

medium-size gouges as appropriate. Take care at the head end to leave sufficient width for the front legs below. Rough out the head, leaving enough wood for the ears, which stick up and slightly outwards.

The body and tail can now be rounded, making sure that the powerful shoulders and hip area show prominently from the narrower chest and stomach. As the shape is curved underneath the body, keep the curves of the crook smooth and notice how the crook gradually narrows towards the acute curve at the end. The lower part of the rear legs projects just a few millimetres from the crook, and can be carved in detail later. On reflection, since the squirrel is almost hanging down it might have been more realistic to carve the rear legs going out backwards (that is, vertically), as when coming down a tree. Either way, from here on we are into microcarving!

Refining the squirrel

At this stage it is worth sanding the crook to provide a smooth contrast to the carving of the squirrel (Fig 6.7). Where the body and legs join the crook, take time to avoid making any stab cuts into the crook, which will be difficult to rectify later. In particular, the wider upper parts of the handle must not get thinner than the stick which is to be attached later.

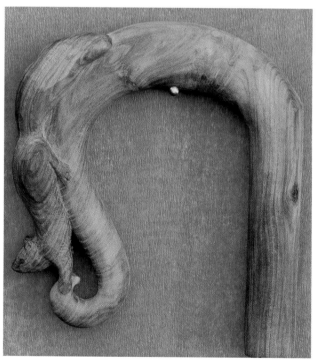

FIG 6.7 *The crook shaped and sanded, and the squirrel blocked out*

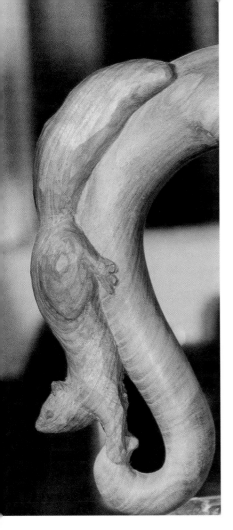

FIG 6.8 *Eye positions, limb and tail shapes set in*

FIG 6.9 *Top view of the squirrel, carving complete*

FIG 6.10 *The completed squirrel with its first coat of sanding sealer*

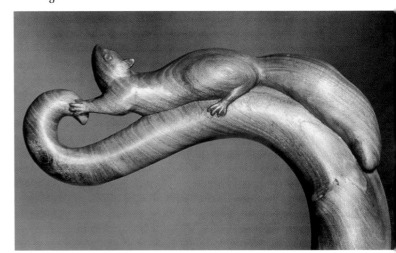

Carefully drill or cut the space between the forelegs, and between the line of the upper chest and the final turn of the crook. Roughly shape the forelegs and paws to stand naturally on the crook, which at this point tapers smoothly around in the shape of a scroll.

The head is approximately acorn-shaped, with projecting ears down just a little on each side. The eye is positioned halfway between the ear and the tip of the nose, on a slight bump. Some care is needed with the shape of the eye, which is oval – almost circular – with its long axis along the line from ear to nose (Fig 6.8). If you have a tiny gouge the size and shape of the eye, this is ideal.

The feet and claws also need great care – being so small, the wood becomes very fragile. If you can give some indication of the knuckles, rather than simply rounding each 'toe' and 'finger', this will look more realistic.

The squirrel can be finished with fine sandpaper or left with the chisel marks, as preferred; the stick illustrated was sanded and finally smoothed with medium-grade wire wool, and the whole crook sealed with two coats of sanding sealer (Figs 6.9–6.11). Traditional makers

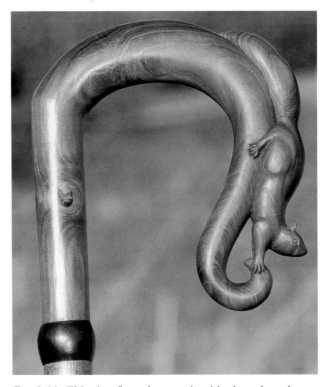

FIG 6.11 *This view from the opposite side shows how the tail disappears round the edge of the crook*

often recommend raw or boiled linseed oil as the sealant, though depending on the timber this may remain tacky for a long time.

Joining the handle to the stick

The completed crook can now be joined to the stick. It hardly needs mentioning that the stick chosen must have been seasoned, so if you have not yet procured a suitable length of hazel and cannot find a supplier, the carving needs to be put away for a year while a newly cut stick dries out. It is not necessary to find an absolutely straight length for the stick; even after seasoning this can be straightened either by prolonged pressure, or, as some professional stick-makers recommend, by careful heating using a hair dryer while bending to shape.

The join between stick and handle often has a spacer of contrasting wood or horn, which acts as a finger grip – particularly in the case of crooks – or simply as decoration. In this case I used African blackwood (*Dalbergia melanoxylon*), which is extremely dense and hard. The spacer is carved (or more easily turned) in the shape of a cylinder with slightly larger diameter than the stick. This is then carved to a convex, barrel-like shape using the inside face of a shallow gouge – trying it frequently against the stick, since the hazel stem is unlikely to be exactly circular. As the stick is covered in bark, the size at the joint is absolutely fixed and cannot be altered, so spacer and handle must be carved accurately to that exact size. From an aesthetic point of view, the straight section of the handle can, if necessary, be tapered very slightly down to the stick (which is also tapered), but not the other way – an upward taper in the handle will spoil the entire piece.

As noted earlier, there are various ways of fixing the stick to the handle, all using a dowel of some sort. For maximum strength a double-screwed metal dowel is as good as anything (Fig 6.12).

If an inserted dowel is used, all the meeting ends (of the stick, handle and spacer) must be accurately cut to 90° and perfectly flat. The dowel hole is drilled through the spacer first. This is then offered up to the stick and handle in turn, to mark the exact position for drilling. Drill these two holes vertically; then everything should be fitted and screwed lightly together. At this point any inaccuracy in drilling or surface angles will immediately become apparent, and can hopefully be rectified before any glue has been applied.

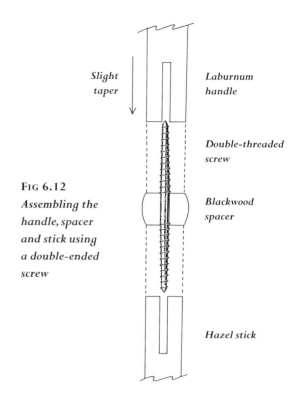

Fig 6.12
Assembling the handle, spacer and stick using a double-ended screw

Slight taper

Laburnum handle

Double-threaded screw

Blackwood spacer

Hazel stick

If linseed oil is used to finish the hazel stick, then after 24 hours it should be rubbed down hard with a cloth to remove any tackiness. Another possibility is simply to seal the completed stick and handle with wax. As a final touch, a metal or rubber ferrule can be purchased and fitted to the ground end of the stick.

A SHELDUCK MARKET STICK

This type is sometimes called a 'block stick', because the whole thing is carved out of one piece of wood. The stick is cut with a section of the 'block' (stock or stem) from which it grew. In this case the stock was growing horizontally and was cut to form a T with the stick itself (Fig 6.13), giving a suitable shape for a market stick. It is more common for the stick to grow diagonally from the stock.

FIG 6.13 *The hazel stick growing from the original stock*

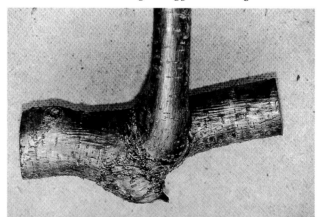

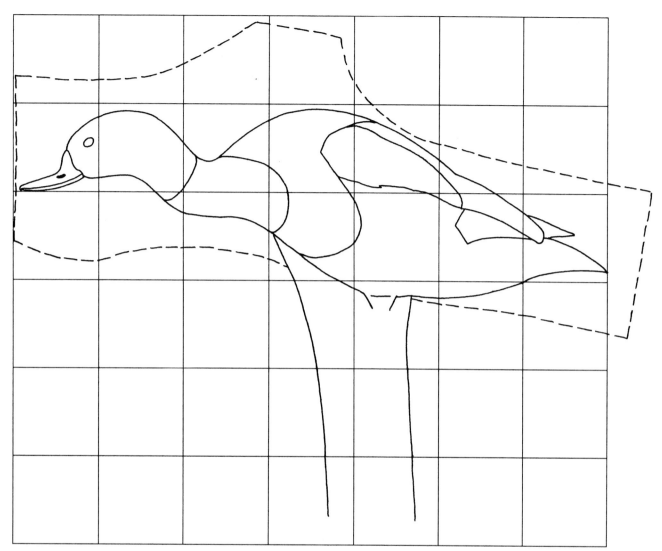

FIG 6.14*a* *Shelduck stick: side elevation*

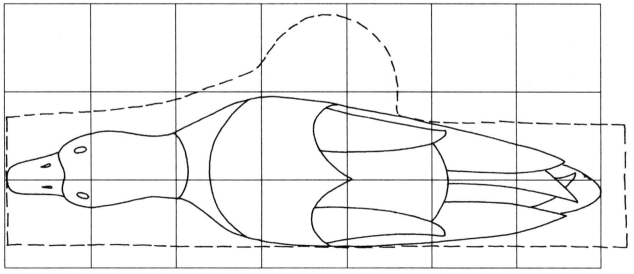

FIG 6.14*b* *Plan view*

Whatever the angle, a suitable subject must be chosen to fit the shape of stock which is to be carved to form the handle. Looking at the piece of hazel I had available, I really wanted to carve a polecat or another mammal, but nothing would quite fit, so what about a bird? It had to be something which worked well in an extended horizontal position, and a shelduck seemed to fit almost exactly.

The shelduck (*Tadorna tadorna*)

This is the largest of the British ducks, and an exception to the rule that drakes are always more highly coloured than ducks. Female camouflage is not required, as the nest is normally made in deep shelter or even in an old rabbit hole. The birds feed at low tide on sand and mud flats, often patting with their feet to encourage small creatures to emerge for convenient consumption. The characteristic almost horizontal position of the head may help the shelduck to see and hear the smallest movements in the ooze; it is also a pose adopted under threat.

Matching bird to timber (Fig 6.14*a* and *b*)

The outline was traced and photocopied to fit the size of the stem, and only slight adjustment of the original picture was required, in the back and leg areas. A template cut out of card is helpful at this stage (Fig 6.15).

The bark is pared away from the stock using a shallow gouge, and the lateral outline marked (Fig 6.16). This is then blocked out by cutting horizontally around the outline, using a saw where you can, and various gouges and flat chisels as appropriate (Fig 6.17). The vertical outline is then marked (Fig 6.18), and blocking out completed by cutting around the vertical shape in the same way. Note how the shape of the hazel stock dictated a slight bend of the head.

Keeping an eye on any photographs or pictures of the shelduck which you have available, remove all the corners to produce the rounded shape required. I tend to use very shallow gouges and flat chisels for this. Working on the body close to the stick becomes quite awkward, particularly if the grain is against you. In these cases a carving knife or a knuckle gouge (a gouge which is bent almost back on itself) can often deal with parts that other chisels cannot reach. On the other hand, the stick provides a useful vice-hold during the whole carving operation, providing it is padded with a folded cloth to protect the bark.

Part of the swelling around the joint between handle and stick may need to be removed, but be careful not to overdo this and weaken the handle. The detail of the junction can be worked out later.

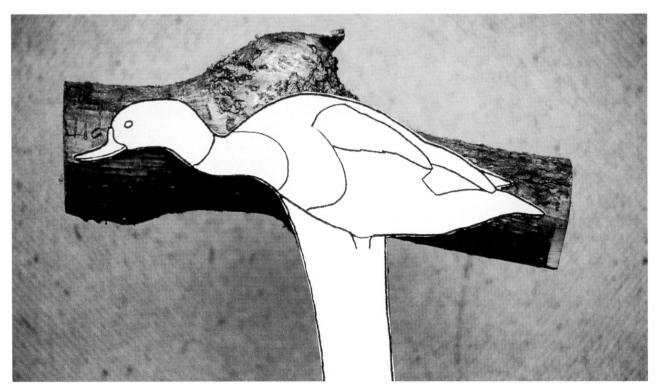

FIG 6.15 *The card template of the shelduck offered up to the hazel stock*

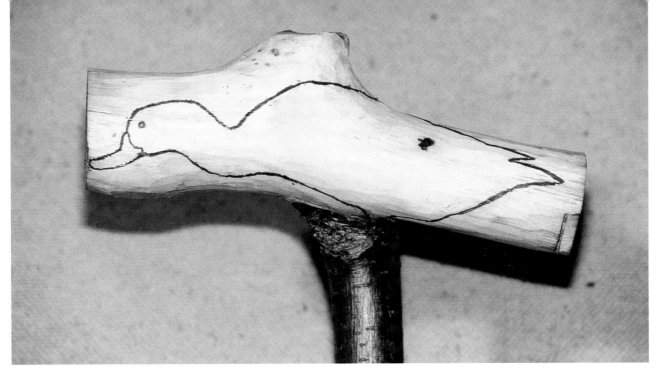

FIG 6.16 *The bark removed and the lateral outline marked on the stock*

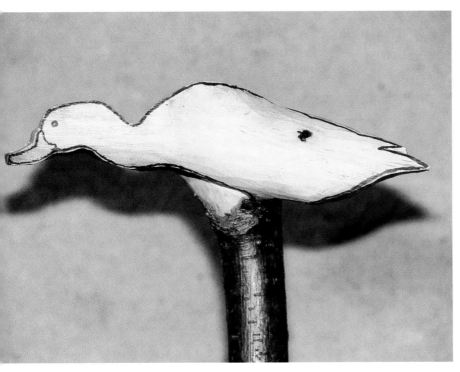

FIG 6.17 *The lateral shape cut out with saw and carving tools*

FIG 6.18 *The vertical outline marked on the stock. A slight curvature of body and neck was necessary, which happens to favour a right-handed grip*

FIG 6.19 *Plumage and other details marked out on the shaped duck*

Leaving the detail of the head and beak area for now, rough-sand the rest of the bird, taking care not to damage any bark on the stick. This sanding will help finalize the overall shape, and facilitate the next stage, which is to mark lightly with a pencil the shapes of the wings, tail and main blocks of feathers (Fig 6.19).

Once you are satisfied with these outlines, check on each one to see which area of feathers overlaps its neighbour, then cut along the lines with a V-tool, about ¹⁄₃₂in (1mm) deep, angling the tool so that the vertical side of the cut is adjacent to the higher area. A certain amount of deeper undercutting will be required around the wing tips and tail area, but this must not be overdone –

remember that the whole bird will eventually function as a handle, and no part of it should be too delicate to handle with a certain amount of pressure (Figs 6.20 and 6.21).

Where the different blocks of feathers overlap, the edges can now be rounded over with small riffler files and fine abrasive paper to give a smooth appearance to the bird. This requires a fair amount of time to get it right.

Head and beak

The lines of the head and beak are critical in any bird carving which is intended to portray a particular species; here we must pay attention to those features which distinguish a shelduck from any other kind of duck. The shape of the head is almost the same as in many other duck species, but the beak is unique in having a vertical protuberance, which is more prominent in the male. The eyes protrude slightly from a shallow groove running midway from the beak and curving down slightly to form rounded cheeks below. The top of the head is narrower than the lower part.

Work on the head and beak together, first with small gouges and then with abrasive paper, to get all the curves right, leaving an oversize bump for the eyes. It is critical that the eyes should be in the right place and at the same position on both sides of the face (see page 153).

The eyes can now be carved very carefully, using a tiny no. 9 or 10 gouge to stab the almost circular outline. At this scale, very small tools are particularly useful to obtain an accurate surface curve on each eye, which can be finally smoothed with 320-grit paper. I had a nasty accident at this point, losing concentration for a second with a

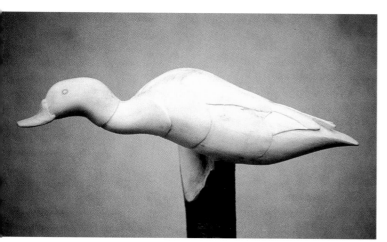

FIG 6.20 *The feather masses defined with the V-tool; note how the joint between stick and stem has been partly cut away to allow the body to be curved round underneath*

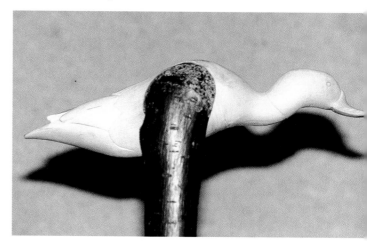

FIG 6.21 *The view from the opposite side shows how the stick bark has been left intact right up to the point where it joins the bird*

delicate gouge cut around the eye and slicing it right off! A new one had to be made from an offcut and stuck on. Shaping a shallow eye just under ⅛in (3mm) across was one of the most exacting tasks I have ever attempted.

Staining

With the carving complete, the bird could simply be sealed and waxed to a natural finish. But a characteristic feature of the shelduck is the vivid contrast of colours, and I felt a monochrome finish, particularly on the nondescript hazel grain figure, would look far too bland. However, personally I do not like painting woodcarvings – no offence to the incredible artistic skills of the wildfowl specialists, but once acrylics have been applied, the piece could just as well be made of plastic, fibreglass or any other material. I therefore decided to try strong water-based staining (Fig 6.22 and 6.23).

Apart from the black and white areas, the other colours may need to be mixed and tried out on scrap wood in order to obtain the correct shade. The stain is then applied with an artist's brush, allowing each colour to dry before beginning the next. It is likely that at least two coats of stain will be needed, along with a steady hand.

When the staining is complete, it can be sealed with a transparent sanding sealer, again using two coats. Cover each colour separately, because surface stain, though perfectly dry, may colour the brush. Sanding sealer is also used on the sections of bare wood where the stick was cut away. If required, the stick itself can be finished with linseed oil.

FIG 6.23 *The top view shows the slight curve of the neck which makes a more comfortable hold, at least for a right-handed user*

CHAPTER 7
Waves

Carving natural subjects is primarily a visual art. The main point of each sculpture – certainly of most projects in this book – is to produce an interpretation in wood of something living. The representation may be realistic, striving to portray the correct proportions and characteristic stance of the subject; or it may be a more 'artistic' one, where certain features are emphasized, others ignored, and detail is on the whole omitted (see for example the large Frog by Chris Coleman on page 164).

However, another important feature of wood sculpture is that it is tactile. Where possible, carvings should be handled (unless they are too delicate), because wood is a warm medium and the sense of touch can often convey more of the feeling of the piece than simply viewing.

This project is very much in the tactile category. In fact, the original idea was to produce a carving for a blind friend. He once asked me what waves on the seashore 'looked like'. While swimming, he had often felt the sudden pressure and movement of waves rolling in, he could hear the crash and undertow on the shingle, but having been blind from birth he had no way of visualizing what was going on. I wondered whether it would be possible to produce some kind of representation of waves in wood – and this was the result.

The resulting sculpture is also visual, particularly in the choice of timber, but the primary purpose is for it to be picked up and felt, even studied in depth (with eyes closed) by those with the precious gift of sight. The design is therefore dictated by the need to produce lines, ridges, swirls, holes, which can be felt in order to interpret the movement of waves to the sense of touch.

Although I have provided a design and described the stages of carving, this project is very much one person's interpretation of the subject. Think of it as an example rather than a pattern to be copied. Each abstract or semi-abstract should illustrate the ideas and interpretation of the person carving. This is discussed further in Chapter 14; for now, the point is that your 'Waves' will probably turn out to be quite different from mine, and I would be fascinated to see some of the results.

DOUGLAS FIR

I have to confess to a certain embarrassment here, as I am only 99% sure that the timber used here is Douglas fir (*Pseudotsuga menziesii*), also known in the USA as Oregon pine. I do know that it came from a structural post rescued during the demolition of a Victorian church vestry and, being over a hundred years old, was particularly well seasoned (Fig 7.1).

Of all the softwoods, Douglas fir shows the most prominent grain figure, due to the contrast in colour and density between the light early wood and much darker late wood. Though normally straight-grained as in this piece, it is sometimes found with wavy or even spiral grain. There is also a significant contrast between the radially sawn surface with close, parallel grain figure and the flat-sawn surface showing an almost random wavy pattern.

Douglas fir is one of the stronger softwoods and is often used in construction work and shipbuilding; it is also used for furniture and in making plywood and decorative veneers. As a carving wood it is not particularly easy to work, being prone to split along the grain, particularly where any delicate features are attempted. It also suffers from a disadvantage common to many pines, where the

FIG 7.1 *The block of Douglas fir ready for carving*

late wood is far harder than the early wood. Sanding by hand is liable to produce an uneven surface, as the soft wood between the darker grain lines is far more easily worn away. Having said that, it is a timber with few knots, and the grain figure on a finished piece can be stunning – particularly suited to this more abstract type of sculpture.

DESIGN (Fig 7.2a–c)

The drawing was done in stages; I began by trying out various shapes and whorls to suggest the surface view of waves and the subsurface movement of the water. Bold, simple lines appear to work best, and although the lateral view is different on each side, only one side is drawn to begin with – the other side can be worked out later during the carving, both to complement the first and to blend in naturally with the overall design. This is almost impossible to visualize in detail at the initial drawing stage. This piece was planned to be freestanding, but with the possibility of mounting on a flat stone plinth later, possibly using slate. At an early stage it became apparent that the long straight line of the base was far too dominant and needed to be broken up by some deeply undercut curves.

Once the rough sketching stage is complete and you are happy with the design, a final drawing can be made

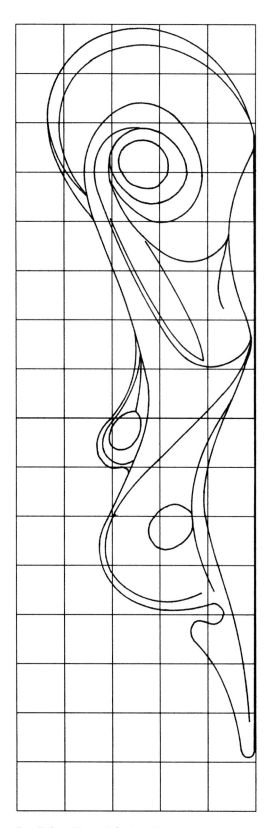

FIG 7.2a *Waves: left elevation*

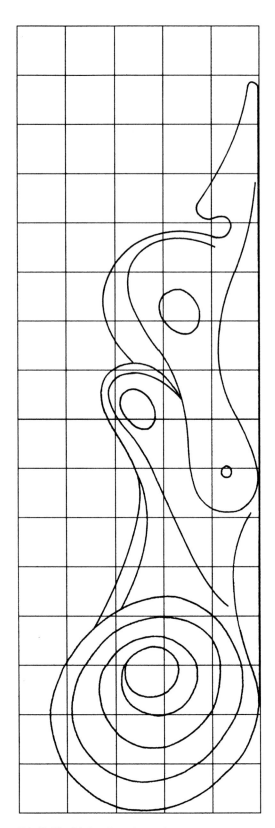

FIG 7.2b *Right elevation*

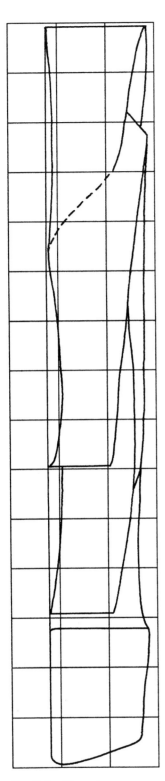

FIG 7.2c *Plan view*

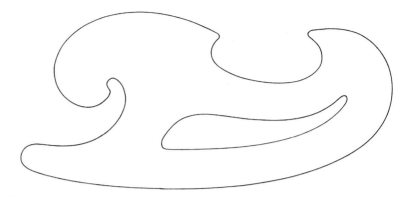

FIG 7.3 *An example of the shapes available from french curves*

using french curves (Fig 7.3). These are indispensable for making accurate and natural-looking curves, and a very good set can be obtained without undue expense.

BLOCKING OUT

A block was cut from the original post, $17 \times 4\frac{1}{2} \times 2$in ($430 \times 114 \times 51$mm), using a section without knots and apparently without nail holes. The block was deliberately cut too long for the design, leaving 3in (76mm) at one end for holding in the vice during carving.

The drawing of the left side (which I think of as the front of the carving) was cut out and placed on the block to mark the outline. Although I sometimes use a felt-tipped pen to mark on timber, this is not a good idea with softwoods, as the ink can stain deeply into the wood. Carbon paper can be useful to mark reasonably smooth timber. Glancing at Fig 7.4, notice the deliberate mistake! The block is not quite high enough, but I did not want to reduce the overall length and decided to adjust the height later.

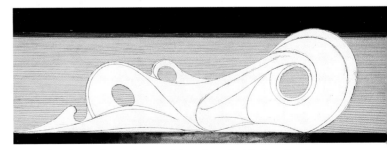

FIG 7.4 *The card template positioned on the block – clearly a little adjustment is necessary at the top right*

FIG 7.5 *The lateral outline cut to shape, leaving a vice-hold at the deep end*

Cut around the outline, using a saw to make vertical cuts down to the line and then a mallet and shallow gouge to remove the waste and trim to within ⅛in (3mm) of the line (Fig 7.5). Take care at this stage to keep everything as near square as possible, and to avoid any splitting through the outline. Because most pinewood is alternately hard and soft, you need exceptionally sharp tools to make a clean cut along or across the grain lines.

BOSTING IN

Although the description below follows the steps I took during this carving, your own design may well be quite different. So, while the general procedure will be the same, the details may need a different approach.

Whatever the design, start by carving the curves and indentations on the front – that is, the lateral view which is facing you. These are done roughly at first (Fig 7.6) to allow for adjustment as the carving progresses. At the same time, cut back as necessary to set out the shapes on the top, where to add interest I decided to drift the waves slightly to one side (Fig 7.7). Most of the carving at this stage is done quite easily by hand, using various shallow or deep gouges as appropriate and taking care always to work with the grain – particularly on either side of the deeper indentations.

Softwoods provide two special challenges to the woodcarver. First, on a curve where the grain changes from one direction to the opposite it is only too easy to split into the curve. Second, you can suddenly find that an area of crush marks appears in the softer early wood

FIG 7.6 *Curves in the front face roughly shaped*

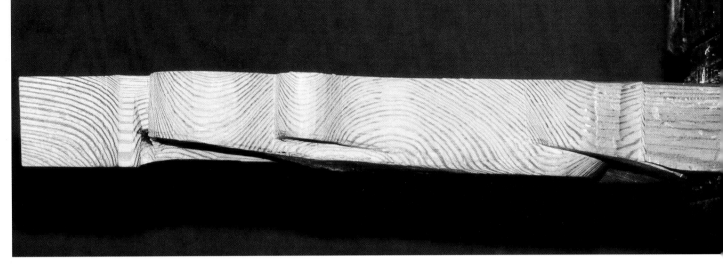

FIG 7.7 *View from the top showing the waves moving to one side*

between the grain lines. These difficulties are discussed further in Chapter 13, page 153.

At an early stage, drill where the holes go right through the carving, using a $^3/_{16}$in (4mm) bit and drilling a series of adjacent holes just inside the marked outline. A waste block clamped to the far side will prevent splitting where the drill bit breaks through. The waste can then be chopped out from each side using a small deep gouge, and then cleaned up as far as possible with gouges of the correct radius for the outline. Inevitably, working here 'inside' the carving and across the grain, it is difficult to clean the edges of the hole with a gouge. But as they will not be disturbed later, the final work can be done now using coarse (120-grit) and then finer (280-grit) abrasive paper wrapped around a circular file or something similar. Remember that the useful life of any sanding paper can be extended by regularly unclogging the grit with a short-wire pad or a brass-wire brush.

EXPECT THE UNEXPECTED

It is not uncommon during carving (at least for me) that, just as everything seems to be going along quite nicely, a problem jumps out of the woodwork. The shallow end of this carving is meant to represent the undertow washing back from the beach. While cutting out the deep groove which separates this from the main wave, I had a mini-disaster, suddenly making contact with the end of a small rusty nail (Fig 7.8) and crunching the edge of a favourite veining tool. The nail was agonizingly removed by cutting around it with tiny gouges and eventually extracting it with small-nose pliers. Unfortunately, like oak, Douglas fir contains acids which over the years attack iron,

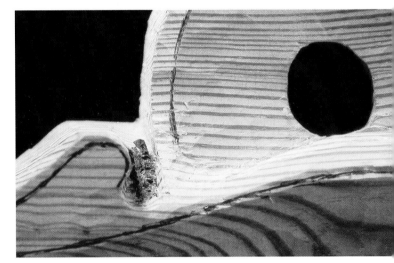

FIG 7.8 *Close-up of the area affected by a rusty nail*

not only rusting nails and screws but also leaving a black stain around them. Luckily, in this case the stain was almost hidden by the deep groove and invisible from the side view (Fig 7.9).

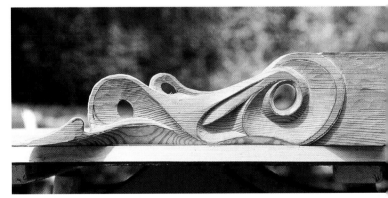

FIG 7.9 *Holes through the carving are now in place. The nail damage at the shallow end is no longer visible from this angle*

FIG 7.10 *Rear view, with the curves complementary to the front view set in*

COMPLETING THE DESIGN

Once the shape of one side has been roughed out, it is time to work on the opposite side, drawing the curves and features to balance those already established (Fig 7.10). Try and include both bold lines and more subtle ones. I included a spiral to suggest a horizontal 'whirlpool' effect, and one other deep hole which also hid a minor defect in the wood at that point. The overall idea is to give a tactile rather than a visual representation of the complex movement of the water – which means you need to *feel* the carving constantly, as well as looking at it, while the shapes are being cut (Fig 7.11).

The final task before finishing is to remove the waste wood at the end which has been used until now as a vice-hold. Most of it can be removed by saw cuts; then clean up with a wide flat chisel or a shallow gouge.

FIG 7.11 *Top view of waves, fully carved and ready for sanding. The shapes should appeal to the touch as well as the eye*

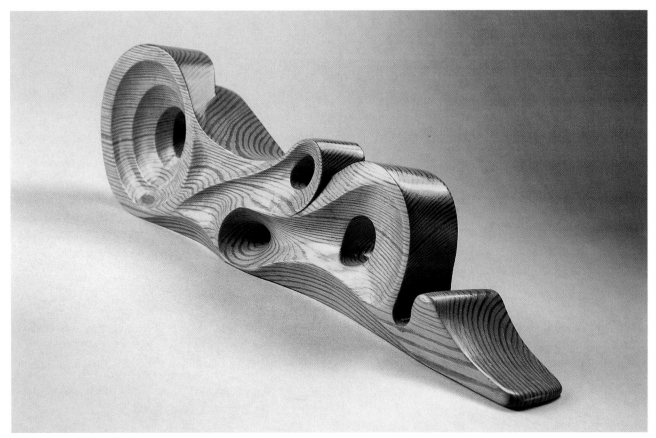

FIG 7.12 *A rear view of the completed carving, finished with yacht varnish to give a suitably smooth surface*

During this operation, and from this point on, if the carving needs to be held in the vice, use a folded cloth or towel to protect the work from crushing and do not overtighten the vice.

SANDING AND FINISHING

Most abstract carvings are finished with a smooth rather than a chiselled surface, and this is definitely required here. However, the danger of sanding is that it is easy to lose clean edges, so a fair amount of care is needed to avoid rounding them over and losing definition. A related problem with softwoods is that the surface very easily becomes dirty, simply due to handling. This is particularly the case during sanding procedures, and one way of avoiding the problem is to sand as far as you can without moving the carving, then seal the finished surface area with sanding sealer. A shellac sealer only takes about 20 minutes to dry completely, and can then be handled confidently with minimal danger of soiling. During the

finishing, riffler files of various shapes are handy for awkward corners.

When the sanding is complete, and one coat of sanding sealer has been applied all over, I would advise leaving the carving overnight. This is not to leave time for the sealer to dry, but to come back to the whole sculpture with a fresh mind. View it from all angles, and under different angles of light, and almost certainly several blemishes, small bumps, perhaps an uneven curve will become apparent. Cleaning up your carvings should never be rushed or shoddy, but with this type of subject, particularly working with softwood, the cleaning-up is paramount.

This is one of the few projects where I would recommend varnish – in fact, I used two coats of yacht varnish (Fig 7.12). Perhaps it turned out glossier than one might like, but the problem with oil finishes and water-based varnishes is that they darken the lighter part of the grain, even after a coat of sanding sealer, so that the beautiful contrast of the two colours would have been diminished.

CHAPTER 8
Cobra

IT SEEMS strange that all over the world a highly successful suborder of land creatures has evolved by dispensing with the universal organs of locomotion – snakes have no limbs. Their movement is more akin to a marine than a land animal, and indeed many are strong swimmers. Over two thousand species of snake

are found worldwide, ranging in length from the tiny 6in (150mm) thread snakes to the record 37ft (11.4m) South American anaconda.

Because of their unique shape and the perceived threat they pose, in many cultures snakes have been held as sacred, as symbols of power or as agents of temptation and evil. This long and mysterious relationship between serpents and mankind requires that any sculpture attempting to portray a snake realistically must try and capture something of these mysterious serpentine qualities. Ideally the finished piece should produce a shudder in those who see it – in fact some may not even be able to touch it!

The cobras, which belong to the family *Elapidae*, form an ideal subject for carving, especially with the dramatic hood or cowl extended to indicate threat or being threatened. In this menacing pose the head and eyes, comparatively so tiny, become the focal point of the whole piece.

DESIGN (Fig 8.1a–c)

The carving, using a two-section construction, is based on an original design by the Kent-based sculptor Bill Prickett. Some examples of his superb work are featured in Chapter 14 (pages 158, 159 and 171).

It's not a bad idea on occasion, if you are particularly impressed by a carving, to study it carefully and learn from it by making your own copy. Carvers are normally very pleased to talk about their work in some detail – in fact the more enthusiastic of our fraternity may be difficult to stop once they get going – some will even write books about it.

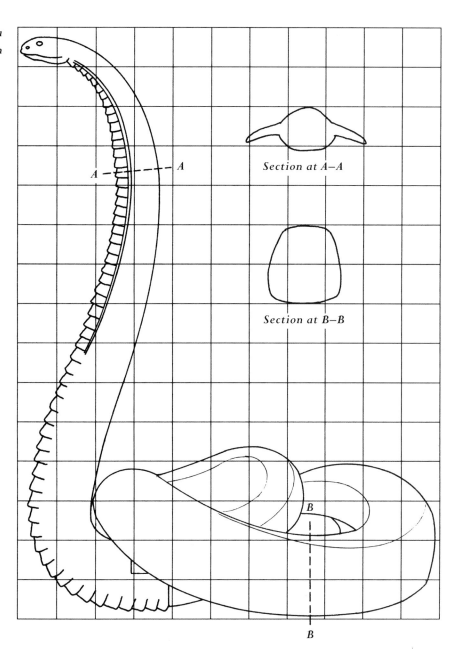

FIG 8.1a
Cobra: side elevation

Section at A–A

Section at B–B

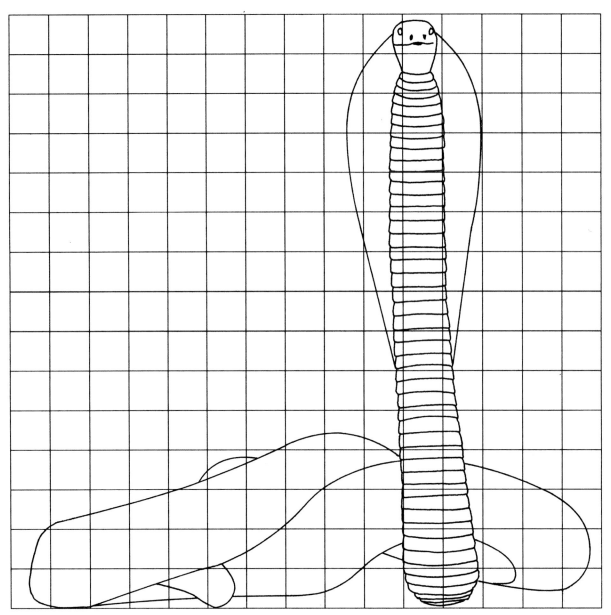

FIG 8.1*b Front elevation*

Equally, don't be afraid to modify someone else's design rather than copy it slavishly; I hope the projects in this book will be modified by any carvers who attempt them. After looking again at real snakes and as many photographs as I could find, I changed various details from Bill's original – not necessarily as an improvement, but to make this my own interpretation of the subject.

I have also been somewhat free with the realism, in the sense of using more than one species as the basis of the project. It is perhaps more like the Indian or spectacled cobra (*Naja naja*) than any other, but again not an exact copy.

Two other preliminary points about this project are worth bearing in mind:

- Although the carving is 15in (380mm) across its greatest width, if uncoiled the snake would be almost 5ft (1.52m) long, so there is a fair amount of work involved, especially in the finishing.
- In the 'threat' position the cobra does not remain stationary, but weaves from side to side while keeping its gaze directly towards the danger (or the intended victim), so the neck has a slight curve rather than being ramrod-straight.

WALNUT

An apology may be required here for using English walnut again (see Chapter 5: the Wren). I have tried to illustrate as many different timbers as carving projects, but since I had a large and beautifully seasoned 10-year-old log of dark-dappled walnut, the thought of searching for something else equally suited to this subject was just too daunting.

Using a section this size, inevitably there will be some shakes to contend with, and if it has been around for some time some areas may be softer or lighter than others, requiring extra care. However, the design is such that it can be made from any dark timber, providing you can find a 10 × 4in (254 × 102mm) beam, at least 20in (510mm) long. Things could be scaled down if necessary, though bear in mind the inevitable loss of dramatic effect as the snake becomes less than life-size.

FIG 8.3 *Preliminary shaping of the body. The external outline has been cut out, except for two flat edges which are left to form a vice-hold. The internal outline has been drilled and cut, leaving strengthening sections between the two straight edges*

CARVING THE BODY SECTION

Mark out the vertical view of the body on to the timber (Fig 8.2). If the neck section is coming from the same block (see Fig 8.1c), mark that outline as well and saw between the sections to separate them, leaving plenty of wood around the neck and head section.

One of the initial problems to overcome is getting the levels right where the body coils over and under itself. These levels are remarkable easy to get wrong, and to avoid mistakes it is advisable first to remove the waste between and around the coils by cutting down vertically. On the outside, much of this can be done with a saw, and

on the inside by drilling consecutive holes right through, making sure each one is accurately vertical. (I have plans one day to purchase a drill stand, which would be extremely helpful for this kind of work.) Before drilling, clamp the block down on to a flat piece of waste board, so that the emerging drill bit does not split off chips from the base. It is also important to leave two flat edges for the time being to facilitate holding in the vice, and to leave a couple of strengthening sections between the coils until all the heavy shaping is complete (Fig 8.3); these will take the strain of crushing pressure from the vice.

Once all the holes are drilled, the waste can be chopped out using a deep gouge – ½in (13mm) or larger – and mallet. The edges can be cleaned up most easily by using a shallow in-cannel gouge worked by hand, keeping the sides vertical at this stage for ease of marking the levels.

Establishing the levels

First be absolutely clear which parts of the coil overlap and which go underneath. Both ends – the tail and the base of the neck – are underneath. Mark the vertical levels of the coils, at this stage allowing ½in (13mm) of overlap where they touch. After marking, check again that you have a continuous snake from one end to the other!

Waste above the lower coils can now be removed. This can be done by simply using a mallet and a deep gouge, or

FIG 8.2 *Vertical outline of the body marked on the wood*

made easier by first sawing down horizontally at ½in (13mm) intervals before chopping out. I found a reciprocating saw (a horizontal jigsaw) particularly useful here, but a small handsaw is sufficient. At this stage continue to keep all the angles square, so that you are still blocking out (Fig 8.4). A Surform file is also helpful to get the external surface curves smooth, and a large V-tool will help where the saw cannot reach. The same process can then be carried out from below, working up to the underside of the upper coils (Figs 8.5 and 8.6).

The cobra, unlike a python, is not a particularly fat snake; nevertheless, leave plenty of wood during blocking out, as with mallet work it is surprisingly easy to cut too deep on occasion. The lateral thickness varies from 1¾in (44mm) at the centre to 1½in (38mm) at the neck area, and 1in (25mm) near the end of the tail.

FIG 8.4 *The vertical levels have been set in from above, still in square section*

FIG 8.5 *View from underneath after the vertical levels have been blocked in from below in the same way*

FIG 8.6 *A side view of the carving at the same stage (upside down)*

FIG 8.7 *Work in progress on rounding the body. Wedges have been glued in to repair major shakes*

Bosting in

Work can now start on rounding the coils. The cross section of the body is not round, or even oval (see Fig 8.1*a*). The backbone near the top produces an almost flat narrowish band along the whole length of the back. The bulk of the body is towards the underside; this swells slightly wherever it lies over a lower coil, and the height is compressed slightly.

Because of the many tight curves, remember that the grain direction often changes along the coil and the angle of cut will need to change accordingly. In order to work these curves, gouges of various depths and widths are helpful, as well as left and right skew chisels, fishtail gouges, a V-tool and whatever else you can use to work the awkward corners; backbent gouges may be useful for finishing the insides of the coils. Forgive the repetition yet again, but watch the vertical levels all the time, viewing from various angles. A mistake here could be very difficult to rectify later.

As carving progresses with a large log, tensions in the wood are released – particularly near the centre – and some shakes may slowly open. Once the body curves are completed, any larger splits can be repaired by inserting and gluing thin wedges cut from waste wood, matching the colour required as closely as possible (Fig 8.7). Hairline cracks can be repaired later.

The neck joint can be shaped at this point or left until later; the technique is described on page 82.

The whole body can now be roughly sanded using 180-grit paper. Although the surface will later be tooled, it

FIG 8.8 *Body shape complete, seen from above. One strengthening section remains*

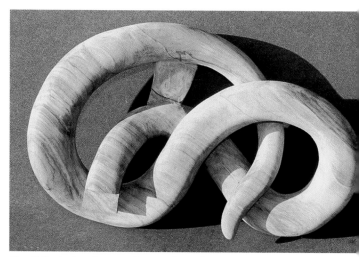

FIG 8.9 *A view from underneath at the same stage*

FIG 8.10 *In the front view, the tail and the neck join show underneath the coiled body*

is important at this stage in finalizing the overall shape to make the coils as smooth and sinuous as you can (Figs 8.8–8.10).

NECK AND HEAD

The body can now be put on one side while work begins on the business end of the cobra: the neck, cowl and head. I seldom use a clay maquette, but in this case the proportions are so critical that it is a good idea to make up a full-size model before starting on the real thing.

Making a maquette
The function of the model is to sort out several problems:
- The length of the vertical 'neck' in relation to the body.
- The double curve of the neck and umbrella-shape of the cowl.
- The shape and details of the head.
- How to set about surface tooling to represent the scales.

Modelling clay can be purchased from any large craft supplier. Stored in a waterproof bag it will last indefinitely, and it can be recycled after use. The wet clay is pliable and therefore needs a solid skeleton to hold it in place. This can be made up with stiff wire and metal rod, as follows.

First cut a malleable metal rod to the length that you estimate for the head and neck together. (Alternatively, filaments of stiff wire can be twisted together.) Bend this

'backbone' along the curves required and offer it up to the neck join under the body coils. Adjust and bend to the required posture (Fig 8.11).

Now make several rolled lumps of the clay and press them round the rod to model the neck and head, leaving them somewhat thinner than required. Press some

FIG 8.11 *A metal rod shaped to the neck and head curves is the foundation for the maquette*

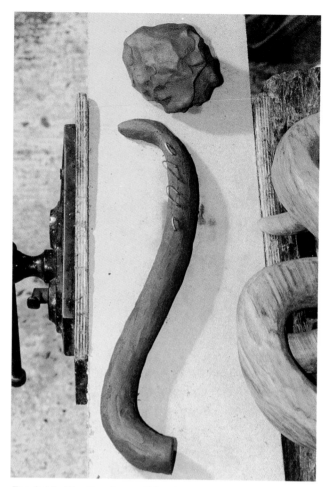

FIG 8.12 *The first layer of clay has been laid over the central rod, and wire 'ribs' set into the clay to support the cowl*

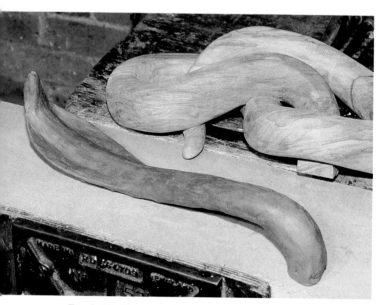

FIG 8.13 *The second layer of clay laid over the neck, and the cowl modelled*

short lengths of flexible wire into the clay where the cowl is to be, rather like a row of ribs. Leave this overnight to harden (Fig 8.12).

If the hardened clay has cracked, mend with new clay and wet the entire surface to give some grip (messy business, this). Add clay to fill out the neck and head to the required thickness, then model the cowl around the wire ribs (Fig 8.13). Leave this to dry, but only until it reaches carving consistency – do not let it get bone-dry.

Now carve the detail – you can use ordinary carving tools, providing they are cleaned thoroughly afterwards. The process is absurdly easy, as there is no grain to worry about, and any mistakes can be chopped out and replaced with new clay.

It was at this stage that I experimented with different techniques for portraying the surface scales. In reality these protrude from the skin, though on a cobra they do not overlap. In some situations it might be possible to make up several metal punches, each with an indented scale of slightly different size. These can be punched into the wood surface, compressing the fibres around each scale; wetting the surface for a while then causes the uncompressed fibres to expand and rise to form a scale. (This technique is known by the Japanese name of *ukibori*.) Unfortunately the technique is not possible with this project because of the coiled shape of the body, where access to many parts is severely limited.

You could also try carving around each scale, but the immensity and difficulty of the task ruled it out for me.

FIG 8.14 *The top section of the completed maquette with scales cut in*

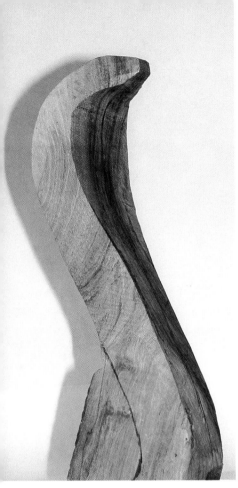

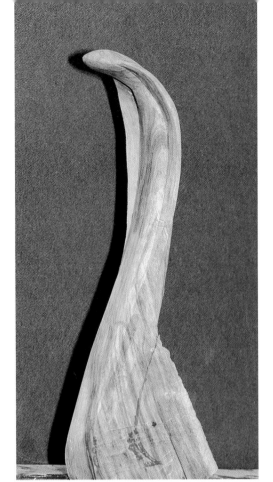

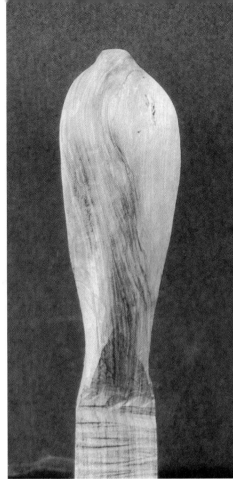

FIG 8.15 *Head and neck section blocked out in timber, leaving a strengthening section at the base*

FIG 8.16 *Neck, cowl and head being shaped from the front. Note how the cowl projects slightly forward of the neck*

FIG 8.17 *Rear view of the cowl, showing woodworm damage at top right*

Eventually I opted for the simple technique of making each scale a shallow dimple, which to some extent fools the eye and feels right to the touch as a slightly rough skin. On the clay model this is done by cutting each scale with a no. 4 gouge, then wetting the surface and rubbing all over with the fingers to give a smoothly dimpled effect (Fig 8.14). For the technique on wood, see below.

From clay to wood

With the completed maquette as your guide, work can now begin on the real neck and head. The outline is marked on to the timber using the maquette. The double-curve shape means that somewhere there is going to be cross grain, and this needs to be borne in mind during carving.

Block out the top two-thirds of the neck and head, leaving a vice-hold and a strengthening section at the base (Fig 8.15). Start rounding the front of the neck with shallow straight and curved gouges. When cutting back the edges of the neck, using a wide V-tool, leave enough

wood for the cowl to project slightly forward (see the neck section in Fig 8.1*a*, and Fig 8.16).

Once the rough shape of the front is in place, begin work on the back. I found that my collage of cobra pictures set up nearby was particularly helpful at this stage, and I was continually offering up the carving at the same angle as the photographs to check progress. The cross-section shape of the neck is approximately the same as the body, except that the back is rounded rather than flat. The cowl is slightly thicker next to the neck than at the edge; reduce the edge thickness of the cowl to about ⅛in (3mm).

Repair

I had a problem with an area of the cowl damaged by woodworm, which really could not be mended except by cutting out the affected section completely (Fig 8.17). The pointed oval shape shown in Fig 8.18 was cut out with a V-tool and shallow gouge, the sides of the hole being sloped to accept a tapered patch. It is almost impossible to

FIG 8.18 *The damaged area cut out ready for patching*

FIG 8.19 *The eye is marked before final shaping of the head*

match the figure of a mottled grain, but the best match will usually be found from a piece of waste. In fact, with any carving it is worth keeping all waste wood (apart from chips and shavings) until the piece is finished. In this case a tapered wedge was carved to fit the hole exactly so that it could be forced in with moderate pressure for the closest possible fit, the thickness being left oversize. The wedge was glued and clamped, then carved back with a shallow gouge flush with the cowl surface, removing all surface glue which had squeezed out. The final size match is good, but the grain figure inevitably shows, though partly hidden by the final tooling of scales (see Fig 8.20).

Head

The head is small, but its shape and features are critical to the whole carving. The top of the head is flat, and the sides at the front are also flat as far back as the eye area; underneath the mouth, the chin is rounded. The eyes are high on the face and can be set in with a tiny semicircular gouge, so that they protrude slightly (Fig 8.19). The mouth is large, to match the snake rather than the head, and curves from the front of the head right round to the cowl. It is shaped using a V-tool so that the upper 'lip' overlaps the chin. The back of the head merges into the neck and cowl; underneath, there is a visible join with the neck scales. Once the head features are complete, it can be carefully sanded to a smooth finish.

Scales

The scales on the underside, and on the front of the vertical neck, are quite large and form horizontal bands, overlapping front to back, which enables them to grip the ground for locomotion. On the front of the neck area about 45 scales are visible, diminishing slightly in width towards the head. In the cowl area these horizontal scales run round to the base of the cowl; lower down, they curve round so as to be just visible on the sides (see Fig 8.23) They are cut with a V-tool and a small flat chisel.

The oval scales are now cut all over the back, and at the front of the cowl, using a ⅜in (10mm) no. 4 gouge. The scales along the entire snake occur in straight lines, each line offset from the next so that the scales also form diagonal lines. The lines are first marked with a pencil (Fig 8.20) and then cut with the gouge along the direction of the grain. Once set in, the whole area is rubbed vigorously in a circular motion with no. 0 wire wool to dull the edges and smooth the entire surface (Fig 8.21).

JOINING THE NECK TO THE BODY

This joint requires a certain amount of strength, so it is made with a rebate and two metal dowels (see Fig 8.26 on page 84). The body side of the join is cut to form a rebated

FIG 8.20 *Lines are marked to facilitate cutting the dimples to portray scales. The patch on the right-hand side of the hood is barely visible at this stage, and will be even less conspicuous when the tooling is finished*

FIG 8.21 *Tooling complete on the front of the neck, cowl and head*

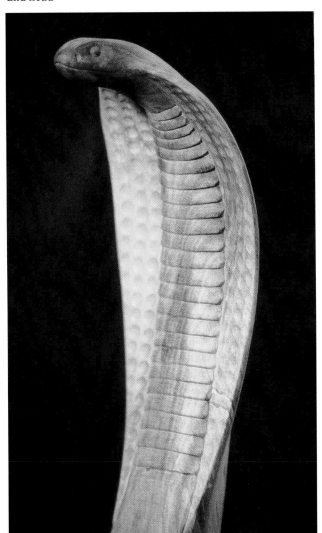

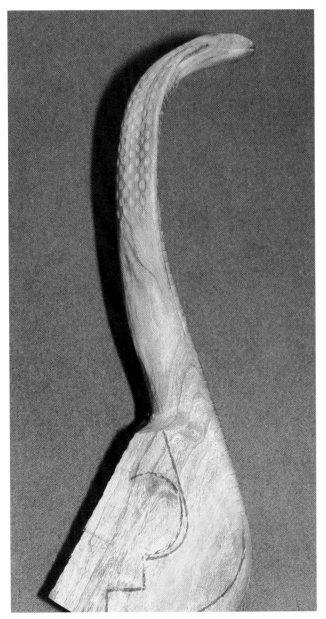

FIG 8.22 *The shape of the body section marked (in green) on the neck piece, by means of a card template. The red lines indicate the final shape of the lower neck*

step, using a small saw and a flat chisel to clean up. Check everything is square and parallel. A card template is made, and the shape of the body piece marked on to the neck section (the green line in Fig 8.22). Cut out the neck part of the joint, and remove the waste which formed the strengthening area at the base of the neck. If the width of one section is slightly greater than the other, this doesn't matter at this stage – it can be trimmed after joining. Ensure that the joint surfaces fit as closely as possible, but before making the actual join it is best to wait until the

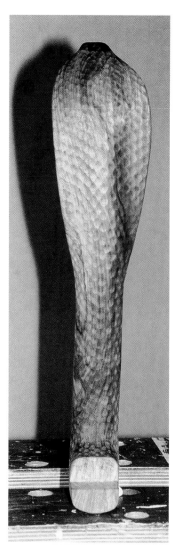

FIG 8.25 *Tooling of scales in progress along the body coils*

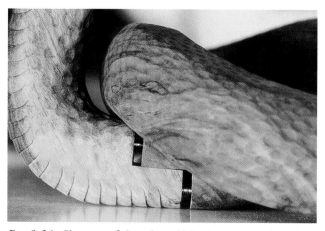

FIG 8.26 *Close-up of the rebated joint between neck and body, partly assembled to show the reinforcing dowels*

FIG 8.23 (ABOVE LEFT) *The lower neck shaped and tooled, with the rebate cut out for attachment to the body*

FIG 8.24 (ABOVE RIGHT) *Rear view of the neck and head at the same stage*

finishing is almost complete. If the scales on the lower neck have not been done, these should be finished now (Figs 8.23 and 8.24).

TEXTURING THE BODY SURFACE

Before embarking on this marathon tooling process, any remaining hairline cracks, caused by release of tension in the timber, can be dealt with. Anything over $\frac{1}{32}$in (1mm) wide should be filled with offcut slivers of wood.

The really narrow cracks can be filled using a wax stick of matching colour.

The entire body section is now dimpled to portray the scales, the size diminishing and frequency increasing towards the tail. Begin by marking both longitudinal and diagonal lines, as before. Later, as work progresses and you become familiar with this long (and eventually tedious) process, longitudinal marks only are necessary. The straight lines along the body are important for the final appearance. Again, smooth the entire area with wire wool; as the body is so long, working in small sections, cutting and smoothing, is less tiring (Fig 8.25). Seal finished sections with one coat of Danish oil when an overnight break is required.

Fainter hearts may prefer to omit the dimpled scaling (several thousand accurately placed dimples are required!) and instead leave a simple tooled or sanded surface – apart from the front of the cowl and neck.

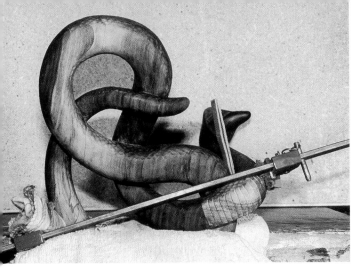

FIG 8.27 *A gimcrack clamping arrangement to hold the two sections together while gluing; various wads of cloth protect the surfaces*

ASSEMBLY

It is crucial that the joint is as strong as possible (Fig 8.26). You are probably working with cross grain here, and the finished carving may well suffer from someone lifting it by the neck. A strong joint is accomplished by using two long metal dowels, made from stainless steel or galvanized screws with heads removed. The technique is similar to that described on page 154, though here we are using longer and more substantial metal dowels than usual. The dowelled joint is glued and clamped, using a sash cramp and packing pieces as necessary (Fig 8.27).

FIG 8.28 *The completed carving seen from the left-hand side*

FIG 8.29 *The front view shows the slight movement of the neck*

FIG 8.30 *The texture of the cowl is prominent in the rear view*

FINISHING

The entire surface may now be rubbed down again with wire wool and one more coat of Danish oil applied. After two or three days, one coat of wax is well brushed in; an hour or so later this can be polished off and the finishing is complete (Figs 8.28–8.30).

CHAPTER 9
Turtle

TORTOISES, terrapins and turtles make up the group of reptiles known as chelonians, instantly recognizable from their distinctive shells. In turtles the carapace (upper shell) and plastron (lower) are never united into a rigid box-shape as in the tortoises. There are seven species of sea turtle (*Chelonidae*), the largest being the leatherback, which can weigh over 800kg (1,760lb); the smallest is the olive ridley, weighing in at just 35kg (77lb). Five of these species are endangered, with numbers of the olive ridley estimated at less than a thousand individuals.

Turtles spend almost their entire life at sea; only the females come ashore once a year to lay eggs on the nesting beaches. Some two months later, when the eggs hatch, the newborn turtles make the most perilous journey of their lives, waddling down the beach at high speed towards the comparative safety of the waves. Even there, as they strike out towards floating mats of seaweed, predatory fish and sharks cruise in the shallow waters, waiting with as high appreciation of the 'toothsomeness of tender turtle' as the proverbial London alderman. Despite its permanent marine environment, and unlike amphibians, every few minutes the turtle must come to the surface to breathe.

The species illustrated is the hawksbill (*Eretmochelys imbricata*), chosen for the beautiful carapace known misleadingly as 'tortoiseshell'. This has always been prized commercially, though fortunately it has now been replaced by plastics to some extent and the species is protected in international law. The shell itself is made up of numerous armoured plates (scutes) which grow over the underlying bone structure, leaving only the limbs, neck and tail to move freely. The hawksbill shell can grow to about 2ft 6in (760mm) long.

DESIGN (Fig 9.1*a–d*)

The shape of a turtle is instantly recognizable, but turns out to be rather more complex than at first one imagines. Features which need particular attention include the insertion of the legs between the carapace and plastron, the small pointed scutes around the edge which join the upper and lower shells, and the details of the head. The various shapes of the individual scutes which form the main shells are also critical for producing a realistic appearance to the carving.

In order to give some idea of movement, the fore left and hind right paddles are set further forward than those opposite. Due to the size of the timber, the fore left paddle had to be carved separately and joined later, which gave the opportunity to set it pointing downwards at 45°.

Free-standing carvings of sea creatures always produce a problem in their overall design, which is only surpassed by the conundrum of how to mount birds in flight. The picture of Brian Faggetter's shark on page 168 shows one way of 'losing' the base; another is to use an arrangement with marine foliage to provide a natural-looking mounting. Yet another is to provide a complete contrast by using a metal rod or rods; see the dolphins on page 161.

I did have the mad notion of setting the turtle in a small glass-topped table, with head and back protruding above the surface, but the logistics proved insurmountable. In the end the decision went to the natural option: using a piece of driftwood, stained and varnished to give the appearance of having been underwater for a long time.

In the case of the hawksbill, most of the shell is covered in an irregular pattern of light and dark shades, providing camouflage in shallow waters or amongst seaweed. The simplest option for the carver is to forget the colouring and go for a nice medium-brown wood, concentrating on the shape alone. If you are trying this project you may well wish to go for this option, because to make a decent job of the staining is an exacting and time-consuming process.

However, if you are going for broke, then a light wood with dark staining is far easier than the reverse. Jelutong, lime, maple, or my choice of European sycamore would all work satisfactorily; American sycamore is generally too dark.

SYCAMORE

European sycamore (*Acer pseudoplatanus*), also known as great maple or Scotch plane, has a fine, even texture, and generally presents a straight grain which is easy to work. Quarter-sawn 'fiddleback' sycamore has a beautiful wavy figure and has traditionally been used for the backs of violins, marquetry, and parquet flooring. For intricate carving sycamore has less mechanical strength than lime, and extra care is needed here when working with the paddle-shaped legs to avoid breaking them off at any stage. One reason for choosing sycamore is that it stains well, and it is often the timber of choice commercially for dyed veneers in a range of colours.

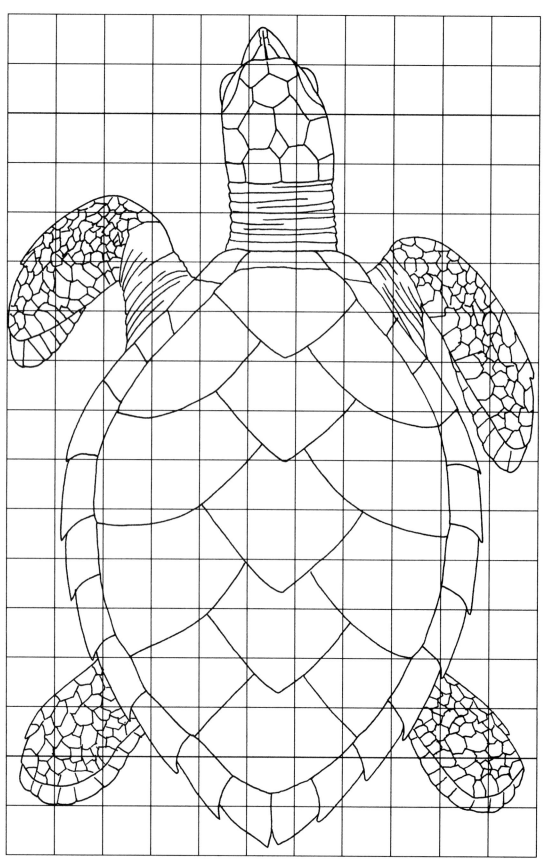

FIG 9.1a *Hawksbill turtle: plan view*

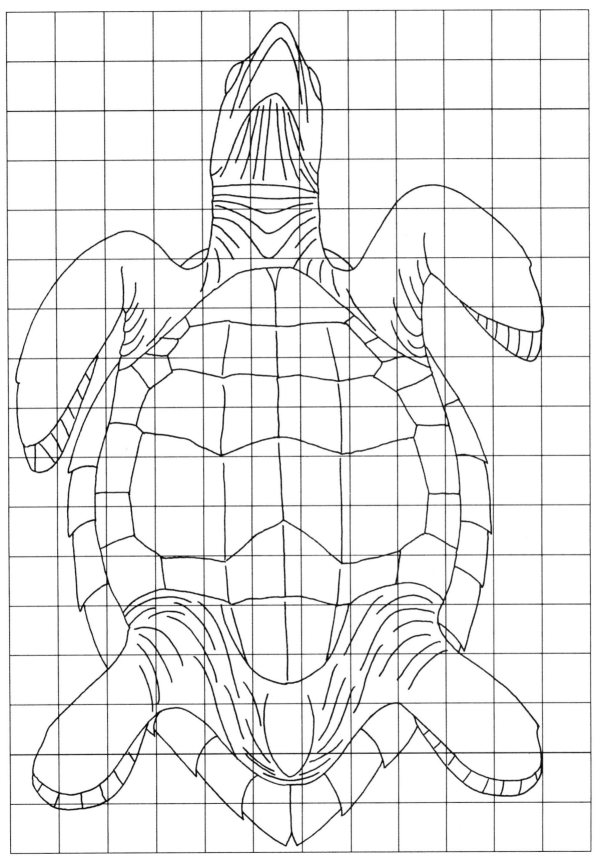

FIG 9.1*b* *View from below*

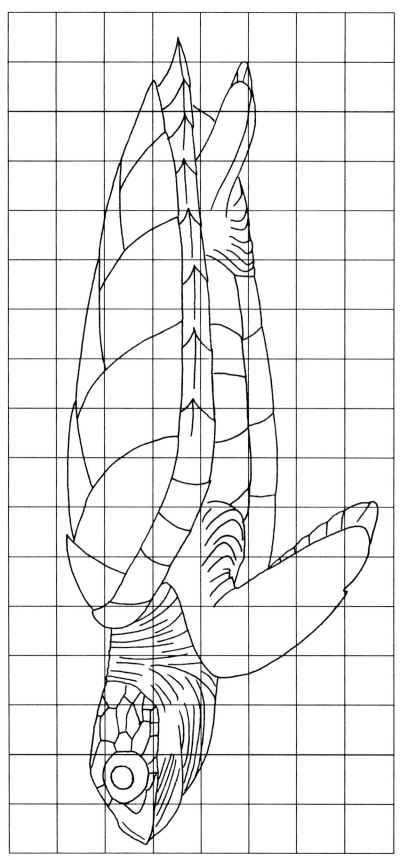

FIG 9.1c *Left elevation*

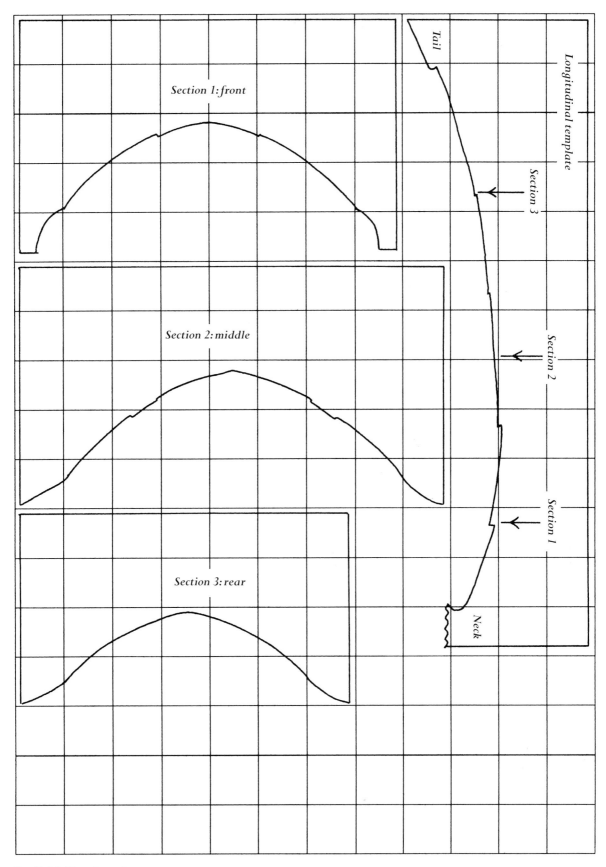

Section 1: front

Section 2: middle

Section 3: rear

Longitudinal template

Tail

Section 3

Section 2

Section 1

Neck

FIG 9.1d Templates for carapace

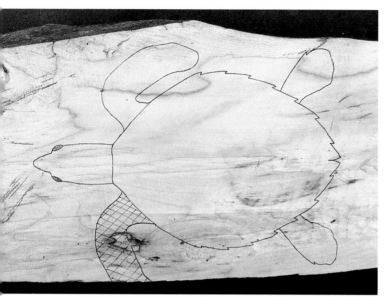

FIG 9.2 *The vertical outline marked on the block of sycamore. The left forepaddle is shown for reference only - this will be carved separately from an offcut*

A fairly hefty chunk is required for this project. I managed to acquire a section 30 × 17in (760 × 430mm), with thickness tapering from 5 to 4in (125–100mm), which had been seasoned for many years in a well-ventilated shed and was virtually shake-free. However, it had been attacked by beetle, and a certain amount of cosmetic repair was necessary at a later stage (see page 98).

FIRST CUTS

Although the section of timber was large, there was insufficient width and depth to allow for all four paddles. From the start it was necessary to plan for one forepaddle to be made separately (Figs 9.2 and 9.3). Mark the vertical outline on the top surface of the block, and if possible leave a 'post' at the rear for holding in the vice during carving. The shape of the turtle makes it very difficult to hold securely in any other way. Saw around the outline, as usual leaving up to 15% – in this case, ½in (13mm) – for any adjustment later (Fig 9.4). After roughing out I realized that the original straight line of the neck and head pointing straight forward would give a rather stiff appearance, and it was later offset slightly to indicate the creature glancing towards the left. It is as well to leave a strengthening connection between the front paddle and the body, as the cross-grain 'wrist' joint would otherwise be vulnerable during the heavy roughing-out process. When blocking out a carving of this size, considerable time can be saved by using a bandsaw or other machine saw – working at this scale with a handsaw is time-consuming and hard work. Either way, a certain amount of chopping out with mallet and stout gouge will be required.

Now mark the lateral outline (Fig 9.5). Cutting out the lateral shape would be extremely awkward with a mechanical saw, but much of the bulky waste can

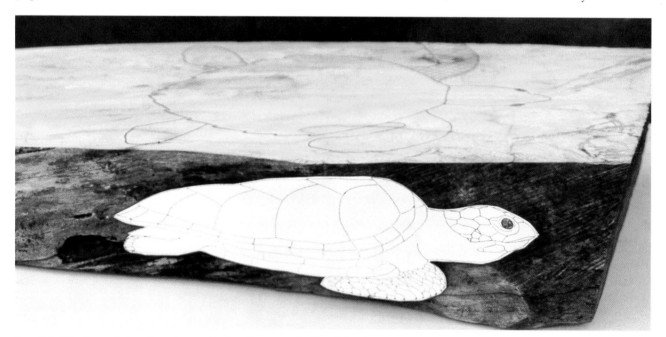

FIG 9.3 *The lateral view drawing applied to the tapered side of the block to check the depth*

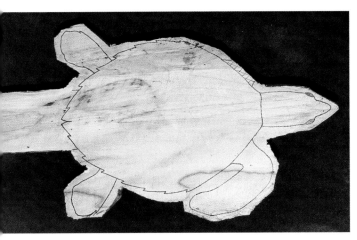

FIG 9.4 *The carving has been blocked out vertically, leaving a projecting vice-hold at the rear end. The right front paddle remains fully attached to the body for the time being*

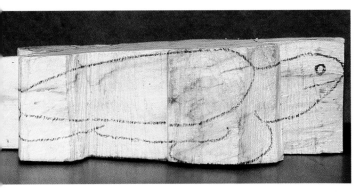

FIG 9.5 *The lateral outline can now be marked on the side*

be removed using parallel handsaw cuts, followed by chopping out with mallet and gouge. Take care that the ends of the paddles project below the lower edge of the body.

BOSTING IN

The form of the turtle is best begun by determining the shape of the dorsal shell. In order to find the curve of the outer edge of the shell, the paddles will first need to be cut down to about 1½in (38mm) thick. So with each paddle, working underneath from the outer end, set in the angle at which the leg slopes upwards towards the body – around 15° for the hind legs, 25° for the foreleg. Then work down from above until the paddle is 1½in (38mm) thick (Fig 9.6).

Mark the edge of the shell all round – the outline will be only approximate at this stage. The centre of the back forms a definite ridge, so mark this central line from head to tail. Remove waste on either side of the ridge down towards the outer edge, leaving ½in (13mm) spare to allow for finalizing the double-curve shape later. Once again, parallel saw cuts chopped out with a gouge will speed the removal of this waste (Fig 9.7) – though some carvers find that an Arbortech machine is the ideal tool for this kind of job.

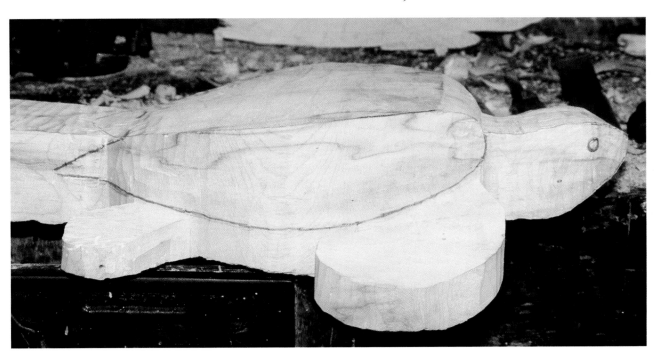

FIG 9.6 *Blocking out complete: the paddles have been reduced to 1½in (38mm) thick*

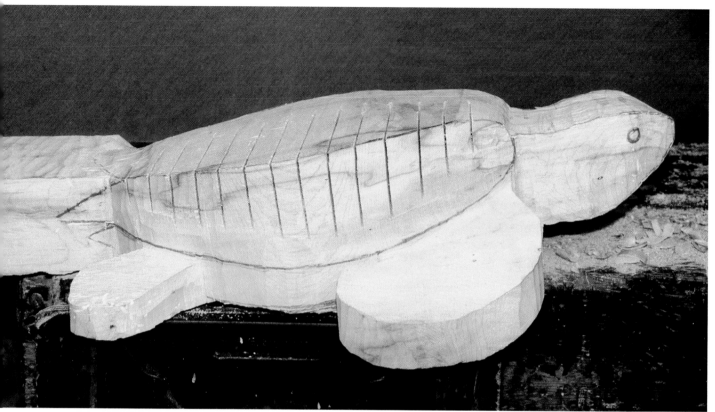

FIG 9.7 *Parallel saw cuts assist removal of waste over the back*

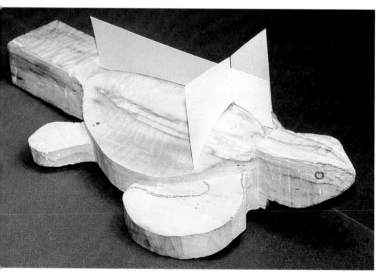

FIG 9.8 *Using card templates to determine the exact curves of the carapace*

In order to assist in getting the final shape of the back correct, templates can be made from cardboard as shown in Fig 9.1*d*. These templates, which were made by reference to a real tortoiseshell, can be offered up

frequently as work progresses with shallow gouges (Fig 9.8). If you are using sycamore, the gouges can be worked accurately by hand, removing wood easily across the grain; harder woods will require the mallet. Remember that there will be a line of smaller scutes around the edge of the shell. At the front these are rounded; at the rear they become thinner and pointed. A curved Surform is useful here to smooth out the long curves.

Most of the top shell can be shaped, except for a small section at the rear where the vice-hold gets in the way; this is dealt with later. Now it is time to shape underneath.

THE LOWER SHELL

The ventral shell is flatter, with two parallel ridges running from front to rear. Points to note are the indented curves around the leg insertion points, the bull-nosed curve up to the neck, and the soft, wrinkled texture of the rear end of the body (see Fig 9.20 on page 100). Clamp the turtle upside down to set in the shell and surrounding areas. Towards the outer edge, the shell and

FIG 9.9 *Lower view after initial shaping of the underside. Part of the strength connection to the front right paddle (shown cross-hatched) is still in place; the front left paddle projects as a short stump to determine the eventual insertion position. The large scutes have been outlined, and beetle damage to the wood is now visible*

FIG 9.10 *The carapace scutes are marked and have been set in on one side. The vice-hold has been reduced*

body curve sharply up to join the edge scutes, more so towards the rear (Fig 9.9); but the tail area must be left until later when the vice-hold is removed. At this stage, with the heavy work largely complete, the width of the vice-hold can be reduced.

The outline of the flattish scutes underneath can be marked and defined with a V-tool, cutting down 1/32–1/16in (1–2mm) so that each scute is overlapped by the one in front. Towards the edge the scutes abut each other, with a shallow groove to mark the join. If you have not yet cut the scutes on the top, do this now, again overlapping front to rear. The first scute behind the neck protrudes significantly, with a sharp central ridge (Fig 9.10).

HEAD AND NECK

Study the head and neck area carefully from the photographs of the finished carving (Figs 9.20–9.25) before beginning work. Notice that the eyes really do poke out sideways and form the widest part of the head and neck area. The top of the head is almost flat, as are the cheeks running down underneath each eye, and the mouthparts are remarkably similar to the beak of a bird – hence the name 'hawksbill' – though chunkier and without a sharp point. Underneath, the chin and neck are rounded and far narrower than the top of the head.

FIG 9.11 *Work commences on the details of head and neck*

PADDLES

The three paddles can now be roughly shaped. The cross section is something like that of an aircraft wing, though a little thicker, and running along the rear of each paddle is a fin-like extension which assists swimming efficiency; there is a small claw on the leading edge. The shaping is done with shallow gouges, using inside and outside cutting edges as appropriate; a V-tool helps with the detail. Near to the body, each leg increases slightly in width.

The missing paddle can now be carved from a large offcut, ensuring that the grain runs in the correct direction to match at the join. While working on the main carving, it is useful to shape a short leg stump to sort out exactly where the new paddle should be inserted. When carving the new paddle to approximate shape, leave plenty of wood around the insertion area.

Set in the eyes and beak, having first taken care that these are drawn in the correct positions before you begin cutting. Small gouges and a narrow V-tool worked by hand will be sufficient to get the shapes right (Fig 9.11). Details of the wrinkles and small plates can be left until later.

ASSEMBLY

Cut back the stump on the body so that its upper edge is almost hidden just below the top shell, and its underside butts on to the edge of the lower shell. Make this joint

FIG 9.12 *Construction of the front paddle: tenon and metal dowel are visible*

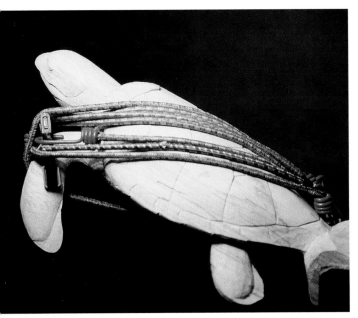

FIG 9.13 *The paddle is clamped using an ad hoc arrangement of strong elastic*

FIG 9.14 *This view of the work at a slightly later stage (with the main carving almost complete and the vice-hold further reduced) shows clearly the delicate fins which extend along the rear edge of each limb*

surface flat, and cut a 1 × ½in (25 × 13mm) mortise into the centre, about ⅜in (10mm) deep. Choose a ⅛in (3mm) brass screw or steel rod to use as a dowel – I prefer a screw, as one end can be screwed into the body and provide a totally solid basis for the dowel. Drill a hole in the centre of the mortise, using a bit slightly under ⅛in (3mm).

Turning to the paddle to be joined, offer it up to the body joint surface at the angle required for the paddle, and mark the joint surface on the paddle, allowing for a tenon protruding ⅜in (10mm) to fit the mortise. The technique appears complicated when described in words, but Fig 9.12 shows what is required.

While working on the joint surfaces, continually offer up the paddle until the fit is as exact as you can make it. The completed mortise and tenon should provide reasonable strength even with the joint dry. Now drill the ⅛in (3mm) dowel hole through the centre of the tenon, insert the dowel and check everything fits together snugly. All being well, the joint can be glued and clamped. Fig 9.13 shows the kind of ad hoc arrangement that may be necessary to provide strong pressure when working with irregular curved objects – it may look terrible, but it works.

The final shaping can now be done on all four paddles, reducing the thickness of the rear fins as far as you dare – in nature these are the thickness of a postcard (Fig 9.14).

FINAL DETAILS

Detailed work on the various body surfaces can now be started, but first the vice-hold must be removed. Using a small saw, cut around the pointed rear end of the body.

From this point on, holding the carving becomes more of a problem. The solution I used was to clamp a large block in the vice, projecting upwards sufficiently so that the flat lower surface of the carving can rest on the block without the paddles touching the bench. A folded cloth is placed on the vice-block, and the carving held with an elastic 'octopus' (an arrangement of strong elastic ropes as used on a car roof rack) wrapped over the body. For working on the underside, the vice-block is set below the level of the vice jaws so that the curved back will rest firmly (again on a folded cloth) on the block and the vice jaws.

WRINKLES

On the turtle all areas of skin where there is underlying skeletal movement show a remarkable degree of wrinkling. In each location, the wrinkles occur in particular directions according to the angles of flexing. It is in fact quite tricky to make realistic wrinkles, and

FIG 9.15 *Wrinkles being set in around the head and neck area*

FIG 9.16 *Scales on the head have been outlined with a V-tool and stained. More work is required to the neck wrinkles*

if they are in the wrong direction, nothing will make them look natural.

Mark the wrinkles in detail before cutting them with a V-tool and a tiny veiner (Fig 9.15). If this is a first attempt at 'wrinkling', experiment on a piece of scrap first until you can produce a reasonably natural appearance. Unless you have a particularly steady hand, the edges of each deep wrinkle will need to be smoothed with a riffler file or abrasive paper.

WOODWORM DAMAGE

This section is for interest only – you are unlikely to be facing the same beetle damage problem I encountered with this project. However, you may well come across it sometime: a large piece of timber which you want to use, and which has small areas showing the telltale holes and grooves of old or new infestation. If the beetle is active you will already have encountered one or more fleshy grubs during the process of carving. Either way, the first step is to make sure any activity is halted by applying a proprietary woodworm treatment, following the instructions on the container. Be aware that on light-coloured timber this may cause local discoloration.

To repair the damage there are various ways to proceed. With the larger grooves along the surface, make them deeper using a tiny drill bit and blow out the dust.

Then shape a sliver of waste to fit the groove, and repair as if it were a small shake (see pages 153–4). Vertical holes can be repaired with a matchstick-sized dowel, though when cut flush to the surface the cross grain of the dowel may show much darker than the surrounding area, and the spotty appearance caused by the repair may look unsightly. Alternatively, use coloured wax to fill the holes, testing it first on an offcut to ensure that the shade will match the wood after the chosen finish has been applied. I used a combination of all three methods, and adjusted the areas of staining later on to help hide the larger repairs.

HEAD AND PADDLE SCALES

By now you should have a reasonable-looking turtle. If you are working with a dark wood and carving simply to produce the right shape and movement, this is the time to start the finishing process and sort out the base.

For those with a hint of masochism, we are going to attempt to carve and stain the tiny scales. Before proceeding, ensure you have the same amount of time as that spent on the carving so far, and be prepared for long hours of close-up work – we are talking detail here! The good news is that if preferred, most of this work can be done in the sitting room rather than a cold workshop.

First, however, the surface should be sanded or scraped to a smooth finish, ending up with medium-grade wire

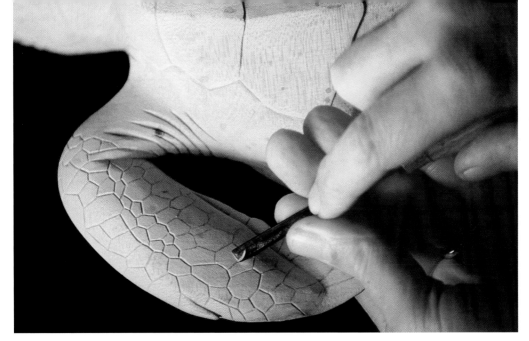

FIG 9.17 *'Chip carving' the individual scales on a front paddle*

wool. The smoother the surface, the less the likelihood of faults while outlining the edges of each scale and staining.

Starting with the head, make three full-size copies of the drawing – one for the top and one for each side. Taking each drawing in turn, use carbon paper to mark through the outline of each scale. A V-tool is used to cut the shallow grooves around each scale. Make sure the V-tool remains sharp as a razor so that the cross-grain cuts are always clean (Fig 9.16). The V-tool was also used to create the hatched effect around the lower edge of the beak, where softer cartilage surrounds the mouth.

Repeat the scaling procedure with each of the four paddles, both above and below. If you have ever done chip carving, this close, detailed work feels very similar (Fig 9.17).

STAINING

We can now begin staining. Acrylic paint would be a simpler option, as there is less likelihood of colour bleeding at the edges of each scale. However, in my experience stain gives a far more natural finish, though certain precautions are required before making a start.

The colour needs to be a mid-chocolate brown. A small, good-quality artist's brush is required, which must work to a fine point. The consistency of the stain must be thick to minimize bleeding, and this can be accomplished by using a shallow container for the stain, spreading two or three small brushfuls over the surface and leaving this to dry out for an hour. Then dip the brush into fresh stain and mix this with the dry to form a waxy consistency.

Experiment on areas of scrap wood until you are happy with the results.

Experiment also with the finish which you intend to apply over the stain, to ensure that it will not cause the colour to run at the finishing stage. This is absolutely crucial, otherwise long hours of work will be ruined in the blink of an eye. For example, an oil-based stain followed by an oil finish is likely to give disastrous results. I opted for an oil-based stain and finishing with shellac sanding sealer.

Once all the parameters are in place, the scales can be stained. Notice that not all the scales on the paddles are dark, particularly on the rear paddles (Figs 9.18 and 9.19), while on the underside very few scales need staining (Fig 9.20). Most scales are dark almost to the

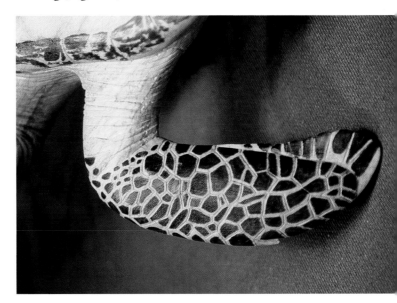

FIG 9.18 *Staining complete on the front left paddle*

FIG 9.19 *Staining on the rear left paddle*

FIG 9.21 *A real 'tortoiseshell' from a hawksbill turtle. The almost random camouflage pattern is not easy to copy realistically*

FIG 9.20 *View from underneath. Here very few scales are dark - from below, looking towards the bright water surface, the turtle requires a light camouflage*

FIG 9.22 *Staining in progress on the carapace*

edge, but some just have a patch of dark near the centre. It is advisable, when one section is completed and the stain is thoroughly dry, to seal that area with finish to avoid any chance of smudging.

The tortoiseshell

The dorsal shell requires a similar technique for staining, except that each of the large scales is covered in an almost random camouflage pattern (Figs 9.21 and 9.22). I say 'almost', because any old pattern will not look right — again, close attention to nature will pay dividends. In

particular, the scales at the edge have a different camouflage from the main shell, and the direction of the 'streaks' on each of the main scutes is also important.

FINISHING

For those who have jumped over the details of scales and staining, now is the time to smooth the surface ready for sealing. A tooled surface would be possible, but a finely sanded surface to most areas will give good results. The idea is to end up with a deep glow (not shine) over the whole carving, most particularly the back.

If you have been involved with staining, most of the surface will already have been sealed in sections as each was completed. One coat of sanding sealer or other finish should now be applied to any unsealed areas. After de-nibbing the first coat of sanding sealer with medium-grade wire wool (if you have stained, do this gently to avoid spoiling detail), apply a second coat all over.

One more session of de-nibbing, and we can apply a final wax finish. If you have used sycamore, the background colour may still be rather pale at this stage. If so, use a wax which imparts a yellowish tinge; otherwise, if you are happy with the colour, use a neutral wax (Figs 9.23–9.25).

The final appearance of the turtle is enhanced by building up a deep patina of wax. Apply each coat using a rag over flat areas and a waxing brush elsewhere, ensuring that there is no build-up of wax in the areas of detail. Allow it to dry for 6–12 hours, then burnish off with a soft rag or (clean) shoe brush. Leave for a further 12 hours and repeat the procedure. After the first three applications, apply any further coats at weekly intervals.

THE BASE

As noted at the beginning of this chapter, quite a lot of thought went into the question of how to mount the turtle. I eventually decided on driftwood, and spent several pleasant days walking the dog along the local river bank and estuary, scouring the area for the right shape. Finally, at the point of despair I happened on a huge stump of elm (Fig 9.26) and, with help, managed to get it home.

Most of the timber was soft and rotten beyond redemption, but part of one side was sound, and from this

FIG 9.23 *All staining completed; sanding sealer and one coat of wax have been applied*

FIG 9.24 *A view of the left side at the same stage*

FIG 9.25 *The front view shows the angles of the front paddles*

FIG 9.26 *The huge driftwood stump of elm*

FIG 9.27 *The base shaped from the driftwood; note the projecting hardwood pegs on which the carving will be located*

I cut out a likely-looking section. With driftwood like this, it is very much a case of following your nose in terms of design. The main thing is to provide a flat, stable base for the reasonably heavy carving. In this case it was a matter of sawing at about 30° to the grain and then planing the base until it was truly flat.

The rest of the work involves tinkering with the shape until it looks right – not so much carving as splitting off small sections at a time with an old carpenter's chisel to leave a natural weathered appearance, and constantly offering up the turtle to ensure that it is going to lie on top at the right angle and that it will not look as if it has been bolted down to the base – there should be as much free space underneath the creature as possible. My original idea was to slope the turtle upwards as though it were coming up for air, but in practice this gave the impression of a rocket taking off! Swimming downwards turned out to look far more natural.

Once the base looks right, the upper surfaces can be vigorously scrubbed with a stiff wire brush to mimic the effect of water penetration; and at this stage, if the driftwood is still damp, it should be left in a warm, ventilated place for some days to dry out thoroughly.

To finish, a darker stain may provide a more realistic underwater colour. As usual, experiment first with a mixture of stains on a piece of waste; when the result is satisfactory, apply liberally with a brush to ensure the rough surface and crevices are all covered.

I seldom use varnish on carvings, as it tends to clog the detail, but here the wetter look of a matt or satin varnish is ideal. Several coats may be necessary – and just for once, no need to rub down between coats.

MOUNTING THE CARVING

The turtle should be able to rest on the base without being fixed, but of course it will be unstable. In order to fix the two together I used simple wooden pegs: four ¼in (6mm) diameter hardwood dowels set into the base, projecting ½in (13mm) upwards, the tops slightly chamfered (Fig 9.27). Holes were drilled in the underside of the turtle to receive the pegs, taking care that the positions were exact and the pegs would insert with a snug but not tight fit.

Final construction simply entailed putting the turtle on the base (Fig 9.28). It could be glued, but I felt it unnecessary, and two removable sections are more convenient for transport, or if further work or repair is required for any reason in the future.

FIG 9.28 *The project complete*

CHAPTER 10
Otter relief

THIS PROJECT is an example of deep relief (or high relief) carving. This technique is halfway between carving completely in the round on the one hand, and on the other using shallow relief, which portrays the subject almost as an embossed picture. Deep relief normally retains the background wood, and may also include, as in this case, a deep base for the practical purpose of standing the carving on a mantelpiece or shelf. The otter itself stands out some $2\frac{1}{2}$in (64mm) from the background, and the base conveniently represents the water from which the animal is emerging. The carving can therefore be viewed from a variety of angles, though if you look at it laterally, almost edge-on, the depth dimension will be somewhat foreshortened.

OTTERS

In the British Isles there is one species of the subfamily *Lutrinae*: the European otter (*Lutra lutra*). They are comparatively rare creatures, and you might make many expeditions to a river or seashore they are known to frequent without catching so much as a glimpse of an otter, apart from finding a few characteristic dark droppings. Thankfully, due to increased conservation work, they are gradually on the increase again, and it is hoped their numbers will reach 1960 levels by the year 2002. Various species of otter occur in many parts of the temperate world.

The otter's shape is designed for the water – streamlined, with a powerfully flexible body and feet webbed between the five clawed toes. The thick fur is in two layers: the outer a coarse, water-shedding fur, the inner coat quite different and comprising a mixture of fine and extremely thick hairs which trap air as a form of insulation.

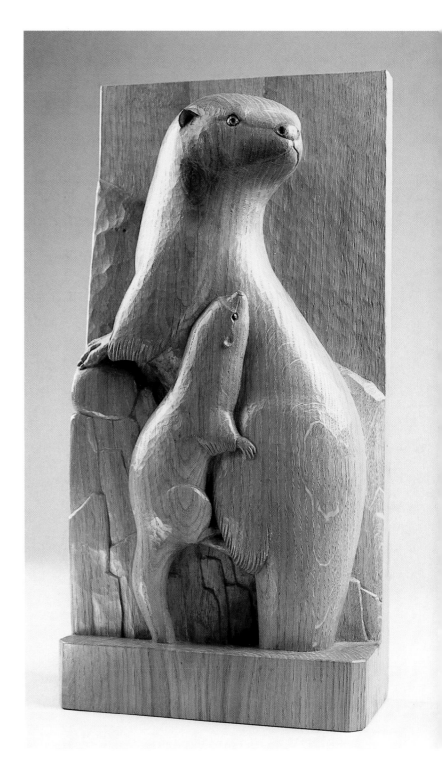

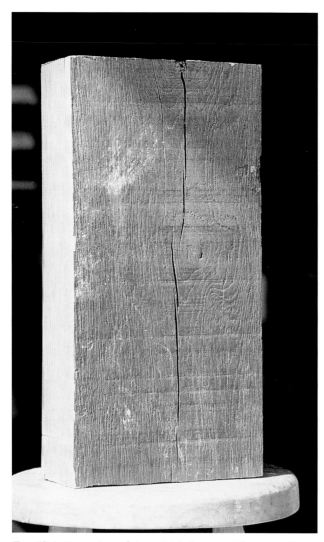

FIG 10.1 *Rear view of the oak block rescued from an old gatepost. The original finish is retained, and the shake will need attention later*

When the otter emerges, water cascades from the outer fur, giving it a distinctive spiky appearance.

For hunting, the otter's eyes adjust to compensate for visual distortion underwater, and the profusion of whiskers around the muzzle and eyebrows helps it to sense the movement of a fish in murky water. Naturally, whiskers are almost impossible to portray in carving and can at best only be suggested, perhaps by cutting fine grooves on the surface.

The cubs remain helpless for many weeks after birth; they are weaned after four months, and grow relatively slowly. They stay with their mother for up to a year, and she will defend them fiercely if threatened. Their first excursion to the water has to be prompted – sometimes

forced – but once they have tried it, the cubs very soon appreciate the endless possibilities of the underwater environment. We could perhaps label this project 'After the first dip'.

OAK

If you were asked to name the royalty of woodcarving timbers, which would you choose? Perhaps the queen would be lime, invariably chosen for decorative work (see Chapter 12), but from a traditional point of view the undoubted king is oak (*Quercus spp.*). Look in any medieval church or great house and the outstanding carvings are in oak: pew ends, misericords, panels depicting Biblical or other historical scenes, chair backs, fireplace surrounds, lecterns and pulpits, even carvings from ships – the list is endless. For its combination of strength, durability, lustrous finish and ability to take detail, oak is king.

Most parts of the oak tree contain tannic acids which make the timber resistant to decay; the heartwood is particularly rich in tannins. The odour is unmistakable in freshly cut timber, and for centuries the tannic acids have been extracted to treat leather. The downside is that tannins react with iron in screws and nails, which eventually disintegrate, producing black 'ink stains'. For this reason wooden pegs have always been used in traditional oak construction, for example in furniture and roofing.

When oak is sawn radially – that is, from the centre to the circumference – the broad silver-grained rays produce an attractive decorative feature prized by the furniture-maker for table tops and panels. Otherwise the timber is yellow-brown, apart from the rare and highly-prized brown oak which is produced by a natural fungus stain.

The piece used for this project came from an old gatepost, 8in (203mm) square, containing some deep shakes. The block size needed is $15\frac{1}{2} \times 8 \times 3\frac{1}{2}$in (390 × 200 × 90mm), so I was able to choose the best area of the post. I deliberately retained one external surface as an original feature for the back of the carving (Fig 10.1). If you cannot obtain a block this size, the thickness of the carving can be reduced a little from $3\frac{1}{2}$in, but then the relief depth will have to be foreshortened further.

The idea for a mother and baby otter design (Fig 10.2a–c) came from a calendar picture which I saw some years ago.

FIG **10.2***a Otter relief:*
front elevation

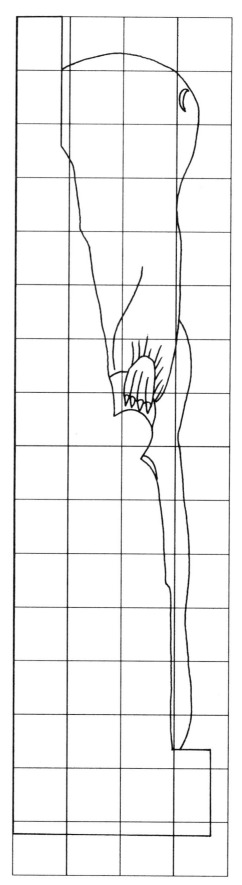

Fɪɢ 10.2*b*
*Right side
elevation*

Fɪɢ 10.2*c*
*Left side
elevation*

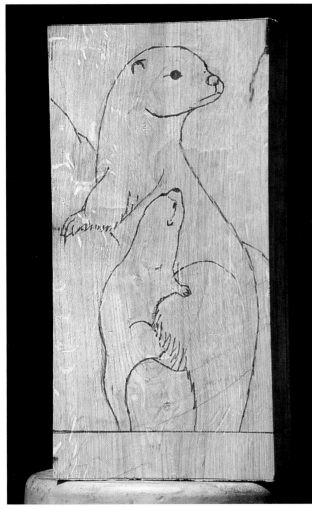

FIG 10.3 *The outline picture marked on the face of the block; the horizontal line near the bottom represents the water level*

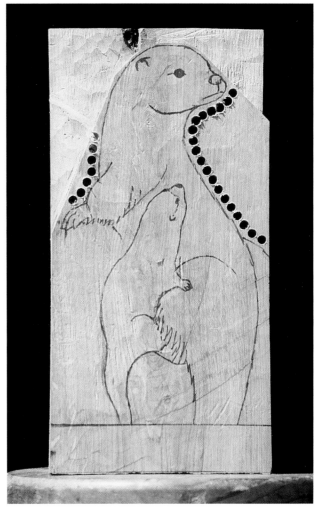

FIG 10.4 *Adjacent holes are drilled around the outline to a depth just above the background level. A nasty knot has appeared at the top at background level; this will be dealt with later*

GROUNDING

'Grounding' is the technical name for establishing the background level. First mark the front view on the face of the block, including the base 'water level' (Fig 10.3). On the sides and top, mark the thickness of the background all round at ⁷⁄₈in (22mm); on the lower part of each side, leave extra wood for the river bank and rocks (this can be seen most clearly in Fig 10.6 overleaf).

Prepare to cut back around the head and shoulders to leave a thickness of 1in (25mm) at the back, the extra ⅛in (3mm) being left to allow for texturing the background later. Use a handsaw to make perpendicular cuts where this is possible, such as around the convex curves of the head and upper body. With a mallet and a large shallow gouge, remove the waste up to these saw cuts; but avoid heavy mallet work, which could send the gouge through to damage the body.

Where the body curves are concave, drill adjacent holes using a bit around ⁵⁄₁₆in (8mm), allowing ⅛in (3mm) for error around the body line (Fig 10.4). Take care not to drill too deep – if you do not have a depth stop on your drill, a small mark of white correcting fluid can be put on the drill bit. Cut away the waste up to the drill holes, this time using a smaller medium-curve gouge (no. 4, for example), then clean up the vertical body line, using a flat chisel for convex sections, and gouges for the concave areas such as under the chin. Straight in-cannel gouges work most efficiently for removing waste across flat surfaces (see pages 151–2).

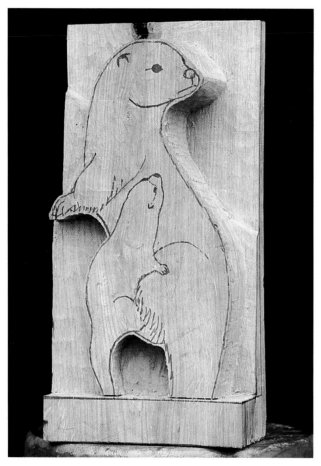

FIG 10.5 *The outline of the two otters blocked out and the various background levels established*

FIG 10.6 *Removing waste outside the lateral outline. The adult head is the highest point and is not disturbed at this stage; treating the cub's head in the same way would be an improvement*

The process of grounding is continued around the adult's front limb and the lower body and tail of both adult and cub. Make sure the background level here is not too deep. The adult's front paw needs to rest on the rock, so the background on the left is quite thick – 2¾in (70mm) from the back (see Fig 10.8). This part of the background then slopes back from left to right; at the right-hand edge it is only 1¼in (32mm) from the back (Fig 10.5).

The section between the tails is a little more challenging. Use the drill technique again, but this time, once the first ½in (13mm) of waste has been removed, a curved or frontbent gouge is required to deepen the recess further – I used a ½in (13mm) no. 15.

BOSTING IN

It is useful during this next section of the work to cut a separate outline of each body from card or thick paper.

Now that the two bodies are blocked out from the background, it is time to sort out the relative depths. The highest (furthest forward) area in my carving is the adult's head. However, on reflection, the finished carving would be better if the cub's head were further forward, as shown in the drawing (Fig 10.2b–c); so cut around both heads at this stage, and cut back everything else by ½in (13mm). (If the original block was less than 3½in (90mm) thick, then reduce the depth levels in proportion to the thickness you are working with). I find the quickest way to remove a layer of this size accurately is to make a number of saw cuts and then chop out between them using mallet and gouge (Fig 10.6). If any knots are encountered, first cut all around them with the gouge and then saw across the knot with a narrow Japanese or similar saw.

Re-mark the body shapes and shade the new high spots: these are the shoulders, haunches and limbs. Elsewhere, the outside edges of the bodies and tails can be rounded (Figs 10.7 and 10.8), but leave any undercutting until later when the curves have been correctly established. Shallow gouges are best for this work. Cut down slowly and carefully around the edges of the cub where it will touch the adult's body, keeping a careful eye on the curves and viewing from different angles as you go. The section around the lower limbs is a little tricky, as you expose the cub leg resting on the adult leg – small gouges, narrow-angle parting tool and skew chisel are needed here.

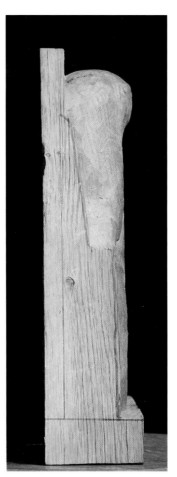

FIG 10.7 *Bosting in: the outlines have been redrawn and the highest areas marked in red. The saw marks still visible from the previous stage will disappear as the body surfaces are modelled*

FIG 10.8 *View from the left side with the background levels set in*

FIG 10.9 *The form of the baby otter has now been defined. Note the rear leg resting on the adult leg, and the tiny protruding ear*

Fig 10.9 shows a detail of this area at a later stage, with the general shapes established.

It is worth noting that in most of the pictures showing the development of each project the work has been cleaned up rather more than usual, for clarity. If your work looks a bit messier, don't worry – so does mine, normally!

BACKGROUND

At this stage or a bit later, the background needs to be textured, and for this carving I have adopted three different stylized surfaces, which can be seen in the photograph on page 103 and in Fig 10.17 on page 113:

- The sky is simply tooled horizontally with a wide shallow gouge (as sharp as possible so as to pare smoothly across the grain).
- The more distant river bank, top and right, is cut vertically along the grain with the same gouge to give a random, irregular surface.
- In order to make the foreground rocks look reasonably authentic, you need to think about them. Apart from heaps of boulders or scree, a rock face will be stratified in some way. Here vertical strata are used, partly because this seemed to work best, but also because the structure leads the eye upwards towards the main focus – the adult head – and to a subsidiary focus in the paw resting on a boulder. Tooling is done with a small flat chisel, shallow gouge and parting tool, except

FIG 10.10 *This detail, with the baby otter almost finished, shows how the tooled rock surfaces are set in to the left and between the tails*

FIG 10.11 *Detail of the adult's front paw resting on a boulder*

between the tails, where it is necessary to use frontbent tools. While working within this cramped space, it is almost impossible not to mark the body surfaces with the tool shafts, which is why the background, here at least, needs to be complete before finishing the bodies. Try to suggest a continuity of background from left to right, including this section between the tails (Fig 10.10).

Once the rocks are complete the front paw can be detailed. Here a selection of the tiniest chisels, skew chisels, parting tool and veiners are used to pick out the five digits, each ending in a claw (Fig 10.11).

THE HEADS

Before working any further on the bodies, it is helpful to get the adult head right. This is the focal point of the whole

carving and will determine all the other curves and relative depths. The head is turned back from the body and ends up three-quarters on, so a front view of the head is seen when the carving is viewed from an angle of 45° to the right (Fig 10.12).

The highest spot from the background is the nose, and we need to work back from there, remembering to leave an uncut area for the ear projecting forwards. It is probably a good idea, before continuing, to touch up the sharpness of all the tools used so far, especially those which have been used with the mallet. From here on, all carving will be done by hand.

Re-mark the positions of the eye, ear and mouth. Using these as reference points, carve the overall shape of the head with a ½in (13mm) chisel and shallow gouge so that it looks right from different angles of viewing, especially face-on. This will require a fair amount of undercutting to expose the left side of the face (the side nearest the background) and the position of the left eye.

FIG 10.12 *The adult head (before cleaning up) viewed from 45°. Note how the left ear 'disappears' into the background. On reflection, the top of the head should be flatter*

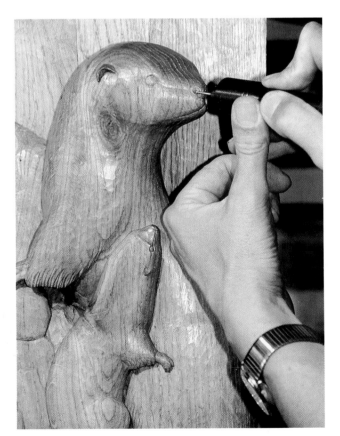

FIG 10.13 *A small burr is used to shape inside the nostrils*

FIG 10.14
Right lateral view, nearing completion. From this angle it is clear that greater depth should have been allowed for the baby's head

The left ear remains permanently out of sight (Fig 10.12).

Once the curves appear satisfactory, work on the detail of the ear, nose and mouth using small gouges and parting tool. The nostrils are inset most easily using a flexi-shaft machine with a small circular burr (Fig 10.13). The eye is shaped by first stabbing with a ¼in (6mm) no. 7 gouge, which will give the correct oval contour for the upper and lower margins of the eye. Curve the eye surface itself with a tiny chisel. The surrounding area is cut down to meet the eye perimeter using a slightly larger gouge. The final touch, if required, is to inset the iris as a tiny shallow bowl – again the flexi-shaft gives the most accurate result for this detailed work.

Once satisfied with the adult head, turn to the cub's head, which, although far smaller, presents several problems: at this scale the eye and ear positions, and the various angles on the face, are rather critical, not to say fiddly. It was at this stage that I wished I had left a greater depth of wood to work with (Fig 10.14) – yes,

quantify authenticity – perhaps it is a sort of instinct etched into the hearts of over-fastidious woodcarvers.

- Leave it and live with it, working on the perspective as best you can in order to fool the eye that the head is not as flat as it really is. This is the option I went for, but it doesn't really help from the side view, which I still find embarrassing.

When both heads are almost complete in shape and detail, the movement of each body can be envisaged more easily. Pare back the various surfaces to obtain long, smooth curves, and where appropriate undercut the body and tail at the junction with the background. The finished surface will be left tooled with flattish gouge marks to indicate the rough fur, completed with smaller cuts on the cub than on the adult. Where the fur hangs from the limbs, a parting tool is used to cut slightly irregular curved lines (Fig 10.15).

A KNOTTY SHAKE

In some of the photographs you can see a badly damaged section to the background, right at the top. Parts of this large exposed knot simply fell out while work was in progress. The knot led to a long, deep crack right down the back which threatened to weaken the entire carving –

FIG 10.15 *The baby complete. The eye has been stained dark. The surfaces of both animals have been left with a gouge-tooled finish; the V-tool was used to define the hanging fur around the limbs*

I know, it shows! What do you do in a situation like this? The options are:

- Reduce the depth of the entire adult – that is, practically recarve the whole thing – a long, tedious procedure, even if it works.
- Chop out and substitute a new cub – not too difficult, but it would be impossible to match the new wood exactly for colour and grain. This would also mean a loss of 'authenticity' – though this may worry the carver more than the eventual viewer. You can't

FIG 10.16 *A new section has been made to replace the knot and part of the deep shake at the rear of the block*

though luckily it did not show through the animal body. Anyway, something radical had to be done.

Having decided to preserve the old gatepost finish on the back, the new section had to be cut from the remaining post and let in to the exact depth. There was no margin for error either in the depth or the side joins – it would be almost impossible to bodge old gatepost surface ('authenticity' again). This meant long hours of carving a section to fit (Fig 10.16). As it turned out, the match at the back was better than at the front, where an invisible join was needed even more. The colour was not an exact match, nor was the grain, which meant that the joins show as tramlines. Greater care in matching the shape of the new piece to the existing background grain would have paid dividends, but in the end life is only so long!

FINAL TOOLING

I tend to leave the final tooling of all sections until the carving is all but complete. There are two reasons for this. One is that inevitably the surface tends to get dirty as you are working, and leaving the tooling till last allows you to ignore this until the final texturing work is done. The other is that at this late stage there may still be some final adjustments to be made in order to improve the appearance or the perspective, and this is annoying if you have already spent considerable time finishing the section in question. In fact, the final cleaning up always takes ages, particularly around the more detailed sections – nose, eye, ear, claw, etc. – on both animals. It is also important to end up with a clean 'join' between the background and the animal body or head, even where this is undercut at an acute angle, as behind the neck. Skew chisels are particularly valuable here.

SEALING

I was tempted to stain the whole thing darker, as freshly cut oak is a remarkably light cream colour; but the contrast between this and the original dark gatepost surface was supposed to be a feature, so – no staining. The surface was given two coats of a shellac sanding sealer, each de-nibbed with fine wire wool. I did succumb to staining the eyes; this was left until after the first coat of sealant so there was no chance of the stain leaching outside the exact edge of the eye. The iris was retooled to remove the sealer and a tiny artist's brush was loaded with some water-based stain (half-dried to the consistency of paint, as described for the Turtle project on page 99) to pick out the iris; normal stain does not take at all once the wood is sealed. The second coat of sanding sealer fixed the stain.

A good coat of neutral-coloured wax was applied with a stiff brush, working the wax into every nook and cranny and avoiding any blobs which might obscure detailed tooling. The wax coat was left to dry for a few hours and then buffed up with a polishing rag, a softer brush being used to polish the deep sections (Fig 10.17).

FIG 10.17 *The carving complete. Verdict: 'E for effort' - the adult head is not as otterlike as I would have liked*

Tools used

It would be tedious to list the tools used for every carving in the book, but this project in particular requires quite a wide range. Glancing at the bench clutter when it was complete, I thought it might be of interest to include all the tools used. Of course, one could get away with a more modest selection, but these are the ones which came out of storage for my Otters.

Description	Sheffield List number	Width		Remarks
		in	*mm*	
Straight chisels	1	½	13	
		¼	6	
		⅛	3	
Skew chisels	2	¼	6	
		⅛	3	
Parting or V-tools	39	⁷⁄₁₆	11	
	41	⅜	8	A selection of different widths and angles is
	45	½	13	helpful for detail and cleaning up
frontbent	43	¼	6	
Gouges	3	¾	19	Used more than any other tool for this project
		⅜	10	
	skew no. 3	¾	19	Home-made from a no. 3 gouge – great for slicing flat surfaces
	4	¼	6	
	6	1	25	
		⁷⁄₁₆	11	
		⅜	10	
	7	¼	6	The eye size for the adult
		³⁄₁₆	5	
	11	³⁄₁₆	5	
Curved gouge	15	½	13	
Frontbent chisel	21	¼	6	The curved and bent tools, including the bent V-tool, are necessary for the recess between the tails
Frontbent gouge	24	¾	19	
Riffler files, various shapes				For finishing detail
Flexi-shaft drill with 2mm burr				For recessed features in eye and nose
Brushes				Stiff wax brush (short bristle) and soft brush for application of the shellac sealer; wash out the shellac brush with methylated spirit (denatured alcohol)
Sandpaper and sanding block				120 to 180 grit, bought in rolls, for the flat surfaces on sides, top and base
Plane				
Set square				
Metal ruler				

CHAPTER 11
Heron

HERONS ARE particularly photogenic birds (Fig 11.1) and a marvellous subject for woodcarving, but be warned – not one of the easiest. The long, thin legs, extended neck and tapering dagger-shaped beak all require the grain to run lengthwise. Unfortunately the beak and legs are invariably found at right angles to each other, so one or the other will need to be carved separately. In this project the bird is standing tall, neck straight and almost

FIG 11.1 *A selection of heron pictures pinned on the wall as a collage, for reference during carving (see page 174). Try to collect pictures from a wide variety of sources, showing your chosen subject in characteristic postures and from as many different angles as possible*

parallel to the legs, so it is sensible to use vertical grain for the main carving, including the legs, and add the beak later (Fig 11.2). Herons also have another characteristic pose for fishing where the neck is bent almost double (see the example on page 179), and in that position it is the legs which are best carved separately, though the leg-to-body join then needs a strengthening dowel of some kind.

HERON SPECIES

This project portrays the grey heron (*Ardea cinerea*), found throughout Europe and across Asia to China, and very similar in appearance to the great blue heron (*Ardea herodias*) of North America. There are over sixty other species of herons, bitterns and egrets worldwide, ranging

in size from the 5ft (1.5m) tall giant heron of Sumatra to the very much smaller and beautifully plumed egrets found all over the world. Apart from the bittern, the grey heron is the only breeding member of the family *Ardeidae* in the British Isles.

All herons are superbly adapted for hunting fish and other shallow-water vertebrates such as frogs and water voles. They are generally gregarious at night, nesting in colonies in nearby trees or reed beds. During the day herons are normally seen standing alone, silent and motionless, head facing down at 45°, eyes focused in total concentration below the water surface. If disturbed by the slightest sound, the bird will stand erect like a sentinel, senses alert to impending danger. It is this latter pose, surveying the wider surroundings, which forms the subject for this project.

Yew

The yew (*Taxus spp.*) is a needle-leaved tree and therefore classified as a softwood – hardly an apt description of this exceptionally hard timber. The botanical name for softwoods, *gymnosperms*, includes all trees which bear naked fruit or seeds. Most of them are conifers, and all have a more primitive cell-structure than the broadleaved hardwoods or *angiosperms*. Some softwoods are physically harder, heavier and stronger than certain hardwoods, while, perversely, the softest and lightest timber (balsa) is a hardwood.

Regardless of its classification as a softwood, due to its slow growth and exceptionally long life cycle, the European yew (*Taxus baccata*) is very hard, dense and difficult to work. In addition, however careful you are with seasoning yew it is prone to extensive cracking – especially during carving, as tensions are released. The many problems found when working with yew, and its comparative scarcity, are perhaps the reasons why some books which list commercial timbers do not include it at all.

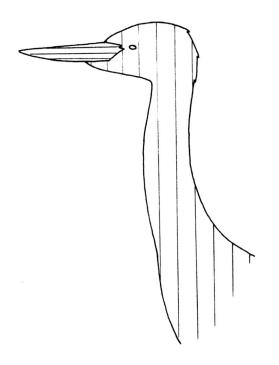

FIG 11.2 *The grain directions adopted for this carving. The grain of the main piece runs vertically for the sake of the legs; the beak will need to be made separately*

Despite all this, the rewards of a finished sculpture in yew can be stunning. Because of its elasticity it has traditionally been used to make longbows (a yew tree in every parish churchyard was not just for decoration), and because of the colouring it is occasionally used in decorative work such as parquet flooring, furniture and lute-making. There was a trend in the 1970s for screwing legs on to large slabs of yew and calling them coffee tables, and this can occasionally be a useful source of supply. The colour range of the wood is remarkable. Within a few inches you can find a variation from deep orange, through browns and purples to a creamy white, and decorated with various stripes and small dark spotted knots. The wood is not resinous, and finishes to a beautiful lustre with a simple coat of wax. The American or Pacific yew (*Taxus brevifolia*) is similar but rather darker in colour, lighter in weight and with a more uniform grain.

Making a start

Whether you feel brave enough to use yew or prefer something a little easier (elm would do well), a log or block of considerable size is needed for this project. Carving a heron, the nearer you can get to life-size the better – too small, and the finished result may be disappointing. Here we are working to approximately three-quarters life-size (Fig 11.3a–c), so the dimensions of timber required are 27 × 15 × 8in (690 × 380 × 200mm) – quite a chunk! I was lucky enough to find a friendly assistant at the local sawmill who helped me trawl through nearly an acre of stacked timber until we found the right piece among a pile of yew logs almost smothered in nettles. I slipped him a fiver, paid £10 for the unsawn timber and got a bargain which I couldn't lift on my own into the car boot (Fig 11.4).

Once home, and inspecting the timber more closely, I found an exceptionally deep groove and two large, almost longitudinal knots, which are not uncommon in yew. Over many years the trunk grows around the side shoots, leaving them almost loose in their 'socket'. The first task with a piece of damaged wood is to cut away all the bad areas and see what's left. In this case it became obvious that some problems would extend into the carving, and so a decision had to be taken: whether to start from scratch, or to continue while accepting that some patching work would be needed later. With some timbers patching can

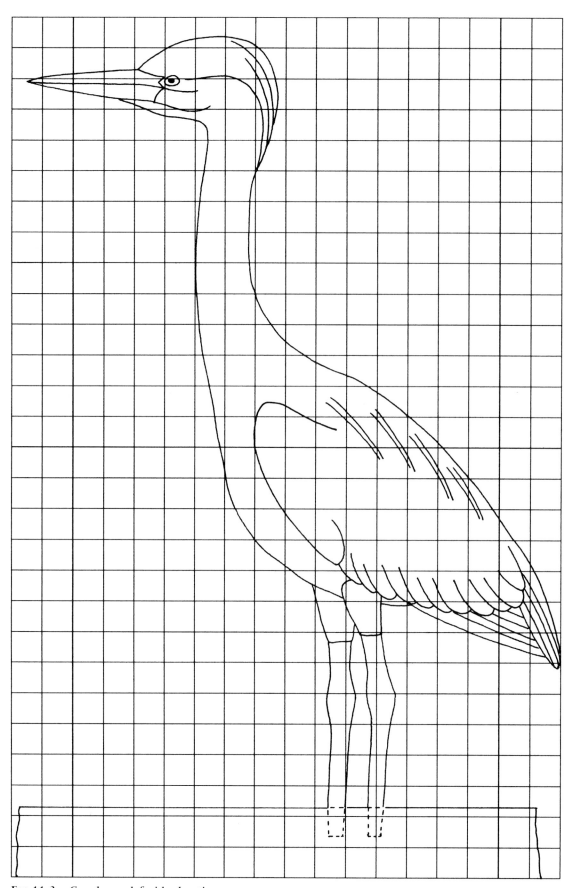

FIG 11.3a *Grey heron: left side elevation*

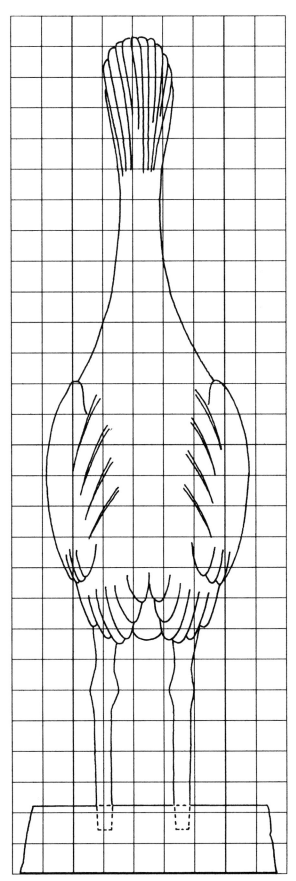

FIG 11.3*b* *Rear elevation*

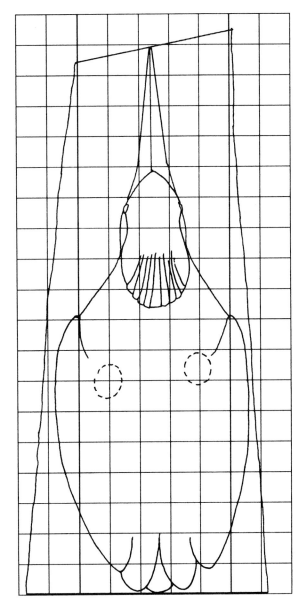

FIG 11.3*c* *Plan view*

FIG 11.4 *The massive log of yew: a daunting prospect*

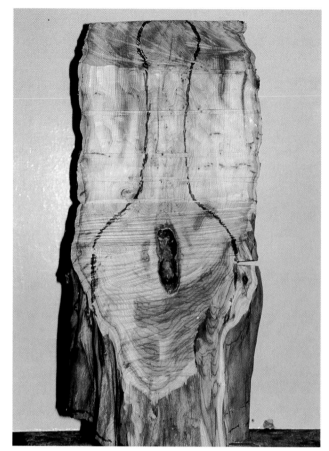

FIG 11.5 *Rear view, showing the back and neck shape cut out with the electric chainsaw and the lateral outlines marked. A significant area of rot has emerged in the centre; the level was reduced to avoid most of this*

be made almost invisible, but there is no way of matching the convoluted grain and vivid colour scheme of yew. Conscious that the project might end up as firewood, I decided to proceed, and was able to repair the damage later with offcuts.

BLOCKING OUT

As usual, the first task is to mark out the lateral view, leaving a generous margin for error all round, and keeping a thick block, 4in (100mm) square, around the legs so that the carving can be held securely in a joiner's vice (see Fig 11.7); a piece this size is impossible to fit on to the average bench-top carver's vice. Mark the lateral profile on to the de-barked log using a card or paper template – a chunky felt-tip pen makes a sufficiently visible mark during the early stages of carving. Now cut the log into block profile. A chainsaw is almost indispensable for this – it would take a mighty bandsaw to do the same job. Bear in mind that

not only will yew blunt all types of blade more quickly than most timbers, it will also produce incredibly sharp chips which fly off at high speed. Protective clothing – and above all an eye guard – is essential. Throughout the carving you will inevitably face hard, sharp edges which can cause abrasions and needle-sharp splinters to unprotected hands.

While cutting out the profile, in places where the saw faces impossible corners, make a number of cuts quite close together down to the marked line (across the grain). The waste can then be hacked out with a large shallow gouge, watching all the time for places where the grain suddenly changes direction to plunge down into the working area.

Next mark out the front-to-back profile (Fig 11.5) and, again using saw and gouges, remove all the waste outside the line. This completes the blocking out (Fig 11.6).

FIG 11.6 *The overall shape blocked out; the marks left by the chainsaw 'slices' are still visible at this stage*

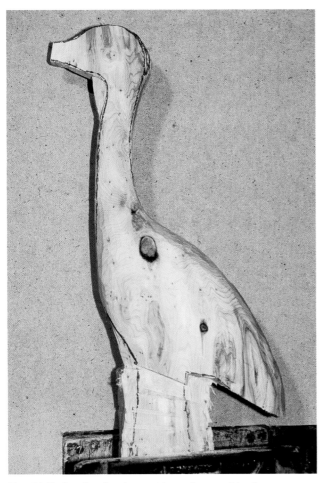

FIG 11.7 *Bosting in: the curves to chest and back are approximately in place. A triangular strengthening piece has been left between head and neck for the time being*

FROM SQUARE EDGES TO CURVES

Now we come to bosting in, where the main forms of the piece are established. The body, neck and head are roughly shaped by removing the corners. This rounding process can be done using shallow or medium gouges, assisted by saw cuts where necessary. You will need to re-mark the profiles from time to time as the carving progresses. It is a good idea to leave a strengthening angle of wood between neck and head for the time being (Fig 11.7), until the head has been rounded to shape. Around the long neck and head section, the mallet is used sparingly if at all — most of the waste can be removed, even on the hardest woods, by working the gouge across the grain, cutting a shallow sliver each time. Other techniques, which are not often found in textbooks, can be used to remove wood over a flat or gently curved area. Perhaps these methods are suspect for reasons which after 25 years I have not yet fathomed; but I find them helpful, and details can be found on pages 151–2.

The general shape of the body and folded wings is that of a rugby ball flattened at the base. At this stage, allow plenty of spare wood on each side so that the wings can protrude by up to ¾in (19mm) (Fig 11.8). The wing shape

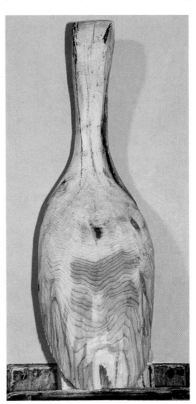

FIG 11.8 *A rear view of the rugby-ball-shaped body. Rot damage is visible to the right of the neck. All the remaining small areas of rot were cut out and replaced with offcuts shaped to match*

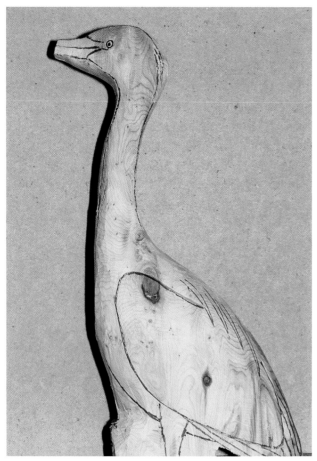

FIG 11.9 *Leg and wing shapes marked, with the larger feathers. The beak tip is not carved, since the whole of the cross-grain beak will be removed later*

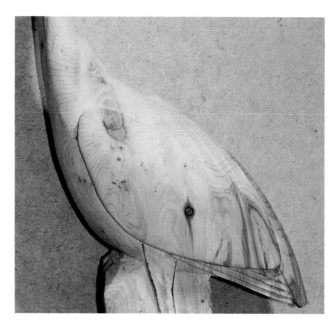

FIG 11.10 *Wing shape complete and primary feathers positioned*

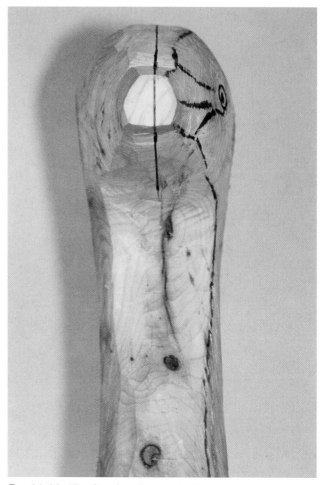

FIG 11.11 *Head and neck roughly shaped, with centre-line mark for reference*

on each side is now marked (Fig 11.9). Along the chest and stomach edges of the wing, cut away about ½in (13mm) using a narrow-angle parting tool with one side vertical along the wing edge, followed by a shallow gouge to increase the curvature of the chest and stomach. Eventually, with undercutting, the curve of the body will 'disappear' under the wings. At the tops of the wings (where they fold on to the body in the first wing joint), the distinctive shape is important to get right. The joint curves round sharply and then gently curves the other way, the projection of each wing fading away into the back feathers (Fig 11.10).

Work on the top section of the body will lead into the neck. Notice that the cross section of the middle and upper neck is not round but oval, with the longer section from front to back – that is, slightly flattened on each side.

As the beak will eventually be replaced by a new section of wood, the main length (which would be cross

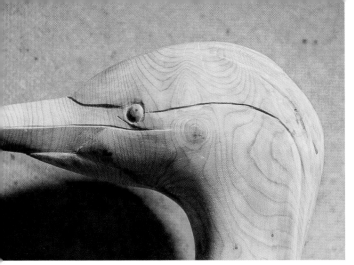

FIG 11.12 *The face area carved and partly sanded, ready for the removal of the temporary beak*

FIG 11.13 *Not a pretty picture! The original beak has been removed and a strengthening splint fitted to avoid damage to the long cross-grain lower 'lip'*

grain) is missing, so it presents a rather odd appearance (see Fig 11.9). There is a temptation at an early stage to carve features of the face and beak in some detail so that you can see the developing proportions of the bird better. However, this is best left until most of the heavier work is complete (Fig 11.11). While a mallet or saw is still being used, it is not difficult to nick or badly damage a section that has been finished too early, even to knock the whole thing out of an insufficiently tightened vice, producing a major problem which it is then too late to rectify.

If you are using yew, as mentioned earlier, there is a continual struggle with the grain which is wildly erratic, particularly around the knots. Even careful work can result in a sudden hole appearing where the grain has swooped downwards.

FEATHERS AND DETAILS

When carving any bird or mammal, a decision has to be taken quite early regarding the amount of detail you are going to attempt with feathers or fur. With this project we are keeping detail to the minimum because the swirling grain largely 'speaks for itself' and fussiness would clutter the final appearance; so only a selection of the larger wing feathers and a suggestion of the long, tapering back feathers will be necessary.

Once all the major removal of waste is complete (apart from the leg area), the head and temporary beak section can be carved in more detail. Mark the position of the eye on each side; take some care with this, as the location of the eye, its size and shape are all critical to the final appearance of the carving. I used a detailed picture of the

head area and marked the timber by pressing a pencil through the drawing. This can be repeated on the opposite side by reversing the drawing. Mark also the lines where the curve of the face is discontinuous, the shape of the beak insertion and the plumage above and behind the head. Although the whole beak section will later be removed, it is important to carve it to shape first so that the curves of both the forehead above and chin feathers below are correct. In cross section the beak itself is approximately diamond-shaped (Fig 11.12).

The features are carved using a parting tool (V-tool) and a small fluter (half-round gouge) to show the lines; small shallow gouges and a flat chisel can be used for the curved surfaces. I have a favourite small flat chisel for this detailed work to finish smoothly curved surfaces: ¼in (6mm) wide with a very shallow bevel on one side only. It is kept razor-sharp and can even be worked carefully against the grain without snagging. However, a tool with such an acute angle of cut is easily blunted or nicked.

THE BEAK

When the head is almost finished, it is time to replace the existing beak by cutting it out and fitting one carved from a separate piece of wood along the grain. This looks and feels like major surgery. The fragile area under the chin is temporarily strengthened using a splint mounted on a soft, modellable material such as Blu-Tack or Plasticine. The old beak is carefully cut out using the smallest available saw – one of the narrow Japanese saws is ideal. The socket is then cleaned up and cut back as accurately as possible to the position of the join (Fig 11.13).

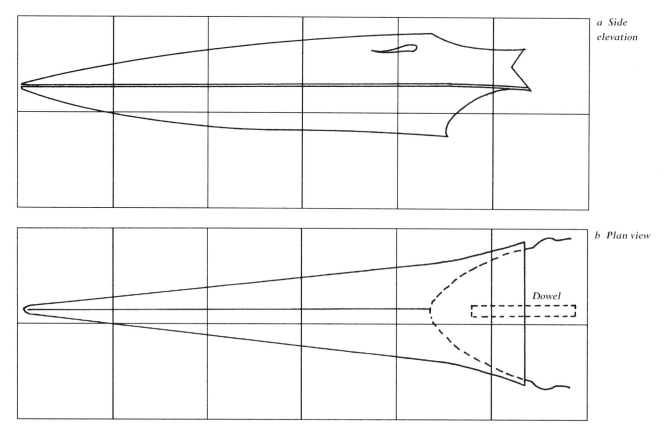

a Side elevation

b Plan view

Dowel

Fig 11.14 *Heron beak*

A new beak (Fig 11.14*a* and *b*) is marked out on an offcut kept from the original chainsawn chunks of waste. Notice how the function of the beak can be clearly seen by its dagger-like shape: it is used by the heron for catching its prey, on occasion by first stabbing a fish which is too large to be gripped easily.

The new beak is carved to shape using card templates of the lateral and plan views, slowly and carefully reducing the socket end until it fits exactly into the mouth area (Fig 11.15). It can be left slightly too wide on each side to allow for final adjustment after fitting. Leave the pointed tip quite blunt for the time being, to assist clamping. The new beak is then fitted using either a steel dowel or a large brass screw – 2 × ⅛in (50 × 3mm) – with the screw head removed. The dowel is not meant to be a secure fixing – this is achieved using wood glue – but as an insurance to hold the beak steady against any future sideways stress. Drill a hole horizontally into the head, centrally between the eyes (see Fig 11.14*b*), and make a temporary short dowel which just protrudes from the hole. Place a blob of paint on the end of the dowel and offer up the beak so that the paint marks the exact position for the hole into the

Fig 11.15 *During carving, the new beak is frequently offered up to the mouth to test the fit*

beak. Remove the temporary dowel, drill the beak, insert the permanent dowel and check the fit. When all is well, the beak can be fixed permanently with glue and clamped overnight (Fig 11.16). Once the glue is dry, the beak can be carved precisely to fit the contours of the face and the horizontal groove separating upper and lower beak set in with a V-tool, merging into the mouth groove under the eye (Fig 11.17).

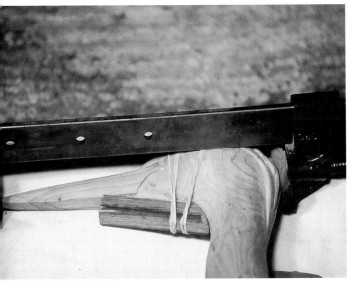

FIG 11.16 *The new beak has now been fitted, glued and clamped*

FIG 11.17 *Detailing of the head complete; notice how the eye looks forward*

In passing, note that when carving different parts of a living creature, it is worth having in mind what function each particular feature of the body has. If it is to appear natural, a beak must look as if it can do what it is designed for in nature: to open and shut, and to grip. For a heron it also acts as a lethal stabbing tool, for a finch it is a crushing tool for hard seeds, for a woodpecker it is a chisel, and so on. This functionality is equally important when we consider the detail of the eyes. Their primary purpose is to look intently ahead along the line of the beak. Each eye socket therefore needs to be tilted slightly forwards. When the central hollow for the iris is cut using a tiny semicircular gouge, it too will be slightly offset forwards, towards the beak (see Fig 11.17).

PLUMAGE

The topknot plumage above and behind the head can best be delineated using small veiners and a narrow parting tool to ensure these rounded feathers are undercut and appear to separate slightly from the head.

With the head and neck sections complete, it is time to stand back and check the main proportions of the head, neck and body so that any final adjustments can be made before starting on the wing and back feathers previously marked. The feathers can now be carved using a small parting tool for edges which overlap, and a shallow gouge

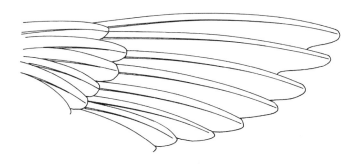

FIG 11.18 *Covert and primary flight feathers, seen from above: each feather overlaps from behind, and the feather shaft is closer to the leading than to the trailing edge*

or flat chisel for the feather surfaces. Note that in nature, on the upper surface of the wings each feather is overlapped by the one behind it in the line of flight (for the secondary feathers, this is also the case on the underside). On a carving where these are picked out in detail, we need to show the shaft of each wing feather offset towards the front, which gives strength to resist the oncoming wind (Fig 11.18). Feathers carved the wrong way round, however beautifully executed, will always look wrong. In this carving the detail is minimal, but we still want to get them right.

The long main flight feathers close to the legs are almost hidden when the wing is folded, but a few of them show, and these tuck under the secondary wing feathers

FIG 11.19 *Flight and tail feathers set in. The 'thigh' shape emerges from behind the wing*

FIG 11.20 *A rear view shows the detail of tail and flight feathers*

(Fig 11.19). At the lower end of the back, the short tail feathers appear between the wings. The tail can be shown here by a simple convex surface between the undercut wing feathers (Fig 11.20).

LEGS

The legs are left until last, because until now the timber around them formed an excellent block for holding the carving solidly in the vice. However, it is now time to work on them, and here there is another compromise decision to be made. The legs of all birds are very thin, and those of the heron exceptionally long. The options are:

- Aim for total realism, with the danger that they will have insufficient strength to hold the heavy carving safely.
- Over-compensate, with the danger that they will look ridiculously stumpy.
- Settle for a compromise width, making them as narrow as you dare and using a long screw to strengthen each lower limb where it enters the base.

Needless to say, we are going for the compromise. (There is a fourth option often used by small-bird carvers: metal legs, which can be purchased in various sizes, though probably not at this scale.)

HOLLOWING OUT

Before working on the legs, in order to reduce the considerable weight of the body it is possible to hollow it out from below. This is not an easy task, but has the additional advantage of helping to prevent the wood cracking due to changing humidity conditions over a long period of time. An opening can be made behind the legs which in the finished carving will be hidden under the lower wings. If you don't fancy trying this, skip the next paragraph.

Using a large bit, drill as many holes as you can up into the body, taking care not to drill too far in any direction. Chop out the waste with a ¾in (19mm) deep gouge. This will produce quite a rough finish, as you are working against the grain. In a sense, it is not necessary to clean up inside the gaping hole, as this will eventually be covered by a flat plate of wood carved to fit snugly over it. If you do want a neater finish, the only way to make a decent job of cutting cleanly inside the hollowed body is to use a knuckle gouge (one which is curved almost back on itself) or a hook knife; both of these cut by pulling (with the grain in this case) rather than pushing. When you have hollowed out the body as far as you dare (Fig 11.21), shape

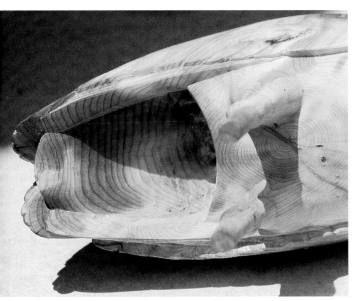

FIG 11.21 *View from underneath showing the hollowing of the body completed*

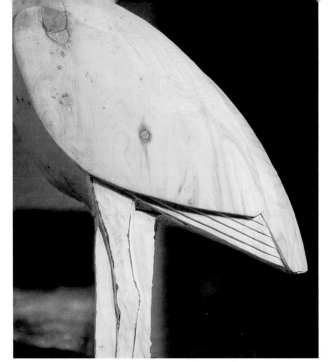

FIG 11.23 *Lateral view of the leg area, with work started on the left leg*

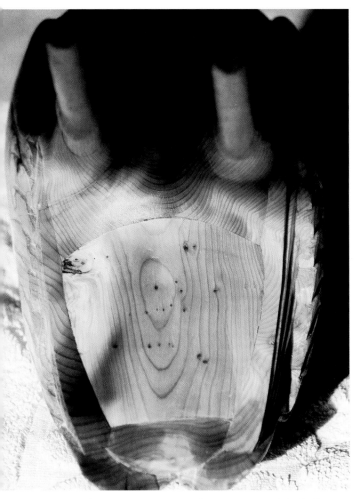

FIG 11.22 *The covering plate fitted to conceal the hollow interior. Using yew, close matching of the grain is impossible*

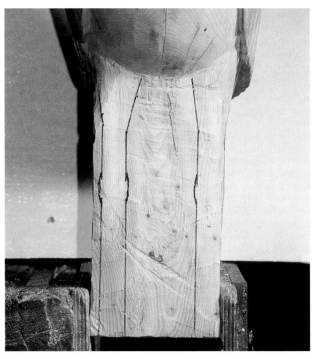

FIG 11.24 *Front view of leg area, with leg positions marked. Notice the tapering 'thighs' and the bulge at the 'knee'*

the covering plate from an offcut so as to fit exactly over the wide entrance to the hole, and finally glue this in place (Fig 11.22).

Mark the outline of the legs on the block (Figs 11.23 and 11.24). Again take some care with this, as the angles are critical for producing a natural appearance. To avoid

FIG 11.25 *The base is a sawn plank of ash with the bark retained. Leg insertion points are chosen to suit the watery grain figure*

THE BASE

For general points about choosing a base for your carvings, see Chapter 14 (page 177). For this carving the base needs to give some impression of water, and therefore requires a timber with a visibly swirling grain. I chose a piece of ash (*Fraxinus excelsior*), though elm, walnut or any suitably grained wood will do. As the design is necessarily top-heavy, the base needs to be fairly solid – just over 2in (50mm) deep – and quite long – about 18in (460mm). If you can find a piece the right size with a stable bark along the sides, this is ideal. The base I used tapered in width from approximately 8in (200mm) at the rear to 6½in (165mm) at the front (Fig 11.25).

FINISHING

Finishing yew is in one sense difficult and in another comparatively easy. The difficulty comes from the erratic grain, and whether you finish with a finely chiselled or a sanded surface, tiny cracks and splinters magically remain in place. This is not at all helpful when applying wax or polishing with wire wool. A fine wire wool will also stain the lighter wood a nasty grey colour; in fact every mark, crack and discoloration is far more visible in yew than almost any other wood. My personal preference is to sand and then scrape very carefully with freshly cut glass to produce a natural finish.

looking like two bamboo stalks, the legs are at slightly different angles to the body, and one is bent a little more than the other (see Fig 11.3*a*). Grip the body upside down in the vice, using an old towel or a folded sheet to prevent the wings and back being marked or the surface crushed. The main sections of waste around the legs are cut away using a saw – an electric jigsaw is ideal for this – and then the resulting squared legs are carved to shape using shallow gouges. Notice how the 'knee' joint halfway down each leg appears quite swollen, and the top section near the body forms a tapering cone which on the real bird is covered with tiny feathers. At the foot end, taper the leg slightly for about the last 1½in (38mm); later this section will fit snugly into the conical holes to be made in the base.

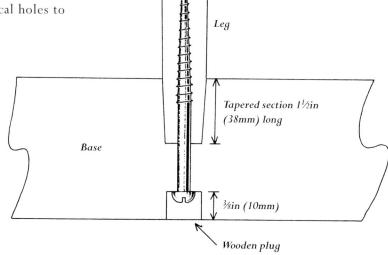

FIG 11.26 *Detail of the joint between leg and base*

The easy aspect of finishing is due to the naturally dense and lustrous surface of the wood. Oil or varnish are not necessary — one or two applications of colourless wax, left for a while then buffed vigorously, will be adequate.

The base can be finished either with two to three coats of Danish oil, followed by wax; or, if a gloss finish is preferred, two or three coats of satin-finish varnish. I know varnish is generally frowned on by carvers, but in a few cases it can work well. For example, if a 'water' surface is lightly tooled, varnish will reflect the light quite realistically to give the appearance of rippled waves. In this case, though, the surface is sanded.

FINAL ASSEMBLY

Mark the base where the legs are to be inserted. Ideally, choose a spot where the grain appears to swirl naturally around the leg (see Fig 11.25). Drill holes the thickness of the narrow end of the leg, 1½in (38mm) down into the base (Fig 11.26). Use a ⅜in (10mm) semicircular gouge to open out the holes into the same conical shape as the tapered end of each leg. Proceed carefully until both legs fit exactly.

Choose two roundhead screws at least 4in (100mm) long and ¼in (6mm) wide for fixing the base to the legs. Drill through from the bottom of the tapered hole to the underside of the base using a ¼in (6mm) bit. Counterbore from the underside to a depth of ⅜in (10mm), to the same diameter as the screw head. Now drill a clearance hole, again using the ¼in bit, through the centre of the leg to about ½in (13mm) short of where the tip of the screw will come, and drill the final ½in with a ⅛in (3mm) drill bit. During this process the lower leg should be temporarily clamped as best you can — the last thing we want is to split the legs at this stage, though the tighter the screw fits, the more strength it will give.

Support both body and base on their side so that the legs can be fitted into the base, test the screws in a dry run almost to complete tightness and make any final adjustments — a reminder here that all the work to the base itself should have been completed before it is permanently fitted to the body. When everything is ready, apply glue to the adjoining surfaces and screw up tight.

Leave undisturbed for at least 12 hours before fitting small wooden plugs to hide the screw heads.

The carving is at last finished (Fig 11.27), and I offer just one final tip: even with the legs strengthened, it is best to support the entire carving whenever it is moved, particularly over any distance, to avoid undue stress on the joints between legs and base.

FIG 11.27 *The finished heron, standing in alert pose to sense possible danger*

CHAPTER 12
Formal leaf design

THERE IS A long tradition of this type of pierced relief carving stretching back to medieval times. It was developed to exceptional perfection by Grinling Gibbons and his contemporaries in the 17th and 18th centuries (see the photograph on page 169) and continues to the present day in the superb work of Rod Naylor, Ray Gonzalez and others. Often used to decorate items of furniture, including the famous fireplace surrounds of architect Robert Adam (1728–92), this style was for many years the

bread and butter of most working woodcarvers. Their work can still be seen in many great houses and in churches where pews, altars and pipe organs were decorated with formal designs or scenes from the Bible.

Personally, I find that pierced carving is easier to execute than high or low relief where the background remains intact. For one thing, you can get at the piece from both sides, indeed from all angles, so undercutting is confined to the subject itself where that is necessary –

for example, where leaves overlap each other. Of course, it is not unknown for pierced work to be fixed later to a background of the same wood, giving the appearance of fabulous relief-carving technique. In fact, many of the classical carvings of the Gibbons school, which look impossible, would indeed be impossible without the carefully crafted hidden joints which may only be found centuries later by the professional restorer.

The price you pay for losing the background is that you also lose the strength. Throughout this project there are compromises to be made between the realism of delicate foliage and the necessity of leaving sufficient timber to hold the whole thing together without breaking.

We can take a cue from illustrious ancestors by carving the piece in four sections which are later joined. It might be possible to do it in one piece, but it would take a consummate skill to attempt this, and also a large width of good timber; which leads us to:

Lime

I suggested in Chapter 10 (page 104) that if oak was the king of carving timbers, lime (*Tilia spp.*) must be the queen. Providing you are not looking for a highly figured wood, or a heavy wood, or a dark wood (though it can of course be stained), lime is without doubt the most amenable of all European timbers to carve. A sharp tool can work lime in almost any direction – with, across and even against the grain (which is wonderful for undercutting leaves). It cuts with a reassuring and satisfyingly crisp 'swish', while tools keep their line almost effortlessly. Features can be detailed to whatever degree your technique can accomplish. Cross-grain strength is remarkable for such a light wood – it seldom splits unless you make a serious error. The finish, whether chiselled or sanded, is smooth, and tooled surfaces show a beautiful lustre.

Need I go on? Small wonder that the first piece of wood handed out to novice carvers is invariably a piece of lime. The tree also goes under other names: in gardens and in classical literature it may be called the 'linden tree', a name derived from Anglo-Saxon days; in New World commercial forests it may be called 'basswood', reflecting the remarkable thick inner bark or bast, used in earlier times for making ropes and mats. North American basswood (*Tilia americana*) is the most widely used commercial lime species, growing mainly in the northern states, while the white basswood (*Tilia heterophylla*) has a more southerly range.

Apart from its long use in sculpture, lime has been used to make all kinds of items which require lightness, strength and detail: hat blocks, shoe trees, engineering patterns, piano keys, bobbins, even artificial limbs. Perhaps the only downside of lime is that it is not durable when exposed to damp, especially out of doors, and is as tasty to infesting beetles as to the discerning carver.

The flora

What we are attempting here is purely decorative, though perhaps with some imagination we could call it a 'Lover's Tryst'. The design is a formalized arrangement of variegated ivy leaves (*Hedera helix*) – which 'entwine and cling so closely' – crowned at the top by leaves from the tropical umbrella-leaved plant (*Heptapleurum arboricola*) – signifying shelter and security – and at the base by a rose – the perennial gift of lovers, in this case the simple Rose of Sharon (*Hypericum calycinum*).

The finished carving can hang on the wall by itself, say in an alcove, or it can be made into a highly decorative surround to something useful – in this case, a mirror.

The design itself (Fig 12.1) is taken from real life: the various leaves and rose flower were picked and arranged painstakingly on a wire framework. Rather than use a long stem of ivy, individual leaves were chosen and tied on separately to give a more formal arrangement. This was then photographed from various angles to get some idea not only of the shape but also the relative heights of the curls in the leaves (Figs 12.2 and 12.3). From these photographs a working drawing was made.

Cutting out the block

The width of this carving makes it unlikely that you can find a piece of lime suitable to work it as one piece. It is in any case much easier to carve in two sections, so I used a block $18^1/_2 \times 10 \times 3$in ($470 \times 255 \times 76$mm). It contained an unfortunate burred knot with small shakes, but the design allowed for this section to be discarded.

The block is first sawn longitudinally with a fine ripsaw to produce two identical bookmatched pieces $1^1/_2$in

FIG 12.2 *The mock-up design using natural leaves and flower on a wire frame*

FIG 12.3 *The mock-up photographed from a different angle to show comparative depths and the way various leaves curl*

FIG 12.4 *The sawn blocks of lime opened like pages so that the knots occur in the central waste area*

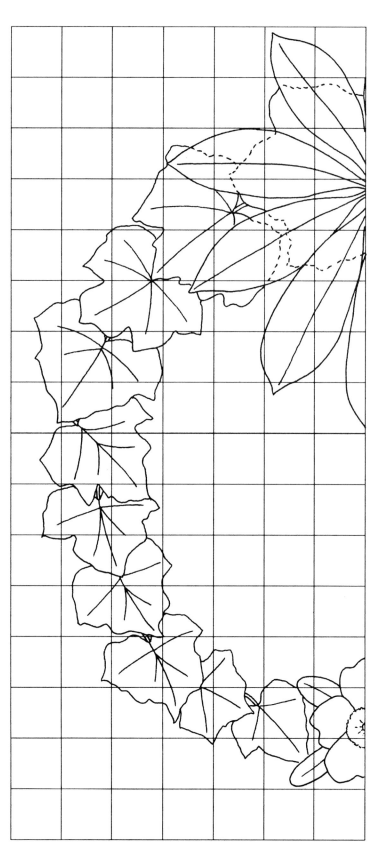

FIG 12.1 *Formal leaf design*

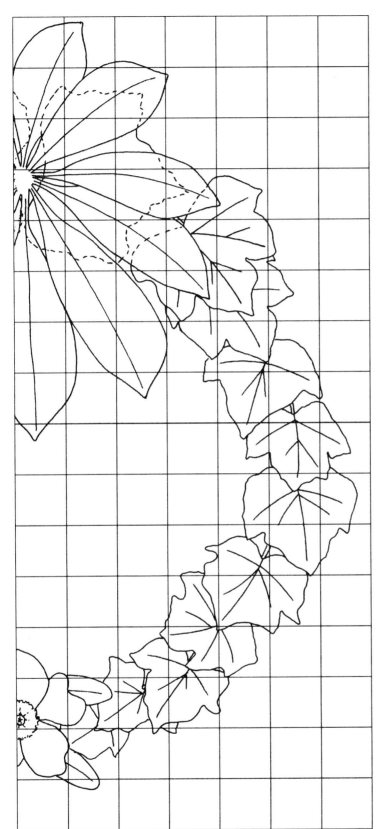

FIG 12.5 *A sash cramp holds the two blocks together for marking out*

FIG 12.6 *Transferring the design on to the clamped blocks*

(38mm) thick, and the meeting edges are then planed (Fig 12.4). The two sections can be temporarily held together with a sash cramp while the drawing is placed over the blocks to mark the outline (Figs 12.5 and 12.6). Each block is then worked quite separately until the final assembly brings the carving together in one piece. A working drawing can be made directly from the photographs of the mock-up, enlarging to full size with a photocopier or using the grid technique (see page 174). With such a complex design this takes a little time, as does marking the timber and cutting it out.

In order to cut round the complex outline of the leaves, a bandsaw is almost indispensable. One

FIG 12.7 *The two sections cut to outline. In the bottom half of the design, the inside edge has been sawn well clear of the final shape, leaving a temporary strengthening area which has been cut down with carving tools to below the level of the ivy leaves*

day I will get one, but meanwhile a friend obliged, and even with a rather primitive machine the task was simplicity itself. At this stage a reinforcing 'web' was left inside the bottom half of the design, the leaf edges in this area being set in with gouges to below the final level of the ivy leaves (Fig 12.7).

Having blocked out the carving in two pieces, there is still further sectioning to do, and this stage is a little tricky. It might be possible to carve the umbrella leaves on top of the underlying ivy leaves, but the techniques required would be so difficult that it is preferable to carve them separately and join them on later.

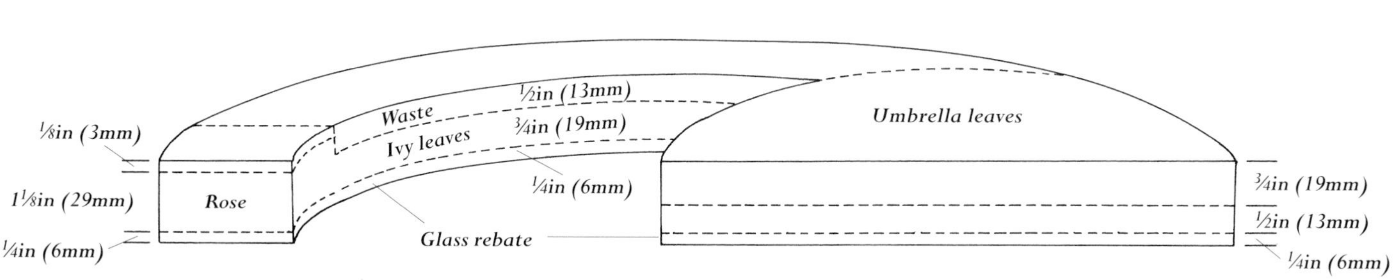

FIG 12.8 *Schematic view of half the carving, showing the different levels required*

LEVELS

We now have to work out some levels. In the following description I will assume that a housing for a mirror is required. If the carving is to be purely decorative, no rebate will be needed and the mirror housing level can be omitted. The levels can be marked on the sides as follows (Fig 12.8):

- **Umbrella leaves** A depth of ¾in (19mm) is marked around the outline of these leaves. The upper surfaces of the leaves can be roughly shaped, and then redrawn. The two umbrella leaf sections can now be sawn off carefully and put to one side for the moment (Figs 12.9 and 12.10).

FIG 12.9 *Sawing off the ¾in (19mm) thick section for the umbrella leaves*

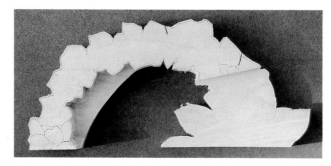

FIG 12.10 *The umbrella leaf section has been removed, so the blank underneath now needs to be redrawn with ivy leaves*

⅛in (3mm)

½in (13mm)

Waste

¾in (19mm)

Ivy leaves

Umbrella leaves

1⅛in (29mm)

Rose

¼in (6mm)

¾in (19mm)

¼in (6mm)

Glass rebate

½in (13mm)

¼in (6mm)

- **Mirror housing** Measuring *from the back*, a depth of ¼in (6mm) needs to be drawn all the way around the *inside* curves only. This will need to be redrawn as carving proceeds, but for now gives an indication of where this level will be.
- **Ivy leaves** Where the umbrella leaves have been removed, a depth of ½in (13mm) remains for the underlying ivy leaves, which should now be drawn in. The rest of the ivy leaves need to have a little more depth to allow for the attractive leaf curls, so mark from the top ½in (13mm) depth all the way round: this will be waste, leaving ¾in (19mm) above the mirror housing for the leaves.
- **Rose** Finally (and before cutting the waste above the ivy leaves), allow at least an extra ⅜in (10mm) depth for the rose, which means marking down from the top around the rose just ⅛in (3mm) of waste.

HOLDING THE WORK

Throughout this carving there is a continual problem with clamping the section you are working on, particularly as the detail appears. The technique I used most of the time was to clamp a flat block of wood in the vice flush with the top, and use one or more quick-release cramps to hold the working piece down flat on the block. When working on the back, place a folded cloth or duster between the carving and the block to protect any surfaces which have already been carved. When working on the sides, particularly of the ivy leaves, it is possible to clamp the piece vertically in the vice, padding one or both sides as necessary. Generally, holding the carving is delicate and fiddly, so experiment with what works best, bearing in mind that you will often want to turn it over or adjust the angle. On occasion you may even need to hold it yourself, as in knife carving, to reach the more inaccessible spots.

THE UMBRELLA LEAVES

These are now in two sections which will be carved separately, though regular notice needs to be taken throughout of the levels where they will eventually be joined together.

To establish the rough shape, cut out the waste between the outward ends of the umbrella leaves with a fretsaw or

FIG 12.11 *A section of umbrella leaves roughly shaped on the top surface and re-marked. The remaining larger ivy leaves, which will lie beneath the umbrella leaves, have been marked and sawn to outline*

fine Japanese saw. Most of the leaves overlap (in nature only some do, but to carve a number of unattached leaves – some across the grain and all on delicate stalks – is beyond most of us). For effect, I have suggested a gap between two of the leaves (at the 10-o'clock position), but this will not be cut through until the sections are finally assembled.

The top surface of each leaf can now be curved downwards from about halfway along towards the leaf tip, using a flat chisel and shallow gouge. Curve down as far as the wood thickness will allow. From the halfway point in each leaf, complete the curve inwards to form a shallow dish at the centre where the stalks will be (Fig 12.11).

By now the marked lines will all have disappeared, so offer up the drawing again and re-mark the leaflet outlines; these should run slightly inside the saw cuts. Do not finalize the shape of the edge until some work has been done underneath. The central veins can also be marked. These run as a shallow groove down the centre of each leaf, and can be set in now or a little later with a V-tool (Fig 12.12). The top surface of each leaf is blended into this groove.

Shaping the underside

Turn the section over to begin shaping the back. Each leaflet will require a central thick 'spine' for strength, particularly those which run across the grain. From the central line the shape then needs to curve outwards to meet each edge at an acute angle – almost flat – so as to

FIG 12.12 *The top surface of the umbrella leaves at a later stage, with carving almost complete. Note the grooves down the centre of each leaf. The working drawing is kept close by for frequent reference*

give a natural leaf-edge appearance about $\frac{1}{16}$in (1.5mm) thick. The 'spine' itself will be almost flat, so each leaf starts thin at the tip and finishes thin at the stalk. On the finished carving it will be practically invisible unless viewed from the side.

Roughly shape the outward half of each leaf to leave this central spine; this can all be done with a shallow gouge by hand (in fact for the whole project it is not necessary to pick up a mallet). Where the leaves overlap, a greater thickness of wood can be left for strengthening. Each carver will determine how thin he or she dares to take the leaves, bearing in mind that before long the delicate stalks will give virtually no support.

Turn the piece over and, if necessary, check that the stalks are all accurately marked. Drill vertical holes right through the intervening spaces. To carve this type of intricate work I like to use not only the expected small V-tool and veiners, but also two $\frac{1}{8}$in (3mm) flat chisels –

FIG 12.13 *Underside of the umbrella leaves, showing the thickened central 'spine' and the triangular section of the stalks*

both sharpened to an acute bevel on one side only, but one with a normal 90° cutting edge and one ground to a sharply angled skew. Remove the waste between the stalks to a depth of about ¼in (6mm) – any deeper and you risk damaging the delicate stalks. Turn the piece over to work from the back in order to clean up between the drill holes. Then carefully reduce the stalks from the back to give a triangular cross section, with its apex running into the leaf 'spine' (Fig 12.13). The intention is to strike a compromise between delicacy and strength.

Completing the umbrella leaves

Turning back to work on the top again, final adjustments can now be made to the shape of each leaf and the surface sanded smooth, slightly rounding each stalk at the same time. Alternatively, you may wish to leave the whole carving with a tooled surface, which is perfectly acceptable and will give a more vigorous appearance to the work. If so, time will be required to clean up with newly sharpened tools chosen to match the surface curves wherever you are working.

If you decide on a sanded finish, bear in mind that limewood has a soft surface, is easily marked, and the fibres can be damaged to some depth by coarse-grit paper. It is best to tool the surface as smoothly as possible and then finish with a 320-grit paper. Fine wire wool can be used to buff to a lustrously smooth finish, but wherever the surface fibres are still rough an unsightly grey staining may occur – it is worth experimenting first on a piece of waste.

As the newly sanded surface is in any case easily marked, even by sweaty fingers, it is best to complete a relatively small area, for example one leaf, and then seal with a coat of clear sanding sealer. This becomes touch-dry very quickly (allowing a short coffee break before continuing). Unless you are a scrupulous perfectionist it is not necessary to sand or clean up too much underneath the leaves, except where the back of the lower leaf tips may be reflected by the mirror. With the example illustrated here I made a definite design fault in allowing the join to cross some of the stalks, rather than running through the centre. This caused extra work and you may be able to adjust your own design to avoid this.

At this stage the unattached stalks to be joined are particularly vulnerable if carved to perfection before gluing. The detail is best left until the joint has been glued and is solid.

Now that one section of the leaf is complete, offer it up to the other half, mark the join levels on the side, also the leaf and stalk intersections above. Repeat all the above procedures on the leaves of the second section, working from these marked levels.

When both sections are complete, the final task is to ensure the joining surfaces are absolutely flat and the vertical angle matches accurately (the joint should be perpendicular). Any small disparity will disastrously spoil the appearance, causing the tips of the horizontal leaves to end up too high or low with respect to the background.

Joining the two sections

With any fragile joint like this I like to insert tiny steel pins to position the join precisely and strengthen it against any later shearing force. Chapter 13 contains further information on setting up these 'micro-dowels' (page 154).

When it comes to gluing, I learnt an object lesson here about the wrong sort of glue! Unthinking, though aware that this was a delicate join, I applied the normal white PVA wood glue with a fine film on both surfaces (the pins were already fitted) and then brought the two halves together, holding them together with elastic bands (Fig 12.14) as there is no way on earth these delicate leaves can

FIG 12.14 *Gluing the two sections of the umbrella leaves together. Pressure is provided by several elastic bands*

FIG 12.15 *View underneath at the same stage: the join line is all too visible*

FIG 12.16 *The umbrella leaves completed; only the small reinforcing 'web' between the two leaves at top left remains to be removed*

be clamped. The problem arose through using such a viscous glue without any real clamping pressure available to close the joint sufficiently. It was not apparent until 24 hours later when the glue was set and the joins cleaned up. The glue was too thick, and how it showed! – as a dark vertical line which was, luckily, worse at the back (Fig 12.15). Clearly a less viscous glue is required. Superglue would be a possibility: it works fine with wood, but allows very little time for adjustment.

Once the glue is set, before removing the elastic bands, clean up around the joins, particularly between the stalks. Then sand if required, and seal with two coats of clear sanding sealer, rubbed down with fine wire wool; there is little danger of this staining the wood grey once it has been sealed. Complete the finish with two coats of clear wax. On complex shapes this is best applied, and later polished, with a short-bristle brush kept specially for working with wax; this prevents the detail becoming clogged (Fig 12.16).

IVY LEAVES

Work can now begin on the ivy leaves in the two main sections. If you are thinking of making the finished piece into a mirror surround, it is possible, before any work is done to the leaves, to cut out the rebate at the back for the mirror housing. However, this reduces the surface of the base so much that firm clamping becomes more difficult. At this stage it is probably easier to remove just enough of the rebate to show where the lowest level for each ivy leaf is situated (Figs 12.17 and 12.18).

FIG 12.17 *Horizontal view of the right-hand section from inside the circle, showing the various levels as they appear before carving begins. The ¼in (6mm) rebate to house the mirror is marked*

Remove the waste above the ivy leaves, which was previously marked (see page 135), then redraw the leaf outlines. You can then proceed either by roughing out all the leaves in turn and then going back to clean up and finish; or by working each leaf separately as far as the first coat of sealant before moving on. I prefer the second way because it is pleasanter to sand a leaf every so often than all together!

While carving, if possible work from nature. Your original ivy leaves may well have gone off by now, but having a few fresh leaves nearby will give an indication of the various natural edge shapes and leaf curls. There will be a fair amount of waste to remove above most leaves, except at the high spots of some of the curls or edges. The strengthening section mentioned before is left for the time being to protect the weaker cross grain near the rose (Fig 12.19).

Between some of the leaves a short length of stem is showing; this is intentional, to enhance the natural appearance. However, carving the tiny triangular holes, which are situated partly underneath the adjacent, overlapping leaf, is tricky. First punch down with a tiny straight chisel and carefully remove up to ¼in (6mm) depth of waste. Where possible, drill right through with a ¹⁄₁₆in (2mm) bit or smaller, and then work from the back to form a cone-shaped hole. This may cut into the mirror housing, but a few gaps will not have any appreciable

FIG 12.18 *View of the underside with preliminary removal of waste at the edges in progress*

weakening effect. Clean up the hole from both back and front; finishing is best done with a triangular file and curved riffler files (see Fig 12.21).

When finishing the top surface of each leaf, remember to undercut the parts overlapped by an adjacent leaf by 45°, or more acutely if you can; the depth of the overlap averages ⅛in (3mm). A ¼in (6mm) no. 3 gouge and small skew chisel are best for undercutting. To complete each leaf surface, the veins are cut in the same way as those on the umbrella leaves to form a rounded groove – though the grooves on the ivy leaves are a little more deeply incised than the others.

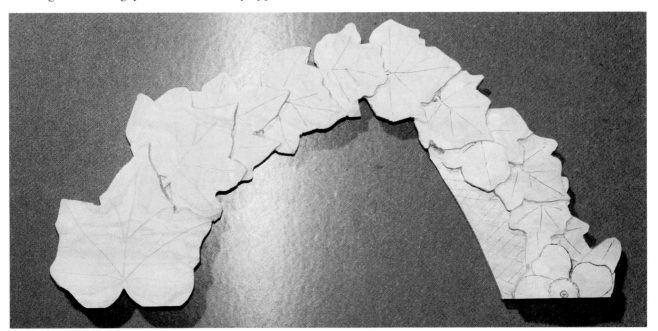

FIG 12.19 *Top surface of the right-hand section with the ivy leaves and rose roughly carved; the strengthening section near the rose is still in place*

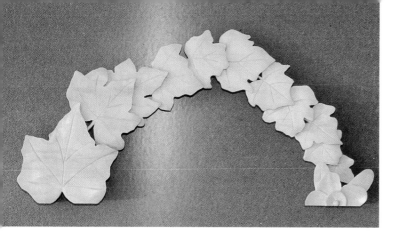

FIG 12.20 *The right-hand section complete and sealed*

THE ROSE

When you reach the rose, remember that it sits on its own small pinnate (feather-shaped) leaves on top of the lowest ivy leaves. Cut out a rose template, re-mark the wood with the outline of petals and leaves, then trim the edges vertically down to meet the ivy leaf beneath. Work upwards to ensure the levels will come right, carving the rose leaves first, before the petals, and finally the central stamens. With this sort of detailed work you will be reaching for a variety of small tools: gouges of various depths, straight and skew chisels, V-tool, and finally riffler files to clean up.

The petals are concave and some have small folds. These need to be finished to a very smooth surface, which is a ticklish job using small folded pieces of abrasive paper.

Carve the central stamen area as a ring – the outside curved like a bicycle tyre and the inside sloping towards

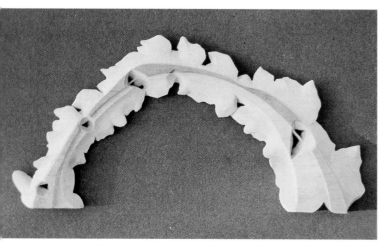

FIG 12.21 *The underside presents an odd appearance. Notice the leaves are undercut, as are the four holes for the stems to show through. The mirror housing rebate forms a recessed ledge inside the darker wood base*

the centre. At the centre leave a semicircular knob protruding upwards, which is the stigma. The stamens are indicated by scoring with the riffler file like spokes of a wheel, and the anthers at their ends are suggested by poking the sharp end of the file in a random pattern around the edge of the ring (Fig 12.20). I completed only one half of the rose at this stage, leaving the other half to be finished after assembly (see Figs 12.24 and 12.25).

CLEANING UP THE BACK

The only way to obtain a mirror the requisite size and shape is to have one cut specially from a template, which I was surprised to find gives no problem to a glass specialist. If you haven't already cut the ¼in (6mm) deep mirror rebate, do this now, protecting the carved top surface with a folded soft cloth while clamping.

The undersides of the leaf edges can now be cleaned up, in the same way as the umbrella leaves, by curving them from the base to an acute angle at the leaf edge. The general rule is to cut back as far as you dare while retaining sufficient strength (Fig 12.21).

JOINING IT ALL TOGETHER

Preparations are now made to join the two main halves of the carving. Place the sections together on a large flat surface and check the fit between the joint surfaces at the top (between two ivy leaves) and at the bottom (between the two halves of the rose). The surfaces are far too small to plane, so use a wide flat chisel to make the necessary adjustments for a perfect fit. It doesn't matter at this stage if the carved surfaces of the petals and the ivy leaves are not at exactly the same level, since that can be adjusted after gluing – in fact the final detail of the carving around the joints is best left until then.

If you are including a mirror, a piece of hardboard can be cut out to the mirror shape and placed in the rebate whenever the two halves of the carving are brought together. This will help to keep everything stable while the joints are set up (Fig 12.22).

As the joints have a very limited surface area, dowels of some kind are needed for strengthening. I decided to use 1¼ × ⅛in (32 × 3mm) brass screws with the heads sawn off, two at each end. Starting with the top join between

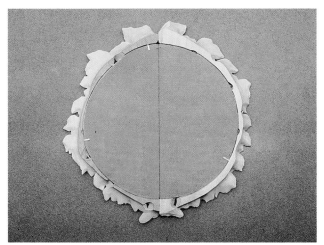

FIG 12.22 *A temporary hardboard 'mirror' is in place to assist final adjustments and gluing. The hardboard can then be given to the glass specialist as a template*

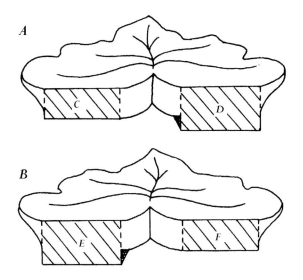

FIG 12.23 *Locating the pin holes for the joint between the ivy leaves at the top of the frame*

the ivy leaves (which is later hidden by the umbrella leaves and therefore not quite so critical), the technique is as follows (Fig 12.23):

On one half of the joint (section A) mark two central points (C and D) where the section is thickest. Drill with a ³⁄₃₂in (2mm) bit to sufficient depth for half the screw. The holes at C and D must be exactly perpendicular to the joint surface. Place the screws in their holes and screw them in to half their length to establish all is well. Take them out, saw off the screw heads and file the sawn ends to remove any burr.

Now cut two panel pins to sufficient length so that when placed in the screw holes, the pointed end will just protrude. Offer up the other half of the carving (section B) to its precise position for the join, thus causing the pin heads to mark the hole positions (E and F) for that side. Drill the holes into the second joint surface at those marks (again precisely perpendicular) using a ¹⁄₈in (3mm) bit, and try the shaft ends of the screws in E and F for size. If the fit is too tight, drill again using the next-size bit.

The screws are now turned into the holes C and D to half their length, using pliers. The two sections are brought together again, fitting the 'dowels' into their respective sockets, and any minor adjustments made for a perfect fit; remember that the entire back of the carving must be flat.

Repeat this procedure for the join at the rose (Figs 12.24 and 12.25).

FIG 12.24 *The three sections ready for assembly, with brass dowels inserted. Several ivy stems are visible against the background*

FIG 12.25 *The left half of the rose, with brass dowels inserted; it has not yet been carved in detail, so it can be adjusted after joining to match the completed right half*

GLUING

Choose a wood glue that is not too viscous – at a pinch, white PVA glue can be thinned very slightly with water. Before gluing, decide how you are going to hold the two sections together under pressure during the drying time. I found strong elastic – such as that used to hold items on a roof rack – to be best; the only other way I can think of is some complicated arrangement using small clamps on a sash cramp, but the elastic seems far simpler – and it works.

Place a thin film of glue on both surfaces and a blob in each dowel hole. Bring the two halves together (using the hardboard mirror template to ensure nothing is out of true) and adjust the elastic to give sufficient pressure on the joints while avoiding undue strain on the delicate leaves. After a final check that the back of the carving is quite flat, leave for at least 24 hours.

Final details of carving around the joints can now be completed, and the wood sealed and waxed (Fig 12.26).

FIG 12.27 *On the underside of the umbrella leaves, five spots mark the contact points for the joining pins. A small area around each one is scraped clean for gluing. The small reinforcing piece noted in Fig 12.16 has now been removed*

FIG 12.26 *The two sections glued together. Both halves of the rose have now been carved in detail*

THE MIRROR AND BACKING BOARD

This section is of course omitted if the carving is to stand on its own, and you can continue at 'One more join' below.

At this stage the whole piece is relatively fragile, so care must be taken not to cause undue stress on the joints. Cover a stable flat surface with a large folded cloth and position the carving face down. Place the mirror into the rebate, also face down – minor adjustments may be needed to the edges of the rebate before it fits exactly. A template is now made from a large sheet of paper, marking the outside position of the back of the frame. Cut out the template and use it to mark a piece of hardboard or thin ply to be used as the backing board. Cut this out to shape and place in position on the carving. At several positions around the edge, note where the base of the carving (outside the rebate) is wide enough to receive screws, and mark these points on the backing board. Using $\frac{1}{2}$in (13mm) no. 6 brass countersunk screws, drill suitable-size clearance holes through the backing board and slightly smaller holes into the carving. Once the backing board is screwed down into position, everything becomes more solid and the edges can be adjusted flush with a small chisel and abrasive paper as necessary to give a reasonably smart appearance to the back (see Fig 12.29).

ONE MORE JOIN

The last stage of construction is to add the umbrella leaves. Place this section on the ivy leaves in its intended position. You will find that several, but not all, of the leaves will touch. Make a small dot with a felt-tip pen to mark these touching positions on top of the ivy leaves and on the underside of the umbrella leaves. These are the points where glue will be applied, so scrape back to bare wood in a ½in (13mm) diameter circle at each position (Fig 12.27). In order to give some strength to the joins, use the pin technique (see page 154), inserting the pins down into the ivy leaves with their points facing upwards. Apply a spot of glue to each position and press down the umbrella leaves on to the pins. These joins are held with small clamps, using protection for the upper leaf surfaces (Fig 12.28).

The carving is now complete, apart from fitting two reasonably strong D-rings for hanging as a mirror, or light hooks or screw eyes if the carving is to be hung on its own (Fig 12.29).

FIG 12.28 *Final stage of construction. The umbrella leaves are pinned and glued, with pressure applied by small clamps*

FIG 12.29 *View from the back of the finished mirror, with strong picture cord attached*

CHAPTER 13
Tools and techniques

Nearly all books on woodcarving include a chapter on tools and techniques, inevitably repeating similar information on types of gouges, sharpening, the structure of timber, etc. There are also excellent publications which focus totally on the woodcarver's equipment, the conversion and seasoning of wood, and so on (see the Select Bibliography on page 180). This chapter takes a different approach. The sections which follow outline some basic areas of concern for the carver and present a number of tips, many of which are not found in the standard textbooks, or are hidden so deep that you may have missed them. This chapter can be read through for general interest, or used as a reference under the following headings:

1 TIMBER

a The raw material

It never fails to amaze me that, courtesy of natural selection, there is such an incredible variety of timber across the world, even amongst the native species of one country. The variations span every quality found in timber – hardness, density, durability, colour, grain regularity and figure – and the possibilities for the carver are endless. Just one tree with a highly figured grain, such as walnut or yew, will provide any number of carving blocks, and no two will be identical.

International trade has enabled the woodworker to choose from a bewildering variety of timbers. Yes, I know that with some of the rarer varieties a reasonable-sized chunk costs a king's ransom, but perhaps that is the way it should be. In so far as purchasers can exert pressure that their timber should come from renewable resources, it will help to guarantee that this rich profusion continues to be available for generations to come.

Many will prefer to focus on timbers from their own locality, where a dozen or more species are likely to be found in good supply. In Great Britain or the United States these include hardwoods and softwoods ranging in colour from rich brown walnut to almost white lime (basswood) and holly, and in texture from open-grained oak and chestnut to dense cherry and yew. Each species takes on a different appearance whether finished with a gouge or sanded smooth, polished or left matt. Wood can be stained to a new shade, not to mention the flamboyant effects available from spalted timber or burr. The choice is enormous.

Every species of wood can be carved, though some are more challenging or more rewarding than others; some can be frustrating, and on occasion disappointing. Apart from reading and listening to advice from experts, the only way to get things right is through your own experience of trial and error. Experience will inevitably remain limited if you confine your efforts to just one or two styles of carving. You can focus closely and become a fantastic painted decoy carver working with two or three species of timber, but then you will never encounter the satisfaction of working on a free-form abstract, or Celtic-design chip-carving, making a relief portrait, restoring an antique lectern, whittling a walking stick – all of which, speaking personally, have given me enormous satisfaction and all kinds of new insights into this fabulous pastime of shaping wood.

It is characteristic of woodcarving that what works for someone else may not work for you. My advice would be to look, listen, experiment, be prepared to fail and on rare occasions chuck precious hours of work on the fire.

b Conversion and seasoning

There are specialist books devoted solely to this subject (see Bibliography), and if you are going to try and season your own timber it is well worth the time to read up on the theory and practice of this difficult process. **Conversion** describes the activity of cutting a log into planks or larger sections so that seasoning can be facilitated. **Seasoning** is the removal of moisture from the timber to match the humidity of its eventual location. As we all regularly use wood which has been seasoned from its original 'green' state, it is worth noting the reasons why this drying process is necessary.

Problems of green wood

Even when sealed, wood will 'breathe', gradually absorbing or expelling water to match the surrounding atmosphere. If a significant volume of moisture is lost from a section of wood, it will inevitably shrink. This shrinkage is not uniform and will depend on the cell structure contained within the wood. In most cases the result is deformation, twisting, reduction of length, and cracks opening where the changed internal tensions have overcome the tensile strength of the timber. Skilled seasoning, whether in the open air or in a drying kiln, is designed to overcome the worst of these problems. During conversion from the freshly felled tree to fully seasoned planks, on average each cubic foot of timber loses just over a gallon of water! This radical change in cell

composition and moisture content has to be managed in such a way as to avoid distortion and undue stress within the timber.

Some figures:
- Air-drying will bring the moisture content down to about 20% in winter, 15% in high summer; kiln-drying to around 10%.
- Central heating will cause movement in any timber above 11%.
- Moulds and fungi need 20% moisture to thrive in timber.

Advantages of dry wood

Seasoning also brings significant advantages in terms of timber quality which are important for most kinds of woodworking. Dry timber has increased strength and reduced weight, glued joints are stronger and more reliable, finishing properties are enhanced, and thermal and electrical insulation are increased – the latter is important, for example, in panelling. And, of course, with well-seasoned timber there is reduced risk of splitting or warping.

Do-it-yourself?

Most carvers try to season some of their own wood, if only because some kind person has given them a tree trunk they want removed from their garden. The following tips will assist successful seasoning, or at least help to avoid 100% failure.

- Cut the trunk into the minimum-size sections you will require for carving. You may wish to retain log-sized pieces, but sections which have been halved or (more usually) quartered longitudinally will season more quickly and with fewer problems. The best results obtained from full logs are with those having irregular grain: elm, walnut, yew, etc. Dense, straight-grained timbers like cherry are notoriously difficult.
- Coat both ends of each section with a waterproof sealant. Various authorities recommend bitumen-, wax- or paint-based products; providing the seal is solidly waterproof I don't think it matters too much. What does matter is that the seal is checked as the seasons change each year, and replaced as necessary. It is a good idea to mark the seal with the date (and the timber species, if you are likely to forget later).

- Store in a dry, well-ventilated area, off the ground. Planks or squared sections should be stacked with a ventilating space around each one, the layers separated by bearing sticks. In fact, whatever the size, try to arrange a free flow of air to all surfaces.
- Check every three months, not only the sealant but also for any kind of rot or infestation. This should be treated, or the worst areas removed as necessary.
- Be prepared to leave the timber seasoning for a long time. The recommended scale is 1 year for every 1in (25mm) diameter. With large sections this becomes an unreasonable length of time for most of us. My own experience is that 1 year for every 1in *radius* is adequate, provided that care is taken during carving if any significantly damp areas are found. In any case, a good rule with larger carvings is to leave them overnight inside a sealed plastic bag. This helps to reduce sudden water loss from newly exposed areas, and the changes of tension will occur less violently.

There is an ongoing debate whether to leave the bark on or remove it for seasoning. The arguments for leaving it on are that it slows down the drying process in the sapwood and therefore reduces surface shakes; and in some cases you may want to use the bark as part of your carving design (see the base for the Heron project, page 128). Unfortunately, sometimes during seasoning the bark will peel away by itself, but this does at least offer a visual guide to progress. The argument for removing the bark is to avoid attack from bark-boring beetles, although these normally do little damage beyond the sapwood. Fungus can also thrive underneath loose, damp bark.

Two more recent methods of seasoning should be mentioned, as some have found them helpful in speeding up the process:

- For small sections it is possible to use a microwave oven, which heats and therefore dries the wood from the inside. This can work well or be a total disaster; if you want to have a go it is worth looking out for articles which give some guidance on settings, safety factors, etc.
- Again for small sections of timber, there is a technique for replacing the moisture content with a chemical called polyethylene glycol (PEG). This requires submersing the wood for some time in a vat of PEG.

Advocates of this method are enthusiastic about the advantages of speed and the fact that carving qualities are unaltered. Again, anyone wanting to try this will need to look up detailed instructions available from suppliers.

Those of us who live by large areas of water may pick up chunks of driftwood from time to time (see the mount for the Turtle project, page 101). This will need drying, though if previously seasoned this may not take long. A greater problem is impregnation with salt from sea water. In this case it is recommended that the wood should be soaked for a few days in fresh water and then dried out quite slowly.

With all driftwood it will be necessary to brush off surface dirt and encrustation. All found and donated wood should also be checked carefully for foreign bodies. In fact, any large piece of timber can contain all kinds of concealed objects: nails, staples, barbed wire, even stones, some embedded deep within the wood and quite invisible until they are hit with the gouge or, worse still, a mechanical saw. There is an apocryphal adage that 'Everyone knows the steel of chisels is superior to that of nails – until the gouge hits a nail.'

c Storage

The conditions for successful wood storage are identical to those recommended during air-drying for seasoning: the store should be dry and reasonably well ventilated, and checks made for any deterioration on a regular basis. Possible problems include:

- **Decay** Symptoms of mild decay include softening of the wood, spalting and staining. More severe forms are sometimes called 'wet' or 'dry' rot, depending on the species of fungus. Neither will thrive if the moisture content of the wood is below 20%.
- **Splits and cracks** Commercial suppliers normally seal the end grain of their blanks with wax. Few carvers will possess the hot-wax bath required for this process, but coating the end grain with gloss paint is worth doing, particularly if your storage area is subject to dramatic changes of temperature or humidity.
- **Beetle (woodworm) attack** Treat any wood that has beetle holes – it is not always easy to detect whether or not the infestation is still active. It may be

worth looking out a well-seasoned scrap section of walnut or sycamore, if possible with the sapwood intact and the surface roughened, to stand near the door or ventilation opening. It doesn't matter if the timber is soft beyond carving – in fact this makes it particularly attractive to the beetles and they will go for the offered bait rather than your precious stock further inside the store. Remove and burn after about 18 months.

- **Knots** In the course of time, sound or tight knots may become loose and eventually decayed.
- **Water damage** Severe condensation or roof leakage can thoroughly soak seasoned wood, increasing the likelihood of fungal attack.
- **Staining** This can be caused by fungi, bacteria, water damage, or by natural enzymes and hydrolysis. Generally there is precious little which can be done about it.

After completion, small carvings can be stored safely in the workshop in empty ice-cream containers, where they are protected from dust, beetles and changes in humidity.

2 THE WORKSHOP

So, how is your workshop? Beautiful? Purpose-built? It is more likely to be part of the garage or a spare room. Whatever the space, it is worth spending a little time planning how you might get the best from it. But before looking at a host of wonderful tips for the perfect workshop, it is worth pondering some words of the late E. J. Tangerman, a prolific full-time carver and writer from the United States, who said: 'I like to use a sturdy card table with two legs folded so that it can rest at a slight angle on the arms of my chair beside the fireplace' (*Carving Religious Motifs in Wood*, p. 10). I am sure he also had a workshop, but the point is made that woodcarving (at least on a small scale) can be done anywhere.

Although the basics of workshop layout can be found in the standard books, I offer the following hints and tips from a variety of sources, some of them directly from personal experience.

a The carving bench

I have the luxury of using a reasonably large garage from which the car is banned, which puts me in the ideal

FIG 13.1 *A chest-high carving bench; gouges are stored in the cabinet beneath*

situation of having room for two benches. One of them is a traditional joiner's bench, bought second-hand and cut down to a length of 8ft (2.45m). It stands waist-high, with a joiner's vice at one end and a small metalwork vice nearby. The other bench is home-made, chest-high, again with a large quick-release vice (Fig 13.1). This provides my favourite carving position: standing without bending the back, with ease of access to three sides. Others will prefer a lower position, or even to work seated, perhaps using a purpose-built carving horse. If you have the opportunity, try various stances for carving before investing in anything permanent. A high bench will require stabilizing with something heavy at the base: either some building blocks or, as illustrated, a sturdy filing cabinet for chisels.

b Lighting

While carving, the quality of benchtop lighting is critical, and it is worth spending time to get it right. There is nothing better than good daylight coming from one direction (though direct sunlight is seldom helpful). Having said that, most amateur carvers will spend much of their time working outside daylight hours, so artificial lighting is a must. The ideal lighting includes:

- General background light, best provided by ceiling strip lights.
- A movable light over the bench which can be quickly adjusted to various angles to facilitate detailed carving. If you can get hold of a second-hand dentist's light to fix from the ceiling, that would be ideal, if a little bulky. (I am still looking for one.) Working on fine detail – feathers for example – is a great deal easier if an angled light source is casting tiny shadows on the undercut.
- One other powerful light (I use a builder's external halogen light) which can be used when further illumination is required elsewhere in the workshop.

c Holding the carving

Here it is a question of personal preference and the type of carving undertaken; a variety of solutions will be needed to suit different circumstances.

- I tend to work mainly with a joiner's vice; sometimes this holds the carving directly, but on occasion I use a hexagonal base fixed to a metal plate to which the carving is screwed (Fig 13.2). The base can be rotated through six positions a total of 360°, and clamped at an angle to hold the carving in a convenient position.
- The same principle is used by the commercially available metal carver's clamp, which is bolted to the benchtop and uses a quick-release universal joint to adjust the base plate. The best makes are excellent; if you buy one, check first that the lock is absolutely solid under pressure, that the bench or vice fitting suits your own requirements, and that the faceplate(s) you require are supplied. For a home-made version, see GMC Publications' *Essential Tips for Woodcarvers*, page 27; no doubt if you have the skills to make one, you can work out how to do it!
- Other holding devices include the traditional carver's chops – a type of high wooden vice which is fixed on top of the bench. If you have one, or use any type of vice, a good tip is to protect the thread of the tightening screw using foam water-pipe insulator,

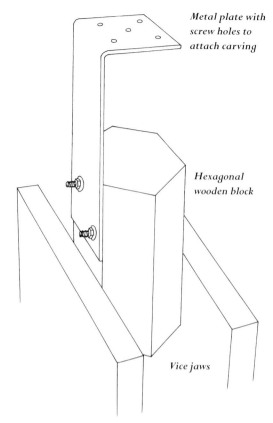

Metal plate with screw holes to attach carving

Hexagonal wooden block

Vice jaws

FIG 13.2 *An easily made adjustable carving stand*

which is widely available and easy to cut and fit. The inside gripping surfaces of a vice or chops can be lined with cork, which grips very well, though it may break down under pressure, particularly when holding a large carving subject to heavy mallet work.

- Another traditional holding device is the carver's screw, which is fitted through the bench surface and screwed into the base of the carving. This, like any faceplate holding method, requires the carving to have a flat base and a suitable place for the screw(s) to be inserted without compromising the finished piece.
- Relief carvings can be held in an adjustable frame on the benchtop, which may be inclined at an angle for ease of carving.
- A relief, or any carving with a flat projecting base, can also be held with a bench holdfast, which acts like a single clamp pressing down on the bench. Its main disadvantage is having a near-vertical chunk of metal close to the carving area.
- Some relief carvers like to glue the piece temporarily to a flat wooden base clamped or screwed to the bench. The method involves gluing with a sheet of

newspaper between carving and base, or using hot-melt glue, or double-sided sticky tape. On completion the carving is prised free of the temporary base using a broad straight-edged chisel. The glued surface will then need to be cleaned, which is less arduous if the glue has been applied only around the frame edge.

- One trick for holding larger carvings as they near completion is to rest the piece on a soft bag filled with rice or sand, which will mould itself to the shape of the carving. This method can either rely on the carving's own weight for stability, or be used in conjunction with webbing straps.
- A final trick used by traditional (and modern) carvers to hold an awkward piece while gluing is to use one or more C-shaped springs cut from old bedsprings. Various kinds of elastic or masking tape can also be used where appropriate.

Whichever holding method you use, it must be able to resist the maximum aggressive pressure you are going to apply to the carving, without damaging your work at the point where it grips. The last thing you want (and we all experience this occasionally) is for a carving to spring on to the floor, breaking off delicate sections which mingle instantly and invisibly with the chips surrounding your bench – an event calculated to generate expletives normally reserved for situations of extreme crisis.

d Benchtop arrangements

A low bench normally has quite a wide area, and the chisels can be laid out parallel to each other, blades facing the carver for quick identification. On a high bench with a smaller surface area, the chisels can be laid out the other way round, the shafts resting safely on a corrugated board at the back, or inserted vertically in a chisel-holding tray which swivels back and forth as required.

There are various ways of colour-coding gouge handles, if you find this helpful for instant recognition on the bench or in the tool roll – you could devise a combination of spots and stripes to suit your own selection of tools. Most of the time you will be using less than a dozen gouges and chisels, and if the benchtop is large enough tools used less often can be laid out further back. The important thing is to protect the cutting edges from each other and from any other metallic benchtop debris – clamps, saws, planes, etc.

It's not a bad idea to get into the discipline of cleaning up every hour or so – remove unwanted tools from the benchtop, brush away chips and sawdust and sweep the floor, removing any piles of highly flammable chips and shavings to a safe location.

If you have plenty of benchtop space, a useful addition is to fit an area of high-density foam somewhere on the bench surface. This is ideal for placing carvings nearing completion, to avoid scratching the base. It can also provide enough grip for gentle work on a relief carving. Again, space permitting, it is extremely helpful to have a totally flat level surface (kept clear of kit) somewhere in the workshop. This can be used to place a carving at any stage in order to check its vertical stance and overall appearance. On larger carvings or reliefs, making the base or the back truly flat can be a long-winded exercise and is best done early on. On such occasions it can save a great deal of time if you can arrange access to a friendly joiner's flat-bed electric planer.

e A few more workshop tips

Any semi-liquid material, such as glue, can be stored in a flexible bottle (for example, a shower soap container) hanging upside down. This must first be thoroughly washed and dried; the stopper or cap needs to be secure, form a good seal and be kept clean. This method provides easy storage and prevents a skin forming on top of an exposed surface.

Heating your workshop with a paraffin or bottled-gas heater, though efficient, will produce substantial quantities of moisture, resulting in corrosion of any metal tools being stored there. Reasonably priced electrical heating will do a better job – notably the type of heat-and-light lamp used by stockbreeders and/or the low-wattage tubular heaters suitable for garage or greenhouse use, which can be left on during the winter to prevent cold and damp getting into everything.

Riffler and standard files clogged by wood dust should be cleaned with a wire brush to avoid damp and rust gaining a hold. Another cleaning method for severely clogged files is to put them in hot water, which causes the wood dust to swell and float away. They should be thoroughly dried afterwards.

If you are leaving your chisels for any length of time, particularly if they are in an unheated area, a thin coat of light oil should be applied with a rag before storage.

3 CARVING

a Tools

Good tools when bought new are expensive. There are a number of reputable firms which specialize in woodcarving tools, and in general the quality of the goods will depend on the price you are prepared to pay. But there is also the option of buying second-hand, and what can equal the fascination of visiting an unfamiliar second-hand tool emporium and exploring the shelves, drawers and cabinets stuffed full of old carving tools (Fig 13.3)? It is enough to make your mouth water and your right hand reach unconsciously towards the cheque book. The shock comes when you find that the price of any half-decent gouge is not far removed from the brand-new equivalent. However, smaller items – riffler files, needle files, rasps, fittings for a dentist's drill, small grindstones, honing wheels (some in shapes you've never seen before, ideal for honing inside a gouge which has never been quite right), handles, drill bits, etc. – will often be down to 10% of the new price. You may have to scratch round endless murky drawers and boxes for an hour or so, but that's half the fun

of these veritable Aladdin's caves. Chisels and gouges which have been abandoned in a shed may sometimes be found unused – you can tell by factory sharpening left untouched. Old steel is often excellent, though sometimes you may need to regrind – it is unbelievable what some people do even with specialist tools, which have been aptly described as 'widows' screwdrivers'.

Often the carving section is only part of a large tool and machinery store; the proprietor may know little about woodcarving, and sometimes an accommodation can be found on price. In my experience the staff are often more helpful than those working in the shops dedicated to new tools. Apart from providing a wonderful afternoon out, some of these shops have shelves of old books on every conceivable aspect of woodworking.

Second-hand tools may also be on sale at open-air wood exhibitions, and can occasionally be found at car boot and jumble sales (yard sales); but if you go to these expecting specifically to find carving tools, prepare to be disappointed.

When contemplating your second-hand purchase, a number of guidelines are worth considering.

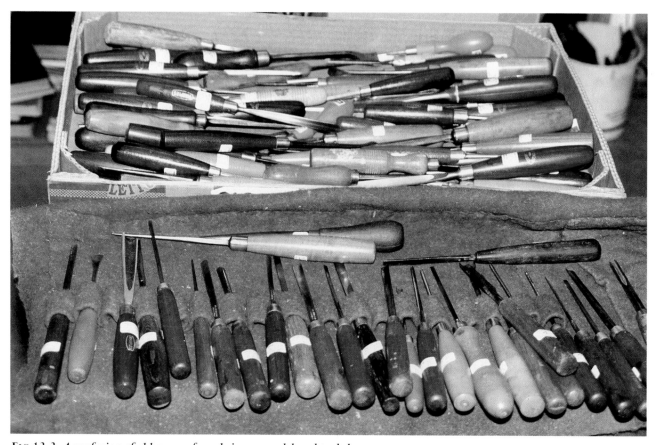

FIG 13.3 *A profusion of old gouges for sale in a second-hand tool shop*

In particular, avoid:

- Any tool with an excessively short blade: remember gouges are only tempered for a short way up the shaft. This is to avoid the whole shaft being too brittle, particularly for heavy use with a mallet. Unless you want to retemper the tool, avoid it. If you are buying a tool with a broken blade, bear in mind how easily the temper can be lost with vigorous regrinding.
- Any tool pitted with rust: a little surface rust can be removed (Fig 13.4), but later grinding may move the cutting edge back into a pitted area which is impossible to sharpen.
- Shafts seriously out of line with the handle: this is indicative of a bent tang inside the handle, and the tool will never work accurately.
- A long tool with the shaft bent, twisted or in any way asymmetric.
- Handles which are split or have their ends bashed to pulp – unless you are prepared to replace with a new handle. Note that though octagonal handles may not suit everyone, they do prevent the tool rolling about on the bench.
- Gouges with a very small or distorted shoulder where the shaft enters the handle. Check also whether the ferrule is intact and serviceable.

FIG 13.4 *A rust-pitted gouge is always liable to provide problems with sharpening, but in this case the pitting is not severe and a small internal bevel (which has many other advantages) should produce a clean cutting edge*

- V-tools with blades of unequal thickness: they will always cause problems with sharpening.

Chris Pye's *Woodcarving Tools, Materials & Equipment* contains everything you could possibly want to know about the care and repair of tools. He points out that some old tools have the name of a previous owner stamped on the handle, which shows that 'you never really *own* a woodcarving tool – you only have custody and care of it. Eventually it will pass on to someone else who will use it and, hopefully, also take care of it and use it to create many beautiful works' (p. 4).

Mallets

Mallet work needs to be restrained in proportion to the size of the gouge, and is very difficult, if not dangerous, with bent gouges, which have too much spring in them; if the task cannot be worked by hand, then the tiniest of mallet taps is necessary, working the blade with a small depth of cut.

Anyone suffering from arthritis or joint disease may find work with a traditional mallet both tiring and painful. If your grip is not a problem, then using a hard rubber mallet will reduce the jarring action on the wrist. The rubber mallet also reduces damage to gouge handles, and reduces noise pollution to your household and neighbours. If gripping the handle is difficult then a palm mallet can be helpful – preferably one with a little-finger grip. In regard to gripping the gouge handle, some have found that wrapping it with water-pipe insulation foam reduces jarring and improves the grip.

b Removing waste

Normally, the quickest way to remove waste and get on to the actual carving is by using a bandsaw, a chainsaw or a power-carving tool such as the Arbortech. **Remember that these must always be used with the correct safety procedures in place before you start, and a final check that fast-moving teeth are not going to touch any nearby metal or foreign body in the timber.**

After roughing out with the saw, there are often occasions when a fair amount of waste still needs to be removed. There are various techniques to speed up what can be a long-winded process.

From a flat or convex surface

The most obvious way is to use mallet and heavy-duty medium-curve gouge, working across the grain. Where possible, making close parallel saw cuts across the grain to just above the required depth will make the chopping out a less tiring exercise (see Figs 9.7 and 10.6 on pages 94 and 108). In-cannel gouges (those with a bevel on the inside only) are excellent for fast removal, but care is needed to avoid digging too deep, and you may not be able to access the flat angle required to use this type of gouge.

For more careful removal from flat or convex surfaces it is possible to use a sturdy ½–¾in (13–19mm) carpenter's chisel. The technique is to angle the chisel slightly, deliberately scoring with one side across the grain, which will spring off chips to the right or left depending which way the grain is running (Fig 13.5).

From a concave surface or deep hole

For deeper sections the most frequently used short cut is to drill a series of adjacent holes around the perimeter, with the drill stopped to ¼in (6mm) above the required depth (see Fig 10.4 on page 107). The waste can then be safely removed with mallet and deep gouge.

For shallow concave surfaces, such as inside a bowl, the task can be speeded up considerably by making a series of criss-cross chainsaw cuts (see Fig 2.4 on page 17). Safety procedures are paramount here, but the technique is easy enough: incline the blade to about 30° and, using the nose of the blade, stroke the cut towards you, increasing the angle slightly as you go. Once the saw cuts are made, chopping out the waste with a gouge takes no time at all.

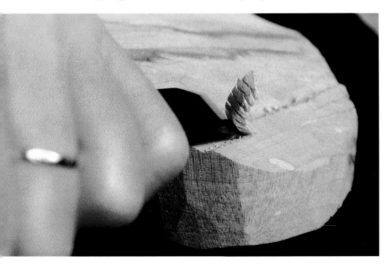

FIG 13.5 *Removing waste by scoring across the grain with a carpentry chisel*

Remember when removing the larger chunks of waste that it is worth retaining these in case matching timber is needed later to fill cracks or effect repairs.

c Overcoming the awkward

A few tips for the 'what do I do now?' situations:

- When a tool becomes stuck in the timber following an over-aggressive clout with the mallet, at all costs avoid the temptation to lever it out by force. More blade breakages occur through inappropriate leverage than anything else, and regrinding is always a long, tedious process. Skew and fishtail chisels are particularly vulnerable to blade fracture. First try careful sideways wriggling (along the direction of the blade). If this fails it may be necessary to excavate carefully around the blade using another gouge.

- Anything else buried in the timber will require similar careful excavation. Apart from metal or stone foreign bodies, you may also come across hard deposits of silica or calcium carbonate. These are normally formed by the tree in an attempt to repair internal damage, and have a tendency to chip tool blades without warning. The only solution is either to try and incorporate a large deposit in the carving, or cut it right out and replace with a section cut from waste.

- If you decide to hollow out the body of a large carving to reduce weight or guard against cracking, in order to clean up once the drilling is done there may be no alternative to working against the grain. The work is helped enormously if you have a knuckle gouge or a scorp, both of which cut towards you by a pulling motion (see the Heron project, page 126).

- Sometimes, while carving well-seasoned timbers like walnut or beech, you will come across a section of friable wood which is impossible to cut cleanly, even with the sharpest tools. If it is not possible to cut this out and replace it, the wood can be strengthened with a dilute solution of a hard-setting glue such as Cascamite. Allow it to penetrate the fibres and leave to dry completely. This will give a firmer surface, but it cannot later be stained, and may finish to a different colour from neighbouring untreated wood.

- A similar problem occurs when working with a softwood such as Douglas fir (Oregon pine), which has closely alternating hard and soft grain lines. You can suddenly find that an area of 'crush marks' appears in the softer early wood between the grain lines. These are caused either by a blunt tool, or by cutting too deep. They can usually be removed by using a gouge sharpened to a more acute angle of cut (say 20° of bevel), taking off very fine slivers along the grain. If the area is accessible, scraping may also work. This alternating type of grain also makes it difficult to sand to a smooth rather than ridged surface; I came across this problem with the Waves project (page 64). A possible remedy is to use a hard backing block (flat or curved as necessary) with the paper drawn tight over the surface.

- Softwoods provide another special challenge to the carver: when cutting out hollows and working inside a concave surface, at the lowest point, where the curve changes grain from one direction to the other, it is only too easy to split into the curve, producing small check marks where the gouge has caught against the grain. Try working up to the change line gingerly with the gouge from each side, leaving a ridge or a line of nicks along the grain change. Then, using an ultra-sharp gouge with slightly tighter curvature than the surface, cut *across* the grain to clean up.
- Finally, a tip to help avoid an awkward result. How often have you carefully carved out a perfect animal or bird eye, only to stand back and find it is not in quite the right position? (Like the rabbit carving which won the nickname Isaiah because 'one eye's 'igher than the other – ha ha'.) The situation can be avoided by using a small sticky index label (or an eye shape cut out from adhesive tape) and experimenting until the position is correct. This spot can than be marked with a pencil. On larger eyes the same process will help to position the pupil in the right spot.

d Repairs

If you are a beginner at carving, don't be daunted when you come across what seems to be an insurmountable problem. Something we tend to forget when admiring other people's carving, or looking through books, is that things almost certainly went wrong for them at some stage during the carving process. The corollary of this is that they were able to overcome it somehow. If you have glanced through the project section of this book you will know that I have not shied away from mistakes – they happen with distressing regularity, and some are discussed in embarrassing detail. The moral is: don't let setbacks and frustrations lead to despair. Apart from the specific problems outlined below, many a setback is caused simply by difficulties in sharpening tools properly.

Common situations which call for repair include:

- Splits in the wood – due to changed tensions caused by removing wood or by loss of moisture – or the discovery of an existing shake inside the timber. It is said that you can detect an internal shake by tapping the log along its length with a chisel handle. Although I have never tried this, apparently the sound changes in the vicinity of a shake or major fault.
- The discovery of an embedded artefact or natural chemical deposit.
- Finding an area of unexpectedly friable wood or a loose or decayed knot.
- Damage caused by the carver.

Before descending into rage, despair or frantic repairing activity, pause for a moment to think about the problem:

- Does it need repair, or can it be left, possibly even complementing the design?
- Can it be carved out, or the design adapted so as to consign the area to waste?
- Can it be repaired, or is it in fact so bad that despite the previous investment of time and energy, the carving is just beyond redemption?

What sort of repair?

If the carving is to be painted, then a wood filler will be fine, as there is no need to match colours or grain – though larger faults may require timber to be replaced.

If a natural finish is envisaged, then there are various options available:

- Use an offcut to fill the problem area. This is most often done with larger splits, or where significant wood removal is required. The grain may be difficult or impossible to match exactly. The minimum amount of glue should be used to avoid an unsightly join.
- To fill shakes, a thinly tapering wedge is carved so that it will produce its own gluing pressure when forced

into the crack. If you have a number of cracks to fill, this carving and matching of wedges can take a considerable time if you are to avoid ending up with a patchwork quilt. Each wedge is left proud until dry. Do not wipe off the glue with a wet cloth as sometimes advised, because this can cause dilute glue to penetrate around the repair, causing finishing problems later. Instead, leave it to dry cheese-hard and then carve it off along with the protruding part of the wedge. (Gluing the wedge is best done early in the day, otherwise it may need attention at 4.00a.m. the following day!) See further tips on gluing in the next section.

- Where the grain is particularly striking, the timber insertion (or other filler) can be stained to resemble a knot, which may appear more natural than non-matching grain.
- Tiny circular holes caused by beetle are not always best repaired with wood: the cocktail-stick type of repair can show (as darker cross grain) as badly as the original hole. The alternative is to use a wax stick of matching colour.
- Coloured wax, shellac or glue-and-sawdust filler are best used in the narrowest shakes and small holes. Wax filling is facilitated if the wax is melted on with a heated knife. The surplus can be scraped off after a few seconds. Shellac gives a harder finish but it is more difficult to apply it and to match colours. Some carvers swear by the glue-and-sawdust mixture, even retrieving some from the dust extraction bag – grit and all! The technique can work well, but try on some scrap first, as it is difficult to ensure a good colour match after finishing.
- Cracks do sometimes open (or close) long after the carving is complete, due to altered temperature and humidity at its eventual location. Wax-filled cracks may even squeeze out and form an unsightly ridge over the surface. So don't be surprised if you are occasionally called upon to make a repair a year or so down the road.
- Small dents are always difficult, as there is insufficient depth for inserting filler. One method worth trying is the Japanese *ukibori* technique, which is simply to apply a wet cloth to the affected area and steam it out with a hot domestic iron. The steam swells the crushed grain and can effect an invisible repair. The technique can also be used deliberately to raise small warts all over the place for a toad or snake skin. Note that this will not work if the surface has already been sealed.

If the repair is needed because of breakage or over-enthusiastic application of the chisel, then normally the separated pieces will require gluing back together. Having said that, just occasionally this particular cloud has a silver lining because the break provides access to areas which are more easily carved *before* gluing everything back together! If so, keep any tiny pieces in a safe place.

e Construction, dowels, gluing

Some carvings require construction from separate pieces to ensure that delicate sections all run along the grain, or simply to fix the carving to a separate base. Most of these joints will need strengthening with some kind of inserted dowel. The dowel can be of wood or metal, though it is best to avoid non-galvanized iron. There are several stages in making up a dowelled joint:

- Decide the best kind of dowel for the joint. Where strength is not critical it is always easier to use a wooden dowel. The tiniest joints (see the Butterfly wings on page 33) will require a pin-sized dowel, and metal is the only option.
- Decide how deeply the dowel needs to be inserted into either side of the joint.
- Drill a hole of the appropriate size into one side of the joint, perpendicular to the joint surface if possible; angled dowel holes are difficult to match accurately.
- Insert a brad, pin or cut-off nail into the drilled hole. This marking dowel needs to be a couple of millimetres longer than the depth of the hole, and inserted point upwards.
- Place the two surfaces together and lightly press the brad point into the undrilled surface.
- Remove the temporary dowel and drill the opposite hole through the point marked by the brad.
- Insert the real dowel and check everything fits together correctly. If not, make any final adjustments before applying glue.
- Apply a thin film of glue to the joint surfaces, allowing a small amount into the dowel hole. Coat the dowel similarly, and glue everything together.
- Provide pressure on the joint by clamping or elastic, and leave for 24 hours.

Wooden dowels can either be carved to size or obtained commercially – ideally with chamfered ends and longitudinal grooves for glue penetration. Very small ones can be made from cocktail or kebab sticks or split bamboo.

Metal dowels can be brass, steel or galvanized iron. They can be made from screws with the head removed, which have the advantage of screwing into one side of the joint (see the Formal Leaf Design, page 140). The tiniest metal dowels are made from needles or sewing pins.

A few dos and don'ts when gluing

- Work out your clamping procedure before gluing up – complex arrangements may require prior experiment, and clamps need to be adjusted to the required opening beforehand.
- Surfaces must be cleared of dirt, grease and dust. Work glue into the wood fibres of both surfaces, leaving very little on the surface.
- Apply adequate clamp pressure and leave it as long as you can.
- Oily woods like teak do not glue well unless the surfaces are given a prior wash with methylated spirit (denatured alcohol).
- In order to hide the thin glue line completely, it is possible to colour the glue with powder pigment. Note that this should be matched to the *finished* colour of the wood – experiment first.
- If you apply glue with a brush, a stiff, fan-shaped artist's brush is ideal (if you can afford it), particularly for penetrating deep cracks. Water-based glues will wash out quite easily from brushes with hot water and soap. Dry with pressure from kitchen tissue.
- If it is necessary to glue to end grain, give the surface a preliminary coat of sizing (thinly diluted glue), and allow to dry.
- Remember that gluing together two different species of timber, or gluing long grain to cross grain, can produce problems later due to unequal shrinkage.

ƒ Sanding

As we approach the finishing stage of any carving, one or two major decisions have to be made, an important one being whether the surface is to be tooled or sanded. In fact, a prior question may provide the answer: is the colour and texture of the natural wood surface required – that is, do you want to show the grain to best advantage? If the answer is no, this is probably because you wish to

finish with paint or deep staining, pyrography, or perhaps stippling or punching the surface. These require specialist advice beyond the scope of this book, but if a natural finish is envisaged then it is a choice between tooling or sanding, or a combination of both.

If sanding is chosen, then this can often take far longer than carefully tooling the entire surface. A smooth surface shows up the tiniest imperfections and therefore needs far more work to complete. As sanding can be such a lengthy and tedious business, a few tips gathered from the experts can only help:

- The purpose of sanding is not to remove a lot of wood, merely to eliminate any marks or surface defects.
- Grades of paper are used in ascending order, normally in steps from 180 to 320. Anything finer than 320 is likely to be less effective because of clogging; beyond this grade it is more efficient to use different grades of wire wool.
- Cheap sandpaper is not an option for the carver – buy the best aluminium oxide or garnet paper you can find. I use strips cut from large trade rolls, which store well and seem to have greater strength than sheets.
- Clean the timber surface between grades with a brush or tack cloth to remove coarser grit particles.
- Offer the beautifully sanded surface up to good daylight, or to a single light source from various angles. The remaining blemishes appear as if by magic. They also appear after the first application of sealer, but at that stage further sanding presents problems of colour matching, unless you remove the entire surface.
- To obtain a soft and smooth finish without losing important detail, try using a 300-grit paper lubricated with linseed oil. Then wipe off all surplus oil, leave to dry, and wax-polish.
- If you are likely to have a lot of sanding to do (as in the Formal Leaf Design, page 130), pace yourself. For any fully sanded carving, the process is likely to take up to a quarter of the whole working time. That means that an 8-day carving requires 2 days' sanding, which is extremely tiring if done all together – far better to sand a section which has been carved, then seal it and move on. This may also help you to see where you are as the carving progresses.
- For sanding in difficult areas such as undercuts, try removing the metal sanding surface from a commercial plastic holder. Cut this into convenient

shapes with tin snips. If necessary it can be glued to a wood or metal backing for easier holding. Some areas of undercut can be cleaned up simply by using a pointed hardwood stick, which will remove stray wood fibres and burnish the surface. A piece cut from a worn hacksaw blade may do the same job, but take care if you are using a vice to snap pieces off – the blades are brittle, and broken chips fly off at high speed. **Eye protection is essential.**

- Inaccessible areas can also be sanded by holding a tiny piece of sandpaper or wire wool in surgical or fishing forceps. The advantage of the forceps is that they are self-locking.

- Inaccessible dust and chips resistant to the tickling of a paint brush, or to blowing hard, can be removed quite easily by using a drinking straw to blow (or suck – but be careful what you might swallow!).

- Cork makes a useful sanding block because it can be cut to shape and has some give. Alternatively you could use the soles of old flip-flop sandals cut and glued together.

- Long sessions of sanding can be particularly wearing on the fingertips. If you can cope with the loss of sensitivity, a thin leather golf glove, leather fingerstall or rubber thimble can provide protection.

- After sanding with the final grade of abrasive, the surface can be moistened with a damp rag and allowed to dry; this has the effect of raising the grain. A final sanding after this will prevent any further raising from occurring later, during staining or finishing.

- Mechanical sanders produce quantities of very fine dust which irritate the breathing passages and with some species of timber can be poisonous. In addition to wearing a mask, you can make a simple dust extraction system by cutting up a large plastic bottle to form a funnel, fixing this to the flexible tube of a household vacuum cleaner and clamping it near the work.

- Instead of sandpaper it is advantageous occasionally to use an abrasive of the same colour as the wood: for example, an old brick for mahogany. The dust from the abrasive acts as a filler and hides small blemishes rather than highlighting them.

- Normally sanding *strips* are more helpful for working on carvings than sanding *sheets*. A strip can also be stretched taut by attaching either end to a springy bow of green wood.

Above all with sanding, make sure you avoid rounding off any crisp detail; this may reduce your work from an inspiring carving to something dull and lifeless.

g Finishing

There are almost as many techniques for finishing as there are carvers, and whole books have been written on the subject. Methods include cellulose or shellac (sanding) sealer, various kinds of natural oils, a wide range of waxes and varnishes, french polish, lacquer, paint or gilding. Some waxes and varnishes come with wood stain or other treatments incorporated.

Prior to finishing, there may be a need to apply water- or oil-based stain, to use a bleach or ammonia treatment, or to finish the surface with pyrography or sandblasting. Various commercial pyrography machines are available, and the technique can be extremely helpful when a fine texture is required for fur or feathers (Fig 13.6).

Each carver will build up a range of favourite products over the years, and apart from reading the specialist books, there is no substitute for personal experience of successes and failures. However, the worst failures can be enormously time-consuming. If a finish has been applied and you don't like the effect, then with a detailed carving you are in for a long haul to strip back to bare wood and start again.

When starting, you can't go far wrong with an oil finish such as Danish oil, or a colourless shellac sanding sealer. Two or three thin coats are applied and rubbed down between each coat; leave for a day or so and finish with one coat of wax, which is allowed to dry and then polished. The only disadvantage with the oil is that it will turn some woods darker than one might wish.

Before committing any finish to your carving, try it out on a piece of scrap and be prepared to adjust or change the finish if it doesn't work, particularly if the colour or surface sheen is wrong. Experiments should be done early on in the carving process so that you are not held up for days at the end. If the finish requires mixing, make sure enough is made up for the whole job, even if some is discarded later. Remixing to a precise colour match is seldom successful.

Before applying any finish, vigorously remove all particles of dust and abrasive, using a clean brush, tack cloth or vacuum cleaner for inaccessible areas.

Most finishes are best applied in a number of thin coats rather than fewer thick ones. Surplus oil, for example,

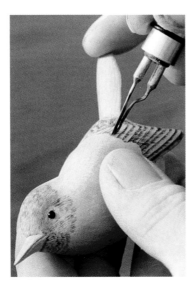

FIG 13.6 *The working end of a pyrography machine, as Geoff Weald textures a wren. Here the scalpel-sharp tip is set sufficiently hot to singe as well as cut. On decoy carvings, texturing is often done at a cooler temperature to avoid singeing, which may show through and spoil the painted surface*

should not be left on the surface for long. Between coats, once the surface is dry, remove any imperfections due to flecks of dust or sealant particles (this is known as **de-nibbing**) with wire wool worked gently over the surface. The hardest, closest-grained timbers need the least finishing. With yew or rosewood, for example, two coats of wax are quite sufficient, provided the surface has been well prepared.

The final coat of oil, varnish, etc. should be left some days before waxing.

Almost any finish will give a yellowish tinge on lighter woods, or darken a strongly coloured wood. The only exceptions are colourless lacquer – which can be difficult to apply evenly – and white (transparent) wax applied without a sealer – more time and elbow grease are required to wax an unsealed surface. Pale woods can also take on a nasty grey tinge if fine-grade wire wool is used for final smoothing. Some recommend experimenting with soap-free scouring pads, but I have yet to find one which is not too coarse.

Two finishing tips

- It is worth keeping several labelled brushes which are each used for one purpose only: applying oil, applying wax, buffing wax, and a clean brush simply for cleaning surfaces.
- It is a fact of life that there is never a clean piece of rag available at the time you need it most. Solution: find a few moments to cut up an old sheet into 9in (25cm) squares and store them in a suitable container (Fig 13.7).

A FINAL NOTE ON SAFETY

If you use nothing but hand tools, the theory is that providing the fingers are kept behind the direction of the blade, all will be well and you will never cut yourself. That's true 99% of the time, but accidents do happen – usually when the carver is tired, not concentrating, or momentarily distracted. Cuts range from a nick on the fingertip (when the greatest concern is to avoid blood stains on your pristine carving) to a deep gash which will require immediate attention to stop the bleeding and avoid infection. A well-stocked first aid cabinet within easy reach is a must.

Other hazards are generated by:

- Power tools, when fingers or clothing touch a fast-moving blade.
- Electrical equipment with faulty or damaged wiring.
- Fire, which can be caused by smoking, naked flames, unsafe electrical equipment, sparks from a grinding machine, and clouds of fine sawdust. It is possible for spontaneous combustion to occur in rags impregnated with dried finishing materials. I have never experienced this, but as a precaution all my soiled rags are promptly disposed of outside in a metal dustbin.

The safety precautions in each case are fairly obvious. Despite all the warnings in textbooks and equipment instructions, accidents invariably happen simply because sensible precautions have been ignored.

FIG 13.7 *Setting up a supply of small rags for future use*

CHAPTER 14
Design and inspiration

Stag in limewood by Bill Prickett, 13in (330mm) high. The antlers are carved separately; otherwise this is all one piece, including the base – which gives strength as well as stability. Body and legs have been fully textured, providing contrast with the smooth head, antlers and hooves. With front leg poised, head turned and upright, eyes wide open, Bill's design has caught the moment of frozen immobility when danger is sensed

MOST CARVING books major on tools and techniques, and few have much to say about carving design (Ian Norbury's books listed in the Bibliography are a notable exception). Perhaps this is because 'design' is a difficult concept to get hold of. In one sense, we all know intuitively when we see a good design, and the top carvers have an innate sense of design which thrills through every piece they make. On the other hand, their experience and depth of study will have been far wider than the average hobby carver's, and it is well worth our taking a little time to think about the principles of design. In this chapter we will be

Triceratops in Russian birch plywood by Bill Prickett, 2ft 6in (760mm) high. This fabulous and massive carving, nearly 5ft (1.52m) long, shows what can be done with laminated plywood – layers can be built up to any size you can manage, with no danger of shrinkage or splitting. The bold, stripy surface appearance would not suit every subject, but it certainly works here

looking at various aspects of carving design under the following headings:

If you are a beginner at carving and some of these sections appear daunting, skip them for now and come back to this chapter later when you have begun to experience difficulties with designing more complex and ambitious carvings.

Hummingbird in limewood and American black walnut by Bill Prickett, 12in (305mm) high. The smoothly curved base and simplified flower stem complement the floating delicacy of this tiny bird. It is supported only by the beak, which has been strengthened using a sewing needle as a dowel

Orang-utan by Ben Harms in sweet chestnut and driftwood with natural objects, 16in (405mm) high overall. This is sculptural design **par excellence,** *including a profusion of foliage, lichen, moss and stones. Notice how the orang-utan blends effortlessly into its habitat and yet is clearly emerging from the trees with distinct purpose*

1 THE THEORY OF DESIGN

The problem is how to hammer the subject into a logical shape. Before getting into practical considerations, and being conscious of the dangers of overanalysing, let's begin by looking at the concept of design under three headings: Art, Science and Faith.

Art

The artistic side is the process of visualizing and working out the overall stance and movement of your carving, designing the right base, and (with a relief carving) sorting out the background and frame. Artistic design will look at the interaction between the various parts of the whole piece (see, for example, the two Otters on page 103), and the areas of maximum focus – the points to which the viewer's eye will be drawn. An impressive carving, whether large or small, will exude good design and encourage the observer to look at it from different angles. On the other hand, you often see an example of beautiful workmanship made lifeless by an unnatural pose, or spoilt by an inappropriate base.

Three dolphins by Brian Faggetter, 11in (280mm) high. Brian has used bubinga wood, which is new to me but clearly finishes perfectly to emphasize the sleek surface of the travelling dolphins. They are supported on a central metal rod (not visible here) and stand on a contrasting sycamore base. The design encapsulates both the speed and the gregarious character of the subjects

Artistic design will also depend on practical technique: working out what is possible in the medium of wood sculpture, and what you yourself can accomplish. Then again, you don't know what you can accomplish until you try. New challenges are the only way of raising our skills to new heights. The process of design will reveal a tension between what the subject looks like, and what you would like it to look like as a carving. You need to consider how far you can achieve this in terms of your own ability, and the timber you have available.

The result will inevitably involve some compromise. In nature carving you may need to compromise on detail: will this bird be textured and painted to portray total realism, or are you planning to suggest the feathers through grain figure, light and shadow? Is the timber you have chosen suitable for fine detail, or could it spoil the overall effect? (See the Heron project on page 115, where a decision was taken at the outset not to detail the feathers.) Are you hoping for a carving

that will be realistic or impressionistic, representative or almost abstract?

In nature carving the design will above all aim to portray the character of the subject – whether it is statuesque, cheeky, threatening, cuddly, vulnerable, etc. Designing the base or mount may make or break all your other efforts (see Section 8 below). And artistic design goes hand in hand with drawing (which in Latin is *designare*), as discussed in Section 6.

One other aspect of artistic design is to ask what the carving is *for*. Will it have a practical use which determines its shape – for example a bowl, walking stick, rocking horse – or will it be primarily decorative?

Science

The scientific side of design focuses on the subject – your observation and understanding of what you are trying to portray. How does the creature move, behave, feed, mate, display, play? What are its dominant characteristics?

Cheetah in limewood by Ian Edwards, 5in (125mm) high and 13in (330mm) long. The great cats when curled up look as smooth and rounded as their domestic cousins, but in movement they display dramatic folds of muscle and bone structure. Ian's cheetah is straining forward like a racehorse, shoulder blades projecting, back arched, the stomach thinner than the haunch. This animal is really travelling. Though the base is large, the rough, dark surface takes nothing from the subject, to which the eye is immediately drawn by the smooth natural limewood finish

Snail in spalted beech on yew by Chris Coleman, 14in (355mm) high. Chris is one of those courageous carvers who can incorporate severely damaged timber into their design and make it look as if it was meant to be like that. Notice the contrasting finishes on the snail's shell and body sections to indicate hard and soft surfaces

Lion in oak by Ray Gonzalez, 8¾in (222mm) high. The essentially defensive pose of this male lion is captured by the turn of the head, open mouth, wide eyes, and the irritation suggested by the curl of the tail. The base is functional but adds particular interest as a cross-sawn section from a whole log

Observation will require some homework on anatomy, both external and internal. Externally: how do the various parts of the body function? What are they for? Are the legs primarily for standing, running, climbing, gripping, tearing prey? How does the creature balance and stay upright? Do the arms, claws, tail, mouthparts, etc. have particular functions? Internally: how do the muscles and bone structure show on the surface? Do the forelegs visibly continue into the shoulder, the rear legs into the haunch? Does the backbone form a ridge or a depression?

Living things are formed by both internal and external circumstances. The internal genetic make-up dictates the animal's basic structure; external pressures determine whether it is fat or thin, full of energy or worn and weary, the coat sleek or dull and patchy. In plants the form alters dramatically with time and the changing seasons, often as an annual cycle; mushrooms, for example, may only be visible for a few days. The design for a plant subject will need to choose one part of the cycle: new growth, full blossoming, autumnal decay or dormancy.

Research material for observation will be based on both pictures and real life, possibly including museum specimens – though these are not always put back together as nature intended. Many carvers build up files of pictures cut out from magazines – my own collection has grown to daunting proportions. Bear in mind that good paintings of natural subjects often reveal more than photographs – the accomplished artist has already done a great deal of observation. But again, beware of artistic licence: always check paintings against real-life photographs. A professional photographer friend pointed out that black-and-white photos are often very useful because there is just too much information in colour – particularly where changes in colour fool the eye into perceiving a change in contour.

Faith

This is far more difficult to express, but concerns the fact that your designs will reflect the way you look at the world around you – how you view your subject in the whole scheme of things. Does this horse have a personality or is it just a bundle of chemicals cunningly put together? Does this bird have a purpose in life beyond the necessities of evolutionary genetics? If so, can you portray anything of

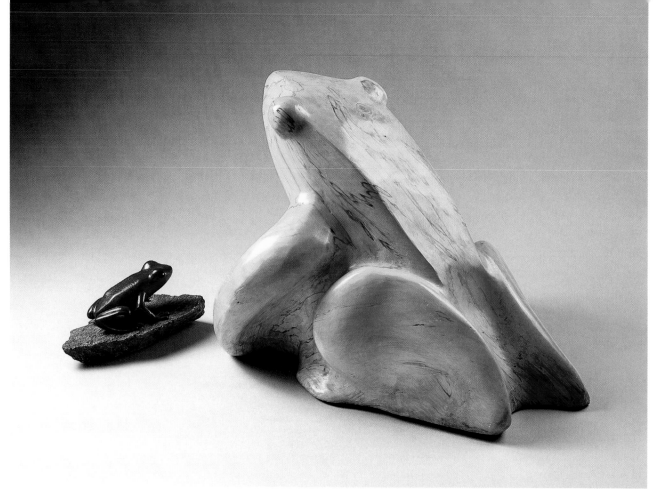

Two contrasting styles: large frog by Chris Coleman and miniature tree frog by the author. The giant frog stands 12in (305mm) high and is carved in a semi-abstract style from spalted beech. Nearly all detail is omitted, allowing the essential froglike form to speak for itself. The tree frog, carved in purpleheart, stands just 2in (50mm) high and is placed on a natural stone base. The colour is natural apart from the eye, which is stained with two coats of a water-based black stain. The feet were shaped to fit the contours of the stone, which has been varnished to look wet

that purpose? Is beauty simply a construct of the human mind or are certain things intrinsically beautiful? It is interesting how a realistic snake carving will produce admiration from some viewers, horror from others. Some will view natural art as simply reflecting the random mutations of a chance universe. For others, that creation reflects the will of the Great Designer through created natural laws, and therefore their art will attempt to reflect something of the Creator's miracles of design.

All this may seem a million miles from your next carving project, but when it is finished that carving will inevitably reflect the things you believe, mainly through the design you have chosen, and what you have been able to capture of the subject. Normally we see ourselves as the centre of the universe; but in order to create and portray something that is not oneself, this viewpoint must change so that our focus is directed totally towards the subject. Slavish copying of other people's work is fine to assist

in learning techniques, but the final aim is to produce your own designs and therefore unique work. The master carver Ian Norbury advises us that 'Designing, researching and creating your personal vision is the great pleasure of . . . carving' (*Fundamentals of Figure Carving*, p. 11).

In previous centuries carvers were faced primarily with problems of function. (What is the function of this carving? Is it to beautify furniture, a house, a church or temple, adorn some practical object, act as a religious symbol?) They were largely confined to a local vision of the world, strongly influenced by their immediate cultural environment. Today we have instant access to every tradition of sculpture across the world, and to every type of subject – in fact we are constantly bombarded with every kind of visual image from which we can draw design inspiration.

The price of this freedom to adopt any style you choose is that there are too many to choose from.

Traditional decoy gull by Bob Pyett, 10in (255mm) high. Bob used reclaimed timber of unknown origin, with an open grain. Before painting with acrylic colours, the surface was burnt with a welding torch to produce the distinctive texture. A carving of beautiful lines and soothing simplicity

Glancing at the chart on page 166, the beginner faces a bewildering richness of technique and subject matter. Where do you start?

2 TRYING TO CARVE FOR THE FIRST TIME

The answer is to begin with a simple design – almost an outline – and start carving. Too much theory at the beginning will swamp the imagination; indeed some professional carvers regularly go back to their roots and produce an incredibly simple design which shows an exceptional beauty through its uncluttered lines and curves (see the Decoy Gull by Bob Pyett, above).

The novice carver doesn't need a workshop full of expensive kit to make a start – far better to begin small,

taking time to get used to a few basic tools and learning to do simple things well. This will give far more satisfaction than failing at something too complex – leading to disappointment, and perhaps giving up after a few initial attempts.

If you have never carved before, avoid a design which requires a difficult timber: lime and (European) sycamore are ideal. Those with more colourful and patterned grain figures, such as elm, yew and mahogany, are beautiful precisely because the grain is irregular, and are therefore more difficult to work.

Good design also involves learning to look at things in three dimensions. If you are carving in the round, the shape of an animal's head is just as important from the top as from the front or side. With certain subjects – such as a bison charging, for example – the top of the head might even dominate the design. It is therefore necessary to sort out the proportions from various viewing angles. For

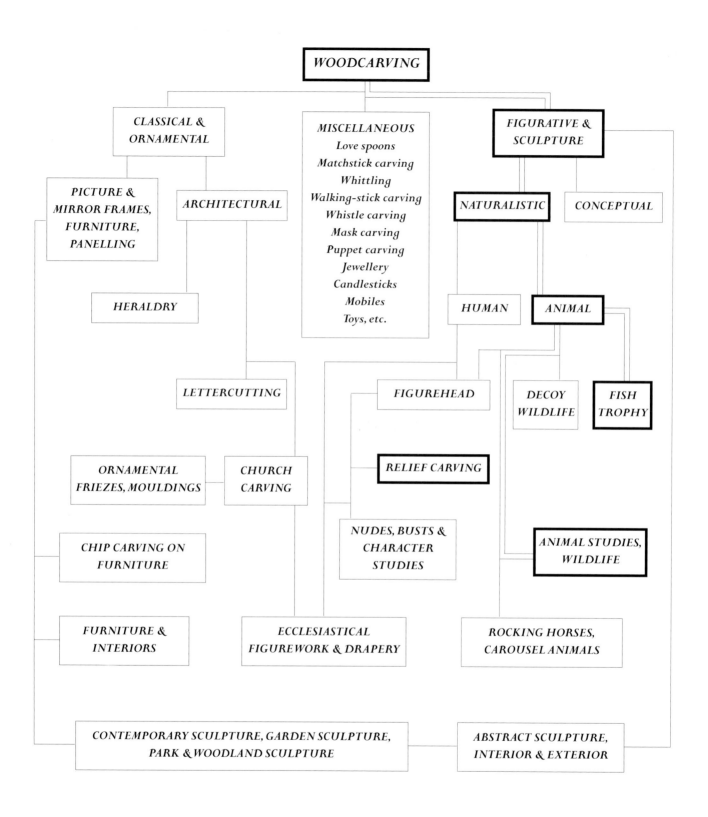

WOODCARVING

CLASSICAL &
ORNAMENTAL

MISCELLANEOUS
Love spoons
Matchstick carving
Whittling
Walking-stick carving
Whistle carving
Mask carving
Puppet carving
Jewellery
Candlesticks
Mobiles
Toys, etc.

FIGURATIVE &
SCULPTURE

PICTURE &
MIRROR FRAMES,
FURNITURE,
PANELLING

ARCHITECTURAL

NATURALISTIC

CONCEPTUAL

HERALDRY

HUMAN

ANIMAL

LETTERCUTTING

FIGUREHEAD

DECOY
WILDLIFE

FISH
TROPHY

ORNAMENTAL
FRIEZES, MOULDINGS

CHURCH
CARVING

RELIEF CARVING

CHIP CARVING ON
FURNITURE

NUDES, BUSTS &
CHARACTER
STUDIES

ANIMAL STUDIES,
WILDLIFE

FURNITURE &
INTERIORS

ECCLESIASTICAL
FIGUREWORK & DRAPERY

ROCKING HORSES,
CAROUSEL ANIMALS

CONTEMPORARY SCULPTURE, GARDEN SCULPTURE,
PARK & WOODLAND SCULPTURE

ABSTRACT SCULPTURE,
INTERIOR & EXTERIOR

*This chart of woodcarving techniques has been slightly adapted (with permission) from a chart by
Ray Gonzalez in* Practical Woodworking *(October 1995). Most of the boxes could be further subdivided
into three-dimensional, high and low relief, carving on turned work, etc. A quick glance will show
the incredible variety of skills encompassed by the term 'woodcarving'. Our concern in this book is
primarily with just a part of one branch, following the double lines.*

Bison in sweet chestnut by Ray Gonzalez. The animal is stationary, but is not going to stay that way long. Every aspect of the stance draws the focus towards the face, as does the inclined base. Who could believe the eye should be nearer the ground than the top of the shoulder? Again the variety of tooled finishing effects is worth study: notice the depth of cut required to indicate the heavy, shaggy coat

example, looking at a face from the front, the apparent distance from nose to ear may be astonishingly different from what appears in the side view. In relief carving, creating the illusion of depth becomes particularly critical for a good design (see Section 7 below). Bad carving can of course be caused by lack of technique, blunt tools, sloppy cleaning up, etc., but just as often the carver is struggling because bad design is causing confusion of line or lack of interesting focus – or reflecting an ignorance of basic anatomy.

It's worth remembering here that the preacher is always speaking to himself as well as to the congregation. Don't take my project carvings as examples of perfect design – some are far from it, and this has occasionally been noted in the text.

3 WHY AM I CARVING?

Your design will reflect your reasons for carving. Is it simply a hobby because you like working with wood, or are you producing objects to sell? The latter will bring commercial pressures to design carvings which appeal to other people. The hobbyist is doing art for art's sake and can carve whatever he or she pleases; the semi-professional must produce what people want, and discerning buyers will be aware of your technical skills, the niceties of cleaning up and finishing, but above all your vision of the subject incorporated in the design.

A word of warning: unless you have exceptional skills, beware of commissions from dog and cat owners, horse trainers, parakeet fanciers, hamster specialists, or anyone

Shark by Brian Faggetter, 17in (430mm) high. The dappled water reflection on the shark's skin is beautifully captured by using a jarrah wood burr. The prey in light sycamore provides a total contrast, and the base is the absolute minimum needed to support a swimming fish – in fact, at first glance you hardly notice it

whose observation of their pet is likely to be distressingly acute. Without consummate skill in capturing not only the species but also the individual poppet concerned, you are unlikely to please.

This leads to a further consideration: do you want to *say* anything through your work? Are you trying to communicate your own skill as a carver, or something of the beauty of natural subjects? Do you primarily want to show what can be done with this beautiful medium of wood? Some would say that in order to get the very best from timber you must be in love with trees, certainly to the extent that you are willing to work *with* the wood and not against it. Carver and author Chris Pye comments that 'There is no need to think in terms of fighting or subduing the material. You have to seduce and cajole, read and listen, direct with affection and be prepared to be directed.' (*Woodcarving Tools, Materials & Equipment*, pp. 292–3)

Remember that although you may be carving nature you are not *bound* by nature – the best designs always owe something to the carver's imagination. The form of a carving appears at first to be 100% your own choice, but is it? You are necessarily constrained by:

- The subject, in all its aspects – that you cannot change.
- The chosen timber, in all its aspects – which can only be changed by starting again.
- The interplay, as the carving progresses, between the timber, the subject and your own skills and imagination. Carving design could be described as a trinity of Inspiration, Craft, and Communication between you and your work (see Section 9 below). For those of a philosophical turn of mind, I would recommend Dorothy L. Sayers's book *The Mind of the Maker*. It is all about the craft of writing, but equally appropriate to any creative art, including woodcarving.

The Kirtlington panel by Grinling Gibbons, lime, 62 × 70½in (1575 × 1790mm). A magnificent example of Gibbons's later work, carved c.1690. In this panel he reached new heights of realism in carving a profusion of natural subjects. The accuracy of observation, matched with flawless technique and exceptional design, has never been surpassed in the history of woodcarving. Photograph by courtesy of the Trustees of the Victoria & Albert Museum

4 THE STUDY OF DESIGN

As the carver's skills progress it is well worth gaining some knowledge of how sculpture and decorative carving have been done in the past – what the experts have found to be possible. Some of this may be beyond our wildest dreams (like the incomparable Grinling Gibbons panel reproduced above), but can still act as a source of inspiration.

Accomplished carver and teacher Dick Onians points out that every specialism has its own language, and you cannot be in any sense proficient without learning the language; our language is that of timber, tools, carving technique and design (*Essential Woodcarving Techniques*, p. 3). The hours spent learning the language will be amply repaid by improved quality in our work.

There is a profusion of books available to illustrate the work of historical and modern carvers. Study can be widened by looking at the real thing in exhibitions, museums, country houses and churches. People may give you an odd look as you are bent double, minutely studying the technique of a cathedral misericord carving, but who cares? Enlightenment is seldom the simple process it might at first appear.

This great carving of a ram is by Anon. and lives at Bentley Wildfowl Centre in Sussex, also a centre for the Bentley Wildlife Carvers Association. Not only is the carving anonymous, the timber and its age are also unidentified, but this massive carving nearly 3ft (920mm) high appears to be made from one piece of wood

5 POINTERS FOR PRACTICAL DESIGN

The need for thorough planning cannot be over-emphasized, the more so if the subject attempts to portray nature in a realistic way. Simply attacking a nice piece of wood seldom produces anything worthwhile.

Here are some preliminary questions which you should consider regarding choice of timber:

- What kind of grain figure is required? Bold grain can enhance the simple, but destroy the complex.
- Is the colour important – light or dark? If necessary, you can arrange to have both by means of different finishing techniques (see for example the Turtle project, page 86).
- Will light and shadow be important, and if so, how will the design facilitate this?
- How much surface detail is envisaged, and will the timber allow this? Even if you try for close realism, you cannot carve every bristle or stamen. Studying other people's work will provide clues on how to give the illusion of reality without the detail becoming over-fussy.

- Does the finish you want require close or open grain?
- Is the timber strong enough to support the weakest part of the carving? If you can't fit the design into the available timber without delicate cross-grain sections, then either:
  - Move the design around until you find an acceptable diagonal compromise.
  - Find a piece of timber which has a convenient swirling or branching grain (see for example the Squirrel stick, page 52).
  - Design in a visible support which looks natural (as in the Wren base, page 47).
  - Design a hidden support or dowel construction.
  - Redesign the whole piece.

Remember that the grain direction is not always as it appears to be and may not follow the visible grain lines. If possible, test any critical area by delicate probing.

Horse portrait in American black walnut by Bill Prickett, 8in (200mm) high. Notice the play of light and shadow over the whole sculpture, emphasizing both major muscle folds and the detailed features of the face, including the tiny veins. Although carved in formal portrait pose, with its pricked ears and watchful eye this horse is alive and alert

When designing areas which involve construction, if possible try to arrange the joints so that they will be hidden (behind an undercut or in shadow, for example), and try to avoid joints crossing wide plain areas. Some joints will need a complex arrangement in order to work to best advantage (see for example the Heron beak, page 123).

It's worth remembering that a natural carving need not always include the whole animal. It could be a portrait (like the horse bust by Bill Prickett on this page), or just the eyes and back of a crocodile showing above a watery base.

Remember that while carving is in progress, the design is not finally fixed. As far as possible, leave your options open – you may want to move away from the exact lines of the drawing if you find that some variation looks better in the round, or with that particular grain pattern (see further Section 9 below).

6 DRAWINGS AND MAQUETTES

Textbooks often urge budding carvers to learn how to draw. Well, I accept that, and believe me I've tried, but the results are still pitiable. I admire the wonderful illustrations in magazines and books and still struggle on as best I can – so don't lose heart if you face the same problem.

The great strength of drawing is that it teaches you to look – even simple sketches require an awareness of form and structure. We are not trying to produce beautiful drawings which are works of art, but rough working sketches which assist the carving process. They can be diagrams or doodles, providing they serve the purpose of putting ideas down on paper (where you can rub anything out) before committing many hours of work to a carving which you then realize has a fundamental flaw in its design.

There is no need to be too self-critical about your drawings – no one need see them – and there are plenty of starter books on drawing techniques available in libraries. There may be occasions where you can draw but not carve, for example on holiday (see the simple Leaf Bowl sketch on page 16). Some will carry a blank-page notebook around to sketch whenever something catches their eye. Others will draw late at night when too tired to carve – five-minute doodles of the family budgie or the cat on the hearthrug.

Shoveler drake by Rob Perrott, 5½in (140mm) high. This is a wonderful example of what can be accomplished when aiming for total realism, right down to the sheen of the head feathers. The timber is jelutong, finely textured and painted with acrylics. The eye is glass

'Oak and Laurel' by Rod Naylor, 10in (255mm) high. This is an exceptionally delicate lime carving. Here an expert tackles a formal leaf design with stems running in all directions, resulting in fragile cross-grain sections. The piece is permanently mounted on a felt-covered board

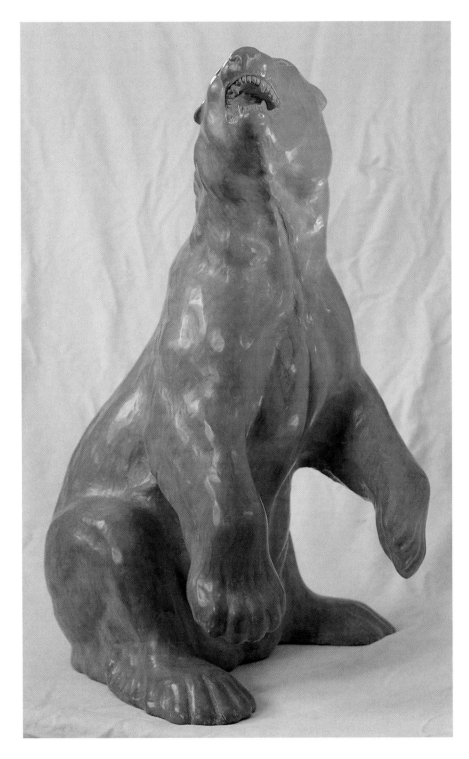

Polar bear in bleached cherry, 20in (510mm) high. This bear by Rod Naylor is pretty big, and carved from three blocks of cherry glued together. It has also been hollowed to prevent shakes developing. The tooled and bleached finish gives a splendid sheen to the surface of the fur

A couple of tips on using drawings

- It is often useful to make a template from your drawing, copying it on to thin card and then cutting round the outline. At the early stages of carving this can be a useful guide and corrective for the overall vertical or lateral shape. Templates can also be made on transparent film, which has the advantage of allowing you to check the positions of features other than the outline.

- If you have the equipment, drawings can be photographed on to a slide transparency, then projected on to the timber to any magnification.

- Copies of drawings and pictures that need size adjustment can be made in a number of ways. The

'An Attitude Problem' by Rod Naylor – pearwood on oak base, 5¼in (133mm) high. The boar's forward movement is emphasized by arranging the two front legs clear of the ground, so a stout fixing is required for the rear legs. Note the hair tooled from head to tail with a V-tool and tiny veiners

easiest is to use a photocopier which will magnify and reduce. More traditional methods include marking a square grid on the original or on a transparent film, then making a new grid of the required size on a blank sheet and copying by hand. The old-fashioned pantograph or map copier will also do a reasonable job if it is held securely.

It's worth remembering the axiom of Mizner: 'When you steal from one author, it's plagiarism; if you steal from many, it's research.' Put another way, woodcarving can be a craft or an art form. The craftsman can accurately copy someone else's design, can restore antique carvings and produce quantities of traditional decorative work for furnishings. The artist, by definition, works from his own designs and produces something which is new and unique. Needless to say, both approaches are equally valid, and a good artist will always need to be an accomplished craftsman.

In addition to the drawings, I nearly always make up a collage of photos and pictures on a board which is mounted behind the bench for ready reference (Fig 11.1

on page 116 shows an example). Pictures from library books can usually be photocopied or scanned, though the librarian's advice should be sought first, and they cannot be used for publication without the written permission of the copyright owner. Your own reference files of pictures can be a life-saver, not only for the carving in hand, but also when you are confronted with the equivalent of writer's block. Browsing through the pictures and old magazines can often stimulate new ideas and inspiration for designing the next project. If you keep the magazines intact, it's worth spending a winter's evening cataloguing and indexing the material.

Maquettes

Just as a drawing can allow you to sort out a number of design problems before committing yourself to a new project, similarly on occasion it can be helpful to experiment with your design in three dimensions, using a soft material. Clay or modelling materials such as Plasticine can be pushed about and changed easily, and are readily available in good craft shops. Professional sculptors in all mediums often make several of these maquettes, as

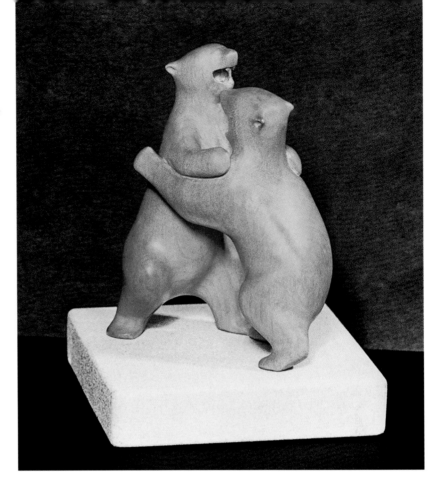

Polar bears in miniature by Rod Naylor, in sycamore with Bath stone base, 5½in (140mm) high. A small carving for a large subject, but notice the wonderful feeling of playfulness. A simple white stone base is ideal here

what appears to work in a drawing may not work out as expected when seen in three dimensions.

An additional advantage for the beginner in carving is that it can be off-putting to find how long it takes to produce anything in wood. The clay model takes far less time, and at least you can see what you are aiming for. If you have never tried any sculpture before, basic lessons in forming simple three-dimensional shapes can be learnt more easily with a soft material. If clay is kept damp, it can be used time and again. Even for the more experienced carver, a maquette may be an indispensable aid to working out a more complex design (see the Cobra project, page 79).

7 DESIGNING A RELIEF

Carving in the round requires the design to be interesting from all angles, and should encourage the viewer to move all round. The viewing angle for relief carvings is far narrower. Relief work is somewhere between drawing and sculpture, between scratching a picture on a flat surface and three-dimensional carving with a background – in fact, a special synthesis of two and three dimensions.

In a relief you are compressing something that is naturally in the round on to a much more shallow area. The lower the relief, the more it is necessary to use the devices of perspective and distortion in order to create the illusion of depth. This is accomplished by flattening the forms of the subject, and by overlapping sections so as to push one into the foreground and the other into the background.

The design therefore has different requirements from freestanding carvings, especially when you bear in mind that the 'picture' may not always be carved on a flat background: relief carving can be done, for example, on the curve of a bowl or on the surface of a vase.

In relief carving the third dimension is always foreshortened. Planes and positions (for example, eye and ear) which are at different depths in the original subject may be at the same level on the relief carving, though made to appear in the right place by the use of perspective and altered proportion; this applies above all to any background landscape. Background detail is best kept to a minimum to avoid fussiness and distraction from the main subject.

There is in fact a host of relief techniques, of which the main varieties are:

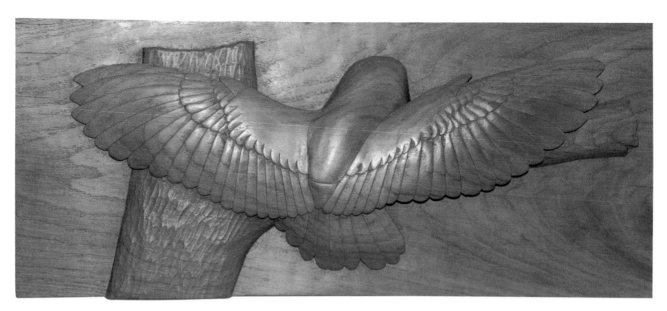

Relief of a barn owl landing, by the author. Carved from an extremely solid piece of English oak and, at 14in (355mm) high, designed to hang on a large wall. The total thickness is 2in (50mm), the wings are undercut to about 30°, and the piece is finished with Danish oil and wax

'Swan Lake' in lime, 7¾in (197mm) high. Rod Naylor again comes up with a unique design, illustrating the reflection of a swan taking off from the water surface. The reflection is less detailed (as in nature), and provides a substantial base

'Brother Gorilla': silverback gorilla in sweet chestnut by Ray Gonzalez, 10in (255mm) high by 24in (610 mm) long. Even at a quick glance you can see a master carver at work: notice the perfect blend of subject and base – you cannot tell where one begins and the other ends – and the variety of tooled finishes to indicate rough and smooth fur, muscle and bone structure, crumpled foliage, etc. And without doubt we are looking at a dominant male gorilla, relaxed, passive, yet frighteningly powerful

- **high relief**, which is almost three-dimensional;
- **low relief**, where the minimal amount of depth is used, normally not more than ¼in (6mm);
- **incised relief**, when the surface only is carved;
- **intaglio**, where there is a negative image, as on a butter pat;
- **pierced work**, which omits any solid background and therefore has a quality of lightness and delicacy.

When choosing timber for any relief work, if possible use a quarter-sawn board, which is less likely to warp in conditions of varying humidity.

8 DESIGNING THE BASE

Many a well-executed carving has ended up on a disappointing mount. Good base design is more to do with imagination than theory, and the best way to find out what works is to look at as many examples of carving as possible in exhibitions, galleries and publications. Good ideas for your own base design will follow.

It hardly needs saying that the base should avoid being too large, thereby overpowering the design; or too small, causing instability. An interesting shape is generally preferable to a rectangle or circle, though on occasion a simple shape can be just what is required (see Rod Naylor's Polar Bears on, page 175). Natural pieces of rock, stone, bark, rough sections of branch, etc., can work very well, as can timber of a contrasting colour and finish. The simplest bases will merely operate as a functional support for the carving; more complex designs will form an integral part of the whole carving. Examples of the latter are water under a heron (page 128), a log under a frog (page 21), ground and foliage under a gorilla (above).

Clearly there are no hard and fast rules, except that from a practical point of view the base must provide stability, and that as far as possible it should complement and add interest to the whole carving – or at least be neutral to show it off to best advantage. Beyond that, it's down to experience and inspiration; and bear in mind some carvers seldom use a base at all (see Chris Coleman's work on pages 164, 178 and 179).

Badger in elm by Chris Coleman, 15in (380mm) high. The stylized design stained with Palette wood dyes looks so simple and yet has a dramatic forward movement. The viewer's eye is drawn forward along the foreleg to the face, where the eye is staring ahead trying to discern what the nose has already found

9 DESIGN CHANGES WHILE CARVING

It is important to leave a safety net of spare wood around the figure while bosting in; in fact, at every stage you should be removing only the amount of waste that is strictly necessary, so as to leave room for later adjustments (see the Turtle project, page 92). Inevitably, as the carving progresses, the options for flexibility gradually close down. The temptation is always to complete the detail you are working on before moving to another section of the carving; as far as possible this is best resisted.

David Esterly encapsulates this ongoing design work and the relationship between the carver and his creation like this:

A carver begins as a god and ends as a slave. With vicious tools, he starts by imposing his will on an undefiled and passive board. As the carving progresses, however, the balance of power shifts. Forms emerge and gather their own potency. Soon the carving begins to make suggestions to the carver; then it makes demands; finally it becomes a pitiless taskmaster, commanding now this, now that detail. The carving is finished when the carver finally loses patience with such thraldom, and removes the carving from the workbench.

(Grinling Gibbons and the Art of Carving, p. 204)

There are in fact two different ways of looking at design. One is the popular view of a Michelangelo working away to find the form which is already inside the marble (or in our case wood). This is the Platonic view, where the idea already exists and the carver's task is to find it, striving to 'finish unseen things because, though invisible to human observers, they are visible to God' (Esterly, p. 199).

Much though I like this approach, generally I find it works the other way round: the carver works not so much by seeing the finished work, rather by continually removing what he or she sees as wrong with the piece at the moment, until finally no more can be taken away without spoiling it. If this rings similar bells for you, it suggests that we are more craftsmen than artists, but so be it; whatever our approach to design, the important thing is to become more proficient at it, and above all to enjoy it.

POSTSCRIPT

Amongst certain peoples, carvers in stone and wood are seen as possessing a form of magic. Their ability to imagine and dream, envisage and create objects which represent the world around and the world of the gods, gives them an awesome quality. They commune with the spirit of the trees, from whom they ask permission before felling.

We may view our craft in rather more mundane terms, but if we lose sight of the magic completely then we are little more than whittlers of wood. If we fail to perceive the living spirit of our raw material then our chipping will produce lifeless forms, however technically brilliant. We may retain an appropriate humility about our talent for

Heron in elm by the author, 20in (510mm) high. This piece is included to show a contrasting style to the Heron project in Chapter 11. Here also the bird is constructed from more than one piece; this time the grain is horizontal, so the beak is integral and the legs added. The feathers are tooled to a more detailed finish (which would not have worked well in yew). The focus is correctly drawn forward to the fish, though the base is less interesting than it could be

woodcarving, but like all talents it is a gift and therefore to be treasured, nurtured as best we can and used with gratitude to produce something worthy of the Giver. Let the wood talk! It has the ability.

Australian poet Henry Rohr puts it like this (in an excerpt from his poem 'A Piece of Wood', in the collection *Set Me Free*, p. 1, reprinted here with permission):

Every possibility is sleeping in such a piece of wood
    It depends on you
    how you look at it
    what you see in it –

        some useless obstacle in your way
        fuel to light your fire
        material
            to build a fence around your isolation
            to build a house – a door – a table.

    OR a challenge
        waiting just for you
            to be set free
            to be called to life.

The woodcarver, the artist sees it like that.

        He takes it in his hands
        and sees the hidden life
        and makes it speak
            Of growth and death
            joy and pain
            all the mysteries of life.

All this is contained
    in a piece of wood.

SELECT BIBLIOGRAPHY

Boultin, E., *A Dictionary of Wood* (London: Thomas Nelson, 1938)

Bridgewater, Alan and Gill, *The Craft of Woodcarving* (Newton Abbot: David and Charles, 1981)

Brown, William, *The Conversion and Seasoning of Wood* (London: Stobart Davies, 1995)

Corkhill, Thomas, *A Glossary of Wood* (London: Stobart Davies, 1979)

Edlin, Herbert, *What Wood is That?* (London: Stobart Davies, 1994)

Essential Tips for Woodcarvers (Lewes: GMC Publications, 1997)

Esterly, David, *Grinling Gibbons and the Art of Carving* (London: V&A Publications, 1998)

Gowan, Leo, *The Craft of Stickmaking* (Marlborough: Crowood, 1994)

Hosker, Ian, *Complete Woodfinishing* (Lewes: GMC Publications, 1997)

Jackson, A., and Day, D., *Woodworkers' Manual* (London: Harper Collins, 1994)

Jones, Andrew, and George, Clive, *Stickmaking: A Complete Course* (Lewes: GMC Publications, 1998)

Lincon, William, *World Woods in Colour* (London: Stobart Davies, 1998)

Magnussen, Magnus, *Lindisfarne* (Stocksfield, Northumberland: Oriel Press, 1984)

Naylor, Rod, *Woodcarving Techniques* (London: Batsford, 1980)

Norbury, Ian, *Projects for Creative Woodcarving* (London: Stobart Davies, 1985)

—— *Fundamentals of Figure Carving* (London: Stobart Davies, 1993)

—— *Techniques of Creative Woodcarving* (London: Stobart Davies, 1994)

Onians, Dick, *Essential Woodcarving Techniques* (Lewes: GMC Publications, 1997)

Pearce, Jim, *Wildfowl Carving, Volume 1* (Lewes: GMC Publications, 1995)

—— *Wildfowl Carving, Volume 2* (Lewes: GMC Publications, 1996)

Practical Tips for Turners & Carvers (Lewes: GMC Publications, 1995)

Pye, Chris, *Woodcarving Tools, Materials & Equipment* (Lewes: GMC Publications, 1994)

Rohr, Henry, *Set Me Free* (Richmond, Victoria, Australia: Spectrum, 1972)

Sayers, Dorothy L., *The Mind of the Maker* (New York: Mowbray, 1994; first pub. 1941)

Tangerman, E. J., *Carving Religious Motifs in Wood* (New York: Sterling, 1980)

—— *Big Book of Whittling & Woodcarving* (New York: Dover, 1989)

CONTACTS

Ray Gonzalez and Ben Harms, Chardleigh House, Chardleigh Green, Wadeford, Somerset, TA20 3AJ

Rod Naylor, 208 Devizes Road, Hilperton, Trowbridge, Wilts. BA14 7QP

Bill Prickett, Brian Faggetter, Rob Perrott, Bob Pyett, c/o Bentley Wildlife Carvers Association, Bentley Wildfowl and Motor Museum, Halland, Lewes, East Sussex, BN8 5AF

Chris Coleman, Valley View Cottage, Litlington, East Sussex, BN26 5RB

ABOUT THE AUTHOR

FRANK FOX-WILSON was born at Byfleet in Surrey in 1946 and went to the City of London Freemen's School at Ashtead. Turning down a degree course in Agriculture, he tried a succession of dead-end jobs before becoming a professional jazz drummer. He eventually settled down as a medical laboratory scientist, qualifying in Bacteriology. Changing horses again, he went off to theological college and to Nottingham University, where he completed a degree in Theology in 1972. He was ordained as an Anglican priest in 1973 and since then has worked in various parishes throughout Sussex. He is presently Rector of four parishes in the beautiful Cuckmere Valley.

He started whittling as a teenager, and has always been fascinated by wood. He has since tried his hand at boat-building, furniture-making and modelling, but has always come back to carving. He has had no formal training in woodwork, but learnt everything from magazines, books, seeing other carvers' work, and years of working out how to avoid making too many mistakes. If asked 'Why woodcarving?', he would find it very difficult to answer in a sentence or two – in fact this book itself is probably the best answer.

He has previously written a local history, *The Story of Goring and Highdown* (1985), but this is his first book on woodcarving.

INDEX